In Dialogue with Reggio Emilia

Listening, researching and learning

Carlina Rinaldi

 Routledge
Taylor & Francis Group

LONDON AND NEW YORK

First published 2006
by Routledge
2 Park Square, Milton Park, Abingdon, Oxon OX14 4RN

Simultaneously published in the USA and Canada
by Routledge
711 Third Avenue, New York, NY 10017 (8th Floor)

Routledge is an imprint of the Taylor & Francis Group, an informa business

© 2006 Carlina Rinaldi

Typeset in Baskerville by RefineCatch Ltd, Bungay, Suffolk
Printed and bound in Great Britain by
TJ International Ltd, Padstow, Cornwall

British Library Cataloguing in Publication Data
A catalogue record for this book is available from the British Library

Library of Congress Cataloging in Publication Data
Rinaldi, Carlina.
    In dialogue with Reggio Emilia : listening, researching, and learning /
Carlina Rinaldi.
        p. cm. — (Contesting early childhood series)
    Includes bibliographical references and index.
    1. Education, Preschool—Italy—Reggio Emilia.
    2. Early childhood education—Italy—Reggio Emilia.   I. Title. II. Series.
    LB1140.25.I8R56 2005
        372.21'0945'43—dc22
                                                    2005007666

ISBN 10: 0–415–34503–0 (hbk)
ISBN 10: 0–415–34504–9 (pbk)

ISBN 13: 978–0–415–34503–3 (hbk)
ISBN 13: 978–0–415–34504–0 (pbk)

To the children, teachers, pedagogistas,
parents and administrators of Reggio Emilia

Contents

Acknowledgements   ix

Note on terminologies   x

Introduction: our Reggio Emilia   1
GUNILLA DAHLBERG AND PETER MOSS

**Carlina Rinaldi: writings, speeches and
interviews, 1984–2004**   23

1 Staying by the children's side: the knowledge of
   educators (1984)   25

2 Participation as communication (1984)   46

3 Malaguzzi and the teachers (1996)   53

4 Documentation and assessment: what is the
   relationship? (1995–8)   61

5 Dialogues   74

6 The space of childhood (1998)   77

7 Issues in educating today (1998)   89

8 Documentation and research (1999)   97

9 Continuity in children's services (1999)   102

10 Creativity as a quality of thought (2000)   111

11 The construction of the educational project: an
   interview with Carlina Rinaldi (2000)   121

12 Teachers as researchers: formation and professional
   development in a school of education (2001)   137

13 The organisation, the method: a conversation with
   Carlina Rinaldi (1998)   143

14 Crossing boundaries: reflections on Loris Malaguzzi
   and Reggio Emilia (2004)   168

15 In dialogue with Carlina Rinaldi: a discussion
   between Carlina Rinaldi, Gunilla Dahlberg and
   Peter Moss   178

   Bibliography   210
   Index   220

Acknowledgements

I would like to thank the many colleagues in Reggio Children who have provided generous and precious support and help over the years and with the preparation of this book, including Paola Riccò, Emanuela Vercalli, Claudia Giudici, Francesca Marastoni and Annamaria Mucchi; Leslie Morrow, Jane McCall and all the other translators who have provided such sensitive translations into English; all the teachers, *pedagogistas, atelieristas* and other colleagues in the Reggio municipal schools who, over the years, have inspired, shared and criticised my thoughts and writings; and finally all my friends, in Reggio Emilia and all over the world, who have accompanied and appreciated my human and professional growth. Finally, I would like to thank Gunilla Dahlberg and Peter Moss for the respect and trust they have shown in me.

Note on terminologies

In this book we have used the Italian terms for the two main types of early childhood service found in Reggio Emilia and the rest of Italy: the *nido* (plural *nidi*) is a centre for children from around 3 months up to 3 years; the *scuola dell'infanzia* (plural *scuole dell'infanzia*) is a centre or nursery school for children from 3 years up to compulsory school age of 6. In Reggio they use the term 'municipal schools' to refer to the thirty-three centres for young children – both *nidi* and *scuole dell'infanzia* – that are either directly managed by the municipality of Reggio Emilia (we use the term 'municipality' for local authority) or managed for the municipality by cooperatives or other non-profit organisations; this term is also used in the book to refer to this network of services. However, the term 'school' (not qualified by 'municipal') is used generically to cover all places of education, whether for children from birth to 6 or for older children and young people.

The staff working directly with the children in *nidi* and *scuole dell'infanzia* are referred to as 'teachers' or 'educators', even though the staff in *nidi* often have lower levels of initial training.

But there are also other groups of workers who play an important role in Reggio's municipal schools. Apart from auxiliary staff, who are discussed in several places in this book (for example, cooks and cleaners), there are *pedagogistas* and *atelieristas*. *Pedagogistas* have a higher degree in psychology or pedagogy, and each works with a small number of municipal schools to help develop understanding of learning processes and pedagogical work through, for example, pedagogical documentation (a method discussed at some length in the book). *Atelieristas*, whose background is often in the visual arts, work alongside teachers in Reggio's municipal schools, often from an *atelier* (workshop) in a *nido* or *scuola dell'infanzia* where they support and develop children's and adults' visual languages as part of the complex process of knowledge building.

One other issue of terminology should be flagged up here, at an early stage of the book: the distinction between the Italian words *programmazione* and *progettazione*. In Italian, the verb *progettare* has a number of meanings: to design, to plan, to devise, to project (in a technical-engineering sense). The use of the noun form *progettazione* by Reggio educators, however, has its own special meaning. It is used in Reggio in opposition to *programmazione*, which implies predefined curricula, programmes, stages, and so on. The concept of *progettazione* thus implies a more global and flexible approach in which initial hypotheses are made about classroom work (as well as about staff development and relationships with parents), but are subject to modifications and changes of direction as the actual work progresses: project work 'grows in many directions without an overall ordering principle, challenging the mainstream idea of knowledge acquisition as a form of linear progression, where the metaphor is the tree' (page 7).

It is not easy to find a term in English that could describe this process precisely as experienced in Reggio Emilia. Some writers in English have used terms such as 'emergent curriculum', 'projected curriculum' or 'integrated curriculum' to describe the overall way in which the Reggio teachers plan and work with children, with colleagues and with parents. But these terms are (as the reader will discover) inappropriate, derived from methods or ways of working developed and used elsewhere; their use renders invisible the otherness of Reggio. We have chosen, therefore, to keep with the Italian word *progettazione*.

Introduction

Our Reggio Emilia

Gunilla Dahlberg and Peter Moss

> Dialogue is of absolute importance. It is an idea of dialogue not as an exchange but as a process of transformation where you lose absolutely the possibility of controlling the final result. And it goes to infinity, it goes to the universe, you can get lost. And for human beings nowadays, and for women particularly, to get lost is a possibility and a risk, you know?
>
> (Carlina Rinaldi: page 184)

This book is about an extraordinary experience as seen through the eyes of one of its leading interpreters. Carlina Rinaldi began working in Reggio in 1970, first as a *pedagogista*, then as the pedagogical director of the municipal early childhood services and, since her retirement in 1999, as a consultant to Reggio Children, the organisation established by the municipality of Reggio Emilia to manage the relationship between the municipal schools in Reggio and the rest of the world. In these various capacities, Carlina has made many speeches, given many interviews and written many papers: this book presents a selection. Through them we can follow how the experience in Reggio Emilia has developed over more than 40 years, in relation both to particular philosophical and theoretical perspectives and to the wider social, cultural and political context.

What is Reggio Emilia? It is a city in Northern Italy, with a population of around 150,000, a prosperous community with a long history which has become, over the last few years, ethnically diverse creating 'a new Reggio' (Piccinini, 2004). The American psychologist Jerome Bruner, an eminent overseas visitor who has become a close friend and admirer of the city and who was given honorary citizenship in 1998, has argued that you cannot understand the municipal schools if you do not understand the city from which they derive: the city of Reggio Emilia, he says, is 'neither confusingly large nor suffocatingly small [and of a size that] favours imagination, energy, community spirit. . . . [I]n Reggio one is given to meeting a rare form of courtesy, a precious form of reciprocal respect' (2004: 27).

Reggio is also the thirty-three municipal schools for children from a few months old to 6 years, provided by the local authority either directly or through agreements with cooperatives. But perhaps most important, Reggio is a unique body of theory and practice about working with young children and their families, produced from a very particular historical, cultural and political context. It is this body of theory and practice and its context that form the subject of this book.

As editors of a series called *Contesting Early Childhood* and as authors of a book in that series titled *Ethics and Politics in Early Childhood Education*, we find the experience of the municipal schools in Reggio Emilia, and Carlina's interpretation of that experience, of the utmost importance. For it seems to us that we live today in a phase of history when the ethical and political dimensions of education, with their accompanying argumentation, are too often neglected issues. The idea of education for all children, including young children, as a shared experience in a democratic society and of schools as part of that society whose citizens take responsibility for all their children is increasingly replaced by another idea. Education is increasingly viewed as an individual commodity and the metaphor for the school changes from the forum or public space to the business, a business competing in a market to sell its products – education and care. Parents become autonomous calculating consumers, supported in their individual calculation by managerial concepts such as delivery, quality, excellence and outcomes. The school is reduced to a site of technical practice, to be evaluated against its ability to reproduce knowledge and identity and to achieve uniform and consistent criteria. The school has become a technology of normalisation.

It is in this historical context that a journey into such a unique educational and cultural experience as the municipal schools of Reggio Emilia becomes so important and urgent. These schools do not dismiss technical practices, nor do they ignore matters of organisation and structure. But they put them in their place: as means to support an educational project that understands the school as first and foremost a public space and a site for ethical and political practice – a place of encounter and connection, interaction and dialogue among citizens, younger and older, living together in a community. We never forget, says Carlina of Reggio, that 'behind every solution and every organisation, this means behind every school, there is a choice of values and ethics'.

For us, Reggio Emilia is an experience that embraces, in the words of the French philosopher Gilles Deleuze, 'a belief in the world' and offers hope for a renewed culture of childhood and for reclaiming the school as a public space of central importance to democratic societies. In the remainder of this introduction, we shall try to make good this claim for Reggio. But in doing so, we recognise we present *our* Reggio, our interpretation of this unique experience resulting from following this practice over the last two decades, by reading, by visiting and by discussion with teachers and others. We feel encouraged to do so because we think Carlina and her colleagues in Reggio would say that interpretation of the world is unavoidable (indeed, in the final chapter of this book Carlina observes that 'Reggio itself is an interpretation of Reggio!' [see page 197]), and that new knowledge is created through putting forward interpretations in dialogue and for contestation.

The story of a pedagogical experiment

The pedagogical experience of Reggio Emilia is a story so far spanning more than 40 years that can be described as a pedagogical experiment in a whole community. As such it is unique; there has, to the best of our knowledge, never been anything like it before. To place this experience in perspective, the single experimental school of John Dewey lasted just 4 years. The American psychologist Howard Gardner has set out the scale of the achievement while reflecting on the Reggio Emilian experience in relation to the history of progressive education in America, where, like in most other countries, the ideals of progressive education are seldom actually realised in practice:

As an American educator, I cannot help but be struck by certain paradoxes. In America we pride ourselves on being focused on children, and yet we do not pay sufficient attention to what they are actually expressing. We call for cooperative learning among children, and yet we rarely have sustained cooperation at the level of teacher and administrator. We call for artistic works, but we rarely fashion environments that can truly support and inspire them. We call for parental involvement, but are loathe to share ownership, responsibility, and credit with parents. We recognize the need for community, but we so often crystallize immediately into interest groups. We hail the discovery method, but we do not have the confidence to allow children to follow their noses and hunches. We call for debate, but often spurn it; we call for listening, but we prefer to talk; we are affluent, but we do not safeguard those resources that can allow us to remain so and to foster the affluence of others. Reggio is so instructive in these respects. Where we are often intent to invoke slogans, the educators in Reggio work tirelessly to solve many of these fundamental – and fundamentally difficult – issues.

(Gardner, 1994: xi–xii)

One reason for Reggio's vigour and longevity has been a willingness to border cross driven by an endless curiosity and a desire to open up to new perspectives. The educators in Reggio have brought in theories and concepts from many different fields, not only education, but also including philosophy, architecture, science, literature, and visual communication. They have related their work to an analysis of the wider world and its continuous processes of change. Loris Malaguzzi, the first pedagogical director of the Reggio municipal schools and one of the greatest pedagogical thinkers and practitioners of the last century, wrote:

It is curious (but not unjustified) how resilient is the belief that educational ideas and practices can derive only from official models or established theories. . . . But talk about education (including education for young children) cannot be confined to its literature. Such talk, which is also political, must continuously address major social changes and transformations in economy, sciences, arts, and human relationships and customs. All of these larger forces influence how human beings – even young children – 'read' and deal with the realities of life. They determine the emergence, on both general and local levels, of new methods of educational content and practice, as well as new problems and soul-searching questions.

(Malaguzzi, 1994: 51, 54)

But the eduactors in Reggio have not just brought in theories and concepts from many places. They have actually reflected on them and experimented with them, creating their own meanings and implications for pedagogical practice.

At the same time, they have always been critical and questioning. For example, an eagerness to follow the latest achievements in science has been tempered by critical analysis and a strong belief that science alone cannot solve what are often questions of value, for example what we consider to be a good life for young children and other citizens in a community, or who we understand the child to be. Science, too, they recognise, offers not only possibilities for good but also possibilities for domination and exploitation. As the Chilean biologist Humberto Maturana observes:

> what science and the training to be a scientist does not provide us with is wisdom. Modern science has arisen in a culture that values appropriation and wealth, that treats knowledge as a source of power, that prizes growth and control, that respects hierarchies and domination, that values appearances and success, and that has lost sight of wisdom and does not know how to cultivate it. We scientists in our efforts to do what we like most, namely, scientific inquiry, frequently fall pray to the passions, desires, and aims of our culture and think that the expansion of science justifies everything, becoming blind to wisdom and how it is learned. Wisdom breeds in the respect for others, in the recognition that power arises through submission and loss of dignity, in the recognition that love is the emotion that constitutes social co-existence, honesty and trustfulness, and in the recognition that the world we live in is always, and unavoidably so, our doing. But, if science and scientific knowledge do not provide us with wisdom, at least they do not deny it.
>
> (Maturana, 1991: 50)

Curiosity, openness and border crossing have left Reggio, time and again, ahead of the game. Theories and philosophies that today start to become widely used in discussions about education, but are still not so visible and embodied in pedagogical practices, have often been visible and embodied in Reggio's practice for some time. Like other radical educational practices in the 1970s, the teachers in Reggio Emilia got inspiration from Piaget's thinking; especially important was Piaget's epistemology and his view that the aim of teaching is to provide conditions for learning. But they also understood that educators, with 'a simple minded greed' had, too often, tried to extract from Piaget's psychology things that he did not consider at all usable in education.

Early on, too, they became aware of certain weaknesses in Piaget's theory, including how Piaget's constructivism decontextualises and isolates the child, something which many constructivists today have remedied. As a result, the teachers in Reggio started to look more critically at certain aspects of Piaget's theory, including:

> the undervaluation of the adult role in promoting cognitive development; the marginal attention to social interaction and to memory (as opposed to inference); the distance between thought and language;

the lock-step linearity of development in constructivism, the way that cognitive, affective and moral development are treated as separate, parallel tracks; the overemphasis on structured stages, egocentrism, and classificatory skills; the lack of recognition for partial competences, the overwhelming importance given to logicomathematical competences; and the overuse of paradigms from the biological and physical sciences.

(Malaguzzi, 1994: 76)

Transgressing the decontextualised idea of Piaget meant that Reggio, in the 1970s, started to experiment with what it would mean to work from another idea: that children's learning is situated in a socio-cultural context and takes place in interrelationships, requiring the construction of an environment that 'allows for maximum movement, interdependence, and interaction' (*ibid.*: 56). In this way, they came to adopt a social constructionist perspective, where knowledge is seen as constituted in a context through a process of meaning making in continuous encounters with others and the world, and the child and the teacher are understood as co-constructers of knowledge and culture.

This perspective opened the teachers in Reggio Emilia to the precious insights of the Russian psychologist Lev Vygotsky. Since then, these insights have been important in their practice, for example the importance he attached to the relationship between thought and language and how action is mediated by cultural tools and symbols. Reggio's very conscious strategies to use other children in the group as a pedagogical tool in the process of co-construction have much in common with Vygotsky's idea about the zone of proximal development.

Another important inspiration was John Dewey, including his view that learning is an active process and not a transmission of pre-packaged knowledge. Knowledge, he argued, is constructed through children's activities, through pragmatic and emancipated experimentation and participation in activities. He also border crossed the dualisms between content and method, process and product, mind and body, science and art, theory and practice: 'Mankind likes to think in extreme opposites. It is given to formulating its beliefs in terms of Either–Ors between which it recognizes no intermediate possibilities' (Dewey, 1938: 17).

Typically, the teachers in Reggio have taken inspiration from theories and theorists, but have not been bound by them; rather than reproducing others' theories, they have used them to construct their own perspectives. Malaguzzi, for example, said that in the beginning they meditated on the work of Maria Montessori, in order to be able to go beyond: 'Montessori – she is our mother, but as all children, we have had to make ourselves independent of our mothers.' The same 'going beyond' was true, as we have just mentioned, of their relationship with Piaget. If Vygotsky and other semiotic thinkers have stressed the verbal and oral language, Reggio has widened the idea of language into what they have called 'the hundred languages of children', what Carlina refers to in this book as 'the fantastic theory' (see page 192). This recognition of the multiplicity of language has meant that they have introduced many new tools as semiotic mediators into their schools, such as video, digital cameras and computers.

Another example of being ahead of the game concerns ideas about knowledge. To understand Reggio Emilia's thinking and practice, for instance the idea of project work, we have to open ourselves to rethinking the mainstream idea of knowledge. Not only do we have to make disciplinarity a permanent question, through keeping open the question of what is a discipline and what is a school subject, we also have to ask ourselves why we have conceptualised and organised knowledge in a certain way.

In Reggio they have questioned and rethought. In one of his speeches, Loris Malaguzzi talked about their idea of knowledge as a 'tangle of spaghetti'. Carlina takes a similar view when she says that 'learning does not proceed in a linear way, determined and deterministic, by progressive and predictable stages, but rather is constructed through contemporaneous advances, standstills, and "retreats" that take many directions' (page 131). Equipped with this concept of knowledge, we can understand why project work in Reggio Emilia grows in many directions without an overall ordering principle, challenging the mainstream idea of knowledge acquisition as a form of linear progression, where the metaphor is the tree – very different to the metaphor of the tangle of spaghetti! Project work in Reggio can be seen as a series of small narratives, narratives that are difficult to combine in an additive and cumulative way.

This, we think, is similar to an image of knowledge as *a rhizome*. This image was developed by the French philosophers Gilles Deleuze and Felix Guattari (1999; see also Deleuze and Parnet, 1987) as a way of transgressing notions such as universality, question and answer patterns, simple judgements, recognition and correct ideas. In a rhizome there is no hierarchy of root, trunk and branch. It is not like a staircase, where you have to take the first step before you move onto and reach the other, which is similar to the tree metaphor of knowledge that remains so prominent in education.

For Deleuze and Guattari, but we think Reggio also, thought and concepts can be seen as a consequence of the provocation of an encounter with difference. They view the *rhizome* as something which shoots in all directions with no beginning and no end, but always *in between*, and with openings towards other directions and places. It is a *multiplicity* functioning by means of connections and heterogeneity, a multiplicity which is not given but constructed. Thought, then, is a matter of experimentation and problematisation – *a line of flight* and an exploration of *becoming*, echoed in Carlina's observation that 'the process of "becoming" is the basis of true education' (page 80).

We can provide a personal example of how the pedagogical work of Reggio's teachers, and their love of experimentation, has put this small city and its municipal schools at the forefront of new thinking and practice. In the late 1990s, together with our Canadian colleague Alan Pence, we wrote a book about early childhood work in which we worked with a philosophical perspective which might be termed postmodern. But the more we worked with this perspective, the more we realised that many facets of the pedagogical thought and practice in Reggio might also be termed postmodern and have been so for some time, for example:

> Choosing to adopt a social constructionist approach; challenging and deconstructing dominant discourses; realizing the power of these discourses in shaping and governing our thoughts and actions . . .; rejecting the prescription of rules, goals, methods and standards, and in so doing risking uncertainty and complexity; having the courage to think for themselves in constructing new discourses, and in so doing daring to make the choice of understanding the child as a rich child, a child of infinite capabilities, a child born with a hundred languages; building a new pedagogical project, foregrounding relations and encounters, dialogue and negotiation, reflection and critical thinking; border crossing disciplines and perspectives, replacing either/or positions with an and/also openness; and understanding the contextualized and dynamic nature of pedagogical practice, which problematizes the idea of a transferable 'programme'.
>
> (Dahlberg *et al.*, 1999: 122)

Hope for renewal of radical politics

For us, Reggio Emilia not only reveals the potentialities of children, it also suggests some directions for the renewal of democratic practice and radical politics in a post-communist world. The origins of early childhood services in Reggio lie in long traditions of collective life in cohesive communities, producing norms of reciprocity and trust and networks of civic engagement, what Putnam (1993) has termed 'social capital'. In this fertile soil, a vigorous left politics grew and flourished. As Carlina says in the interview that ends this book, 'the roots of our experience are in the socialist ideas that took hold in our area of Italy in the late nineteenth century and early twentieth century' (page 178). From similar political origins have also grown other innovative local experiences in Northern and Central Italy in the field of early childhood education, Reggio being, as Carlina readily acknowledges, 'one of many places which expresses the vitality, wealth and quality of Italian pedagogical research . . . and courageous investment by municipalities in services for early childhood' (page 102). Though, as Carlina also illustrates, despite much exchange and sharing, important differences emerged between many of these local experiences, making for distinctive identities.

But left politics was not the only ingredient. Reggio is also a women's story, the product of women's active participation in the struggle to improve not only their rights but the rights of children; and the story of a determination to prevent a re-emergence of fascism and a desire to break the monopoly of the Catholic Church on education for young children. Subsequently, Reggio has shown a readiness to come to a new collaborative relationship with the Church and to criticise secular education. Malaguzzi (1994) could be scathing of state-run schooling, 'sticking to its stupid and intolerable indifference towards children, its opportunistic and obsequious attention towards authority, and its self-serving cleverness, pushing pre-packaged knowledge' (42). Instead he, and his colleagues, wanted to recognise the right of each child to be a protagonist and to sustain each child's spontaneous curiosity at a high level; and to create an amiable environment, where children, families and teachers feel at ease – 'to give a human, dignified *civil* meaning to existence' (*ibid.*: 50).

The contribution of Reggio to a renewal of radical politics comes in two ways. First, there is the forging of new relationships of interdependence between individuality and collectivity, difference and solidarity. We are all different, all individual: but equally important, indeed vital, 'for the future of humanity itself [is] the relationship between the individual and others, between Self and Other' (page 139). In Reggio, the individual can never assume the liberal guise of autonomous subject, but only acquires full subjectivity – through construction as a unique and unrepeatable subject – in her or his relation with others: 'I can discover this individuality because you exist. Thank you! And because we are interdependent' (page 188). In the importance it attaches to relationships, Reggio provokes us to choose 'between societies oriented toward the individual in competition and societies based on the individual constructed with others, who seeks out others. . . . [A] political and economic choice that can influence the entire educational system but also the social system' (page 139).

Second, they have challenged the calculative rationality of neoliberalism and the necessity of public service renewal based on managerial practices, the operation of markets and investment rationality. They view this 'economic thinking' as at odds with values that are precious to them, in particular dialogue and relationships of cooperation – not competition – not only between individuals but also between municipal schools that function as a network. They believe in the importance of choice in public services, but choice as political and ethical decisions made in relationship with others, not choice as decisions made by individual consumers.

> Pedagogy like school is not neutral. It takes sides, it participates in deep and vital ways in the definition of this project whose central theme is not mankind, but his relations with the world, his being in the world, his feeling of *interdependence* with what is other than himself. So pedagogy implies choices, and choosing . . . [it] means having the courage of our doubts, of our uncertainties, it means participating in something for which we take responsibility.
>
> (page 170)

The first and most basic of these choices has been in answer to the question 'what is our image of the child?' – of which more later.

The early childhood services of Reggio Emilia insist on the importance of viewing public services as a collective responsibility and offer us an understanding of the school as first and foremost a public space and as a site for ethical and political practice – a place of encounter, interaction and connections among citizens in a community, a place where relationships combine a profound respect for otherness and difference with a deep sense of responsibility for the other, a place of profound interdependency. In their work, the teachers of Reggio have struggled to realise the emancipatory potential of democracy, by giving each child possibilities to function as an active citizen and to have the possibility of a good life in a democratic community.

In this way, radical politics are completely enmeshed with democratic politics. Participation, by children, parents, teachers, the wider community, is a central value and integral to the educational experience: participation meant not as a means of governing more effectively through 'educating parents' to adopt a certain official perspective, but as 'active, direct and explicit participation . . . in the formulation of the educational project' (page 27) and the construction of meaning – an idea caught in the repeated use by Carlina of the word 'protagonist' to describe all participants in the Reggio project. Through participation, the municipal schools have provided new sites for democratic politics, while at the same time extending the scope of politics to new areas.

Their social constructionist approach has meant that Reggio Emilia has been engaged in what can be termed a *politics of epistemology*. They have contested modernity's idea of knowledge as an objective representation of a real world, in favour of knowledge as 'an interpretation of reality that is constantly evolving' (page 125) that is socially constructed by each one of us in relation with others. For Carlina and her colleagues,

> learning does not take place by means of transmission or reproduction. It is a process of construction, in which each individual constructs for himself the reasons, the 'whys', the meanings of things, others, nature, events, reality and life. The learning process is certainly individual, but because the reasons, explanations, interpretations, and meanings of others are indispensable for our knowledge building, it is also a process of relations – a process of social construction. We thus consider knowledge to be a process of construction by the individual in relation with others, a true act of co-construction.
>
> (page 125)

This has also meant that they have problematised the idea of predetermined goals, opening up instead for the exploration of alternative and marginalised ways to think and give meanings to the world in which subjectivity, surprise, amazement and openness to doubt are all important values. Significant here, as we understand it, have been Bateson's cybenetic ideas on self-regulating systems in a process of continuous reciprocal change (Bateson, 1972); Dewey's view that learning is an active process and not transmission of pre-packaged knowledge; and the thoughts of the Chilean biologists Maturana and Varela (1992) on 'languaging'.

Like phenomenologists and others, Maturana and Varela question objectivity. They suggest that we relate ourselves to the world as if it was possible to be objective, but at the same time realise that we can never be objective! What the observer does in language as a human being explaining her or his experience cannot refer to anything deemed independent of what the observer does. You are always part of the context, a participant in the system you are observing and interpreting; the world that we live in is always our doing – and unavoidably so. We are constituted through language which means that we cannot live outside language: 'Life happens to us, experience happens to us, the worlds we live happen to us as we bring them forth in our explanations' (Maturana, 1991: 49). A shift is proposed, from language as an abstract thing, a noun, to languaging as an act, a verb. Languaging brings forth a world created with others in the act of coexistence which gives rise to what is human; and every human act has got an ethical meaning because it is an act of constitution of the human world: 'the notion of ethics has to do with our concern for the consequences of our actions on the life of other human beings that we accept in coexistence with us' (*ibid.*: 43).

Reggio's constant questioning has provoked a *politics of education and learning*. Reggio's adoption of a 'pedagogy of listening', so often referred to by Carlina and discussed further below, contests an increasingly dominant idea of education as transmission and reproduction; while the process of pedagogical documentation, also appearing frequently in Carlina's work and discussed below, provides a means for democratic participation in the discussion and evaluation of pedagogical practice.

Through Reggio's politics of education and learning, the meaning of the school comes up for democratic attention. It is, Carlina argues, a place for both the transmission and the creation of culture and values. It is a place that recognises children as citizens. It is a place of possibilities, where knowledge and identity are co-constructed and learning processes are investigated, always in relationship with others – a forum, a place of encounter, a construction site, a workshop and a permanent laboratory are just some of the metaphors used by Carlina. And it is a place which is both a community in itself as well as an integral part of a wider community: a Reggio school, Bruner comments, 'is a special kind of place, one in which young human beings are invited to grow in mind, sensibility, and in belonging to a broader community . . . [I]t is a learning community, where mind and sensibility are shared. It is a place to learn together about the real world, and about possible worlds of the imagination' (1998).

Last, but not least, a *politics of childhood* has been stimulated by that simple but powerful question to which we have already referred and which some might call the hallmark of Reggio – what is your image of the child? For them childhood is a value-laden construction, which they have seriously taken notice of in order to open up new possibilities. Or as Carlina has said, 'childhood does not exist, we create it as a society, as a public subject. It is a social, political and historical construction.' This makes us think of Michel Foucault's work on how knowledge and power are intertwined in dominant discourses, the one legitimising the other – and of how in Reggio they recognise, confront and deconstruct that relationship (see Dahlberg *et al.*, 1999 for further discussion).

The answer to the question for Reggio has been the 'rich child', an image based on the understanding that all children are intelligent, meaning that all children are embarked on a course of making meaning of the world, a constant process of constructing knowledge, identity and value. Following on this social construction, they have struggled to show the potentialities of each child and to give each child the democratic right to be listened to and to be a recognised citizen in the community. This has been a very strong message, a provocation, as young children and their lives have not really figured much in public discourse; and when they do, they are readily devalued and marginalised as the 'poor', 'weak' or 'innocent' child, spoken of in terms of deficit, immaturity, fragility or cuteness.

To make another choice, to adopt the image of the rich child, to insist on the idea of all children being competent and intelligent has been intensely political: not only to insist on a better deal for children but also on the need to see children from a different perspective, to recast the *problematique* and redefine the critical questions. Reggio's politics of childhood has challenged our dominant discourses and taken-for-given assumptions about the child, for example the categories of developmental psychology which have governed what we think a child is, can and should be, replacing politics with scientific truth claims.

Reggio's experience has come out of what might be termed traditional politics, that is, the municipal schools and their pedagogical work have been created and supported by a local authority, elected by the adult citizens of Reggio; it is an example of how such politics can still have an important part to play in innovative experimentation. But the latter part of the twentieth century has seen the spread of other political forms, what Melucci (1989) has called new social movements in the public arena. Well-known examples include the peace movement, the women's movement, the environmental movement and the movement against global neo-liberalism.

These movements open up for a widening of democracy in postmodern times – calling for engagement, collective action and the proliferation of public spaces or forums, in short a new political culture. These movements, often crossing nation state borders, have both contributed to bringing forth new political topics on the political agenda, and challenged established forms of political action and organisation. They question the meaning of concepts such as politics and democracy in our times. Viewed from this perspective, Reggio can be said to be a social movement on childhood and its schools new public spaces for democratic practice.

Schools as a loci of ethical practice

Reggio, we have already suggested, re-asserts the school as being, first and foremost, a place of political and ethical practice. We have considered the political, but where does the ethical come in? Partly through the high priority paid to values. Schools in Reggio are seen as places for building values, values such as friendship, solidarity, respect for differences, dialogue, feelings, affection.

But to understand the place of ethics in Reggio, we must also ask what ethics? For us Reggio's pedagogy of listening provides an important clue to answering this question. In our earlier book in this series (Dahlberg and Moss, 2005), we argued that their active listening to children's theories and meaning making are inscribed with a particular ethical approach: Emmanuel Levinas's concept of the ethics of an encounter. Levinas argues that there is a strong Western philosophical tradition that gives primacy to knowing. Through this will to know, we grasp the other and make the other into the same. An example is concepts and classifications such as developmental stages, which give us as teachers or researchers possibilities to possess and 'comprehend' the child. With grasping through the will to know, alterity disappears and singularity and novelty are excluded, to be replaced by 'the totalitarianism of the same'. The ethics of an encounter attempts to counter this grasping through respect for the absolute alterity of the Other.

Listening also connects Reggio to the powerful ethical vision that Bill Readings sketched in his final book – *The University of Ruins* – of how universities and other institutions for education and learning have the possibility to be 'sites of obligation' and 'loci of ethical practices' rather than 'sites for the transmission of scientific knowledge'. For, he goes on to argue,

> the condition of pedagogical practice is 'an infinite attention to the other'. . . . (and) education is this drawing out of the otherness of thought. . . . [It is] *Listening to Thought* . . . Doing justice to Thought, listening to our interlocutors, means trying to hear that which

cannot be said but that which tries to make itself heard. . . . It is to think besides each other and ourselves to explore an open network of obligation that keeps the question of meaning open as a locus for debate.

(Readings, 1996: 161, 162, 165: original emphasis)

A 'pedagogy of listening' – listening to thought – exemplifies for us an ethics of an encounter built on welcoming and hospitality of the Other – an openness to the difference of the Other, to the coming of the Other. It involves an ethical relationship of openness to the Other, trying to listen to the Other from his or her own position and experience and not treating the Other as the same. The implications are seismic for education.

Working with the ethics of an encounter in a pedagogy of listening requires the teacher to think an Other whom she cannot grasp, which challenges the whole scene of pedagogy. For a pedagogy of listening means listening to thought – the ideas and theories, questions and answers of children and adults; it means treating thought seriously and with respect; it means struggling to make meaning from what is said, without preconceived ideas of what is correct or appropriate. A pedagogy of listening treats knowledge as constructed, perspectival and provisional, not the transmission of a body of knowledge which makes the Other into the same. For each question one has to open oneself to Otherness – to welcome the stranger, which means an affirmation, a *yes, yes, yes* to the Other, the stranger. Or even broader, an affirmation of the Alterity of existence (Derrida, 1999).

In the pedagogy of listening, Reggio's municipal schools have pursued the aspirations of their founders, whose experience of fascism had 'taught them that people who conformed and obeyed were dangerous, and that in building a new society it was imperative to safeguard and communicate that lesson and maintain a vision of children who can think and act for themselves' (Dahlberg *et al.*, 1999: 12). Hence politics and ethics come together in an approach to education which rejects the regulatory bonds of developmental classifications and education as transmission and normative outcomes, and which emphasises the importance of otherness and difference, connectedness and relationships.

The power of pedagogical documentation

Running through the work of Reggio Emilia, as it does through the chapters that follow, is the practice of pedagogical documentation. Most simply expressed, pedagogical documentation is a process for making pedagogical (or other) work visible and subject to interpretation, dialogue, confrontation (argumentation) and understanding. It embodies the value of subjectivity, that there is no objective point of view that makes observation neutral; but at the same time, it insists on the need for rigorous subjectivity, by making perspectives and interpretations explicit and contestable through documenting in relationship with others, be they children, parents, educators or other citizens: documentation fosters a conflict of ideas and argumentation, not a cosy search for consensus, it is a way to capture subjectivities interacting in a group. The value of subjectivity also means that the subject must take responsibility for her or his point of view; there can be no hiding behind an assumed scientific objectivity or criteria offered by experts.

Pedagogical documentation, as it is discussed by Carlina, is a multipurpose tool. It visualises children's learning processes, their search for meaning and their ways of constructing knowledge. It enables the connection in everyday work of theory and practice. It is a means for that professional development of the teacher on which Reggio places such great importance, not least through the teacher being understood and treated as both researcher and learner. It promotes the idea of the school as a place of democratic political practice, by enabling citizens, young and old, to engage with and argue about important issues: childhood, care, education, knowledge and so on. It is a way to open up a public space or forum in civil society, where dominant discourses, and the way we have constructed ourselves as subjects – governed ourselves – through these discourses, can be visualised and problematised.

It is also a method for assessment and evaluation, 'an extremely strong "antibody" to a proliferation of assessment/evaluation tools which are more and more anonymous, decontextualised and only apparently objective and democratic' (page 62). Rating scales and similar normative tools that evaluate against a set of criteria assumed to be stable, uniform and objective represent one 'language of evaluation' (the language of 'quality and excellence'). Pedagogical documentation represents another language (what we have termed elsewhere the language of 'meaning making' (Dahlberg et al., 1999): one that assumes we must take responsibility for making judgements, on the basis of confronting the actual practice, struggling to interpret and make meaning of what we see, and relating it to the values we deem important – and always in relationship with others, in dialogue with our fellow citizens, as part of the collective who have taken responsibility for this practice, as part of a true act of democracy.

Otherness, dissensus and provocation

We might sum up our preceding discussion by saying that the importance of Reggio for us lies in its difference, its otherness, its alterity. This is not to say it is unconnected or autonomous, for as we have seen it has developed its thinking and practice always in relation to the wider world, co-constructing its knowledge, identity and values with many disciplines, places and people. But the result of that co-construction is something particular, an active singularity. We would go further and say that Reggio is an island of dissensus, a provocation to an increasingly dominant and smothering discourse about early childhood education in particular and education in general, a largely English-language and highly instrumental discourse that views schools as places for governing children through the application of technologies to produce pre-determined, normative outcomes. By so doing, Reggio provides a powerful, collective example of critical thought, vividly described by Nikolas Rose as 'introducing a critical attitude towards those things that are given to our present experience as if they were timeless, natural, unquestionable: [standing against] the current of received wisdom ... introducing a kind of awkwardness into the fabric of one's experience [and] interrupting the fluency of the narratives that encode that experience and making them stutter' (Rose, 1999: 20).

By its existence, its provocation, its critical thinking, Reggio reminds us that education, learning, knowledge, childhood, teacher, evaluation and much else besides have many meanings. We face political choices not technical necessities. We have to think and we have to take responsibility – we cannot await an expert telling us 'what works'.

Reggio's theories are rich and provocative, not least the pedagogy of listening and the hundred languages. But at the same time, Reggio challenges 'the arrogant idea of the continuing separation between theory and practice' (page 100), arguing that they are inseparable – one without the other is inconceivable. By so doing, Reggio also revalues the practitioner, indeed questions the very term as implying that there can and should be a distinction between those who practice and those who theorise. Furthermore, by the importance they attach to teachers as researchers they undermine yet another distinction, between the practitioner in the classroom and the researcher in the university. Research, they argue, can and should take place as much in the classroom and by teachers as in the university and by 'academics': 'The word "research", in this sense, leaves – or rather, demands to come out of – the scientific laboratories, thus ceasing to be a privilege of the few (in universities and other designated places) to become the stance, the attitude with which teachers approach the sense and meaning of life' (page 148).

Here, Reggio is rejecting dualistic thinking – but also everywhere else. For example, hoary discussions about whether more attention should be paid to process or outcome become nonsensical in Reggio's discourse. Can we divide life up in this way, are we not always in the middle, always becoming, how can we differentiate except by an artificial fragmenting of life?

Before ending this section, we want to raise two other provocations that have a particular appeal for us, and which figure in particular in our dialogue with Carlina with which this book ends. First, doubt, uncertainty and feelings of crisis are seen as resources and qualities to value and offer, conditions for openness and listening, as requirements for creating new thinking and perspectives. The other side of this coin is being 'against all pedagogy whose purpose is in some way to predict the result, which is a sort of predictor that pre-determines the result, and that becomes a sort of prison for the child and for the teacher, and for the human being' (page 181). Nothing could be further from much of today's early childhood research and policy that strives for certainty through the search for and application of technologies that will ensure predefined outcomes and exclude the possibility of being surprised and unsettled.

Second, there is a recognition that Reggio's idea of education requires a certain time, not only a certain quantity of time so as not to be 'time governed' but also a certain concept of time that is not 'the time of production'. Positivistic researchers may attempt to define what quantity of time spent by children in early childhood institutions produces the best normative educational outcomes; policy then can respond to this prescription inscribed with the idea of 'the time of production'. In Reggio, however, time is something else, a necessary element for creating relationships, an offering that the school gives: 'time to children, time to teachers, time for their being together. There has to be the possibility in schools, of any kind, the possibility in any group, to create connections but also to live differences and conflicts' (page 207).

Reggio: longing, hope, utopia, dream

Reggio is both an intensely local experience, an example of a community which has embarked on a long-term process of social experimentation, and a global phenomenon. Every year thousands visit the city to learn about its experience. Since 1981, the Reggio exhibition – 'The Hundred

Languages of Children' – has travelled the world, accompanied by speakers from Reggio: in this time, it has had well over a hundred showings in more than 20 countries. There are 'Reggio networks' in 13 countries, including Australia, the United States, Korea, the United Kingdom, Germany, the Netherlands and all five Nordic countries. Why this appeal? How can we understand this example of 'glocalisation', a local experience with global appeal? What of the future?

The appeal, in part at least, arises from the alterity of Reggio, and the provocation it offers. We think that the worldwide interest in Reggio reflects a reaction to the increasingly dominant discourse about early childhood education to which we have already referred. This discourse is inscribed with highly instrumental and calculative neo-liberal values and assumptions and managerial practices. It is a discourse that treats early childhood services as sites for applying 'human technologies' to produce pre-defined and normative outcomes, to better govern the child to serve as a redemptive agent who will save us from the uncertainties and inequalities of the world – a technical solution which will avoid us having to confront the political and ethical problems that are ruining our world and its peoples.

Reggio speaks to those of us who long for something else, another belonging. It gives comfort and hope by being different, by showing the possibility of different values, different relationships, different ways of living. For example, visitors to Reggio Emilia are usually coming home with a strong feeling that children, parents and politicians are really participators in the schools, that Reggio has managed to involve them and created an interest and participatory engagement. To create such an interest, pedagogical documentation has been a fantastic mediator and tool. In Reggio, they have managed to make children's schools important in a democratic context, something which counteracts apathy and disinterest, which often is the result of not being listened to and taken seriously – 'It does not matter what I do. The important questions are anyway decided by others.'

Reggio offers a sense of belonging to people longing for other values, relationships and ways of living. At the same time, it erodes, even in a small way, the confidence of the dominant discourse, its critical thinking putting a stutter in that discourse's arrogant narrative of necessity and absolute truth. By doing so it offers something very precious and in short supply today – hope.

For many, the future seems to be unimaginable, catastrophic or just depressing. There is an absence of utopian thought and energies that can guide us, give us something to strive for, and give occasional achievements.

Without an idea of the future which is neither a continuance of the present nor a catastrophe, politics is reduced to arguments about the best way to manage the status quo. Utopian thought, by contrast, both provokes and enables radical critique of what exists and it can give direction for future change through the exploration by imagination of new modes of human possibility that can help us to reinvent the future. It both deconstructs the present and reconstructs the future. It provides a provocation to politics and ethics through the act of thinking differently, and, hence, enables us to construct a new horizon of possibilities and new directions for future change.

However, utopian thinking is not enough by itself to bring about radical change. It needs spaces which enable thought to take place and a willingness to act, spaces where there is an openness to experimentation, research and continuous reflection, critique and argumentation – and to crossing boundaries. In this way, utopian thought and action can be in constant relationship and subject to revision in the light of experience, learning and dialogue. But these spaces do not need to be on a grand scale, they can be local.

For us, Reggio Emilia is a local place that is engaged in both utopian thought and action through a process that might be called 'a local cultural project of childhood'. But what has happened is that this local project has dispersed geographically and become a global network – it has constructed 'a new cultural geography', as Carlina has expressed it. This network is an opening towards the possibility of exploring new modes of human possibility.

In her dialogue with us at the end of the book, Carlina prefers to talk of Reggio as a dream rather than a utopia, 'because utopia is something very good but perfect, but dreams are something that you can have one night' (page 197). This is a warning against the danger of utopias becoming set in stone and uncontestable, with all the dangers of any 'final solution'. For us, there needs to be a constant relationship between utopian thought and action, which keeps utopian thought 'on its toes', subject to revision in the light of experience, learning and dialogue – utopia as a provisional dream perhaps.

Reggio is not a model, a programme, a 'best practice' or benchmark (not least if 'Reggio is an interpretation of Reggio'). The municipal schools and the work in them arise from a particular context, a particular history and particular political and ethical choices. Reggio's relationship to others, therefore, is not a commercial one of having an exportable product. It is, as we have outlined, a relationship of hope, a utopia or dream or both. It offers a sense of belonging and a standing provocation to those who look for different values and ways of thinking to those they find around them.

But Reggio is, in Carlina's words, 'a place of encounter and dialogue, and not only with Reggio but with many related protagonists. So Reggio makes room for people to dialogue, it provides an excuse to do this' (page 197) Through this dialoguing, it enables people to enter a learning process, a process of co-constructing their own knowledge, values and identity; a process that is in relationship with Reggio, but in which it is possible for the protagonists, those in dialogue with Reggio, to retain their 'otherness' without Reggio seeking to grasp them and make them into the same; a process, moreover, as the quotation that opens this chapter reminds us, which promises transformation and the risk (or possibility) of getting lost, losing control over where things go.

The question for us, which Carlina touches on in several places, for example in her discussion of curriculum, is whether some of those who enter into dialogue with Reggio may, unwittingly, attempt to grasp Reggio. By not working with the ethics of an encounter, by not listening, they may deny Reggio's alterity. They may make Reggio instead into something which they are able to know by applying to this singular experience their own concepts and their own systems of knowledge and values – 'oh yes, that's rather like we do only a bit better', 'what is the evidence of your outcomes?', 'what type of curriculum do you use?'.

There is growing awareness today about the need to maintain and increase bio-diversity, in the face of global trends that threaten our material environment to an unprecedented extent. In the same way, we need socio-cultural diversity, both as a value and out of self-interest to ensure our future. Reggio is an important example of that diversity, which needs protecting both from its enemies – the advocates of neo-liberal rationality and managerial practice – and from its friends, who may smother it with love. We also need more Reggios, not in the sense of Reggio clones, but of other communities which are prepared to embark on local cultural projects of childhood, to combine utopian thought and action, to dream about the future, to hope for a better world.

What follows?

The rest of the book gives voice to Carlina Rinaldi. Carlina has made a selection of her presentations from over the last 20 years – some writings, but mostly speeches. There are also three interviews, the third, at the end of the book, with the two of us, which Carlina insisted (in keeping with her perspective) on calling a dialogue. A few pieces have already been published in English, but most have not.

Selecting from her past work, Carlina says, has been rewarding but also sometimes difficult: 'because it is hard for me to re-read what I wrote without changing it, I often feel a sense of dissatisfaction and incompleteness' (personal communication). It seems to us as editors, however, that it is important to offer these documents unchanged, as traces of the past, since they offer insight into Carlina's thinking over a period of time, both the changes of emphasis and the continuities of themes and values. She has also written, especially for this book, introductions which offer the reader insight into the particular context of each article, speech or interview.

The reader should always remember that Carlina's voice is Italian. Some of the work that follows was originally presented by Carlina in English, the rest was translated into English. Either way, Carlina is working and thinking through the medium of the Italian language. In some cases, this presents particular issues of translation, since some words and terms do not transpose well from one language to another. But language and culture are closely connected and different cultures have some different ways of thinking about and conceptualising the world. The reader should perhaps be prepared on occasion to struggle with the unfamiliar and resist too ready an attempt to equate it with what is familiar.

In Dialogue with Reggio Emilia is the title of the book and dialogue is a relationship and value that runs, like Ariadne's thread, through the papers that follow, as it does through the pedagogical work in Reggio's municipal schools. We hope this book can give further inspiration for a wider and deeper dialogue with Reggio. A dialogue that can help to open up a process of transformation towards a new social, cultural and political landscape where we can find new possibilities for childhood and parenthood, education and schools, families and communities – and, as Carlina says, this is both a risk and a possibility.

Carlina Rinaldi

Writings, speeches and
interviews, 1984–2004

Chapter 1

Staying by the children's side

The knowledge of educators (1984)

This piece was written for the national conference of the *Gruppo Nazionale Nidi* which was held in Venice in 1984. For a better understanding of the reasons for this talk and the one that follows, but especially the themes they deal with such as relationships, communication and participation, it is necessary to take into consideration some contextual elements.

That year, 12 years had passed since approval of the national law 1044 promoting the funding and construction of *nidi* throughout Italy for children aged three months to three years. According to this law 2,500 *nidi* were to be built around the country within the first five years. Yet by 1984 only a few hundred centres had been built and nearly all of these were in central and northern parts of Italy.

So the law had not been applied and more and more obstacles were created by national governments, especially economic. Only some municipalities continued investing money from their own resources to make up for the State's lack of investment, and these municipalities were particularly aware of the importance of *nidi* because of their political orientation; most were in the regions of Emilia Romagna, Tuscany, Lombardy, Lazio and Veneto, and most were governed by the left at that time. The task they faced was both to extend network of *nidi* in particular and services in general (developing the welfare state) and at the same time to guarantee quality for the children, families and teachers. In order to support this search for quality and also to co-ordinate the political struggles which were emerging more and more among teachers working in *nidi*, the *Gruppo Nazionale Nidi* (now known as *Gruppo Nazionale Nidi Infanzia*) was started up in Reggio Emilia.

Amongst the aims then of the *Gruppo Nazionale Nidi* were the expansion of *nidi* and the consolidation of a concept which at that time was culturally innovative: the young child's right to quality schools. From a proposal by Loris Malaguzzi (*pedagogista* and fundamental inspirer of the pedagogy and experience of the municipal schools of Reggio Emilia), the *Gruppo Nazionale Nidi* promoted (and continues to promote) national conferences and local seminars for the professional development of teachers. These are times for exchange about experiences, sharing reflections and constructing awareness of cultural and political commitment by those working in early childhood services.

This was the background to the 1984 Conference, organised in collaboration with the Commune of Venice. The topic I chose was actually agreed on by Loris Malaguzzi and the organisers. The theme of participation and organisation in the *nidi* was particularly urgent and of interest at the time because it was extremely difficult in many places (and still is) to understand that family participation was not a choice but part of the identity of the *nido*, the children's right besides being the parents' right.

Defence of and expansion of services could only come about with family understanding, solidarity and support, achieved by parents coming to the *nido* not to be instructed and educated on parenthood but to bring their parental knowledge. They would then see the *nido* as a place where value could be attributed to them and they could attribute value to childhood as a social and cultural heritage.

Forging the educational project in the community

Twelve years after law 1044 was passed and having got as far as the 5th Conference of the *Gruppo Nazionale Nidi*, in which we have often discussed (as we have in other venues and on other occasions) the significance and the role of parents within the *Nido* experience, I will start by recalling all the things we have accomplished, at least at the theoretical level, and consolidated together. In the second part, I will look beyond the consolidation of what we have already accomplished and try to understand more fully and define more accurately our thoughts and actions, so that we can identify and pursue the areas for future advance, thereby gaining collective impetus and achieving new targets, though being aware of the fact that new ideas (and the participation of families in the management of education institutions is something new) always require substantial amounts of time to become established in our country, particularly when they introduce new cultural and political processes.

The accomplishments which I think it is important to recall (for a 'historical' – group – memory that allows us to advance our level of reflection) are as follows:

(1) This is the century in which the quality of the parent–children relationship has emerged for the first time as a theoretical proposition (though tampered with, in practice), and as a public topic and issue, i.e. of a social and cultural nature. More particularly, it

is the first time that a public education institution (i.e. the *nido*) has sought the *active, direct and explicit participation of parents* in the formulation of the educational project. [*Added by CR when editing the book:* usually parents are expected to delegate responsibility to the teachers and rarely discuss choices which have been made for fear their children may be made to pay for questioning teachers' decisions. For us, this was to be avoided at all costs.]

(2)   Therefore, over and above the frequent accusations of its limitations and ambiguities which do require urgent change, law 1044 represents a very advanced step even today, at least as far as participation and social management are concerned. It is advanced because it sanctions a public institution for the *healthy child* (not only the handicapped or sick child), and because of the definition and recognition it gives to the municipality as the managing body of socio-educational institutions. But most of all, it is advanced because it underlines the centrality of the *nido* not only in the relationship between educator and child but also in the interaction between family environment and *nido* environment. It does so not through illusory simplifications of theories of educational continuity, but by highlighting instead the dialogic nature and permanent dialectic quality of the relationship. [*Added by CR when editing the book:* here I am underlining, for the *nido*, the centrality placed not only on the relationship between child and teacher but on the relationship between the child, teachers and parents. The meaning of the *nido* lies in the interaction between these subjects, in encouraging these relationships. The *nido* is a place of relationships and communication, a place where a way or culture of teaching is constructed.]

(3)   The *nido* is therefore *a communication system that is integrated in the wider social system*: a system of communication, of socialisation, of personalisation [*Added by CR when editing the book:* I mean valuing the subjectivity of each person, child and adult], of interactions in which there are three main interested subjects affected by the educational project, i.e. the child, the educator and the family. These three subjects are inseparable and integrated; in order to fulfil its main task, the *nido* needs to be concerned and deal with the well-being of staff and of parents as well as with that of the children. The system of relations is so integrated that the well-being or malaise of one of the three protagonists is not only correlated but interdependent with that of the other two.

(4)   This well-being is closely associated with the quantity and quality of: (a) the communication that takes place between the parties, (b) the

knowledge and awareness which the parties have of their mutual needs and satisfaction, and (c) the opportunities for meeting and getting together which arise in a system of permanent relations.

(5)

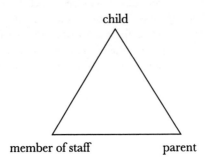

The identity of the *nido* therefore hinges on this system of relations-communications in which the active participation of the parents (both social participation and management) is considered an integral part of the educational experience.

(6) As we have often stated, if all this is to go beyond the purely conceptual and abstract, there needs to be a strong commitment at the organisational level – which is itself subject to constant appraisal and adjustment – and at the functional, methodological and political level. Everything else develops automatically from this, e.g. the architecture of the *nido* (the spaces and furniture), the methods and timeframes of communication, the working hours of the staff, the concept of collegiality and educational freedom, and the meaning and contents of professional development. From exchange and dialogue with families, new concepts emerge which define the very idea of participation and of the *nido*. [*Added by CR when editing the book:* a participatory *nido* is a school where one learns to listen, where the competencies of each person (child and adult) can be expressed and find appreciation, where *progettazione* is preferred to *programmazione* [see discussion of these terms on page xi], where the concept of democracy is not based on who has the majority but on the construction of consent, of agreed meaning, of mutual consent.]

(7) Finally, it seems to have been accepted that these processes of relations-communication, particularly between staff–parents–local community, need organisation, conceived and implemented with the same flexibility as well as with the same skill and commitment

required by the kinds of relations-communications and interactions we have with the children.

These theoretical assumptions, which have been developed, discussed, compared and enriched over the years, have become the convictions of many, but the customary practice and action of few. The reason is both because of the conceptual and cultural complexity of these propositions (since they break down and overturn beliefs and attitudes that are quite widespread and widely shared); but also because of a series of events and phenomena of a political, economic, cultural and social nature which have hindered their practicability to the point of raising doubts on their validity.

I will mention only a few of these events/phenomena which have characterised this century:

- a distinguishing feature of the historical moment in which we are living is change, movement, and becoming. In Italy this has given rise to a large-scale and profound transformation of an economic and technological–social–institutional–moral nature and with a political dimension. This, in turn, has produced numerous and sometimes dramatic problems, the management of which has turned the attention of political forces away from the problems of education in general and of school in particular (where reforms have never been completed). As a whole, schools in Italy are seriously behind in comparison to other countries in responding to changes and new requirements and are undergoing a painstaking process in their search for a new role and a new identity;

- the policy of the welfare state has been massively attacked on many occasions in words and deeds (economic), as has, on the whole, the policy of decentralisation and participation, with criticisms that are sometimes well-founded but also with prejudiced criticisms. This has caused a reaffirmation of the centrality of power and a rejection of every form of decentralisation. In practice this has led to a serious weakening of services both at the economic level and at the cultural, social and political level;

- all those many organisations which talk of participation, but do not make it possible for the real actors to act and decide by taking on responsibility, are going through a period of crisis. At times, there has been too much emphasis on participation but without a sufficient focus on its contents and on the participation processes, whose key players have not been properly analysed and have often been sacrificed between the quest for consensus and centralising trends.

Nidi (and *scuole dell'infanzia*) – though not in all cases – may actually be one of the rare exceptions where an attempt has been made to apply concretely the concept of participation as a way of forging, promoting and organising the educational project.

It should not be forgotten, however, that participation (meant not only in terms of the staff–parent relationship but also in its more extended form that creates a real network of relations that includes staff–parents, parent–parent, staff–children and parent–children relationships as well as the children–staff–parents–local community organisation–local administration relationship, etc.) is not an independent variable or an optional choice which may or may not be adopted. As we stated at the beginning, it is an expression of important values, it belongs physiologically to the concept of the *nido*, it is biologically innate to the very age of these children and it is decisive for affirming the educational concept of the *nido* (and not only the *nido*). This is why the *nido* cannot merely complain about falling participation and it cannot afford to renounce participation, particularly the dialogue with families, with parents and with the community: its very existence and survival would be undermined.

It is, therefore, not just a question of reiterating forcefully the basic accomplishments we were referring to earlier, reaffirming their validity and effectiveness at the cultural and political level. We need to take them forward as we have perhaps never done before through an analysis of facts, methods and actions. While we are perfectly aware that today everything is more complex than it was in the past – or perhaps just different – and requires greater intelligence and new interpretative frameworks, safeguarding and practising participation (we will clarify this concept later) means safeguarding the survival of the *nido* itself. It means reappraising and re-establishing the role and meaning of the *nido* in a society which, at least on the surface, would appear to be no longer interested in the *nido*. It means bringing the *nido* to the attention of politicians, administrators, movements and associations, trade unions and citizens.

We need a better interpretation of the facts, events and context that surround us. We have to analyse and understand the new subjects of the *nido* (parents–staff–children), who are still the same but, in truth, are always so different, depending on each situation. We need to avoid generic statements, slogans, words which are too all-embracing (such as 'family needs', 'fostering relationships', 'communicating', and so on) and make an effort to conjugate them and grasp their many facets. It means understanding new (and old) needs in order to construct new answers, though fully aware that there is nothing final about them. It takes a major effort to do all this, but it must be attempted. I will begin to do so by relying not only on my own reflections but also on those of my colleagues in Reggio Emilia who are engaged in this permanent search. This, together with your contributions, should help us to leave this meeting not only equipped with more knowledge, considerations and issues, but also with suggestions on strategies to think about and apply. It is important to understand not only the subjects but also their behaviour, the links that connect them, their ways of interacting, the fields in which they are situated and operate, the power which keeps them together and separates them, and their constant change and transformation.

The family and the social context

If we apply the type of thinking we should always adopt in order to gain a better understanding of the new phenomena which characterise modern families, we need to start out from a number of considerations regarding the context (the setting) in which this family lives and operates, i.e. society, and go on to examine some of the many aspects which appear to be interesting 'indicators' for our reflections.

Our society has often been defined as the 'fragmented society' because it has shifted toward situations and mechanisms which are so different and multidimensional that they have also suggested the term 'indistinct society', in which it is impossible to perceive important differences: for example, in terms of employment (millions of people entering and leaving the job market every year), the structure of groups and social classes (increasingly undifferentiated), consumer patterns (we hear of consumer polytheism), the use of time (recovery of night-time) and leisure time, and the management of power.

One other term which may help us define the character of our time is the 'segmentation society', i.e. an increasing differentiation between subjects according to the experiences which define and characterise them. This makes categories and generalisations increasingly difficult to apply, for every act of 'exchange' (whether communication-based or not) is not a simple matter. An increasing amount of time has to be spent on 'arbitration' exercises dealing with exchanges, particularly verbal exchanges. In the so-called age of communication, communication between individuals appears to be increasingly difficult.

The unavoidable consequence is the desire for self-determination and for the personalisation of one's individual experience in the social context, with respect to the selection of information, the choice of services, and the planning and use of leisure time. This has led to the great range of opportunities being offered by the market (especially the private market which has taken possession of and hugely magnified this desire) which should enable a good choice to be made. The public services (including the *nido*) are not excluded from this analysis; they must seek to avoid offering a standardised response which is insufficiently attentive to the particular needs and preferences of the individual.

The family has shown an extraordinary ability to withstand and adapt to such deep and rapid processes of social transformation and to practise organisational flexibility in response. Any other kind of generalisation, however, is impossible since today, more than ever before, we have to talk about families and no longer of the family, because of its increasingly varied and complex make-up. Here are some considerations that are helpful to understand the complex geography of the family:

- household diversity: there are increasing numbers of one person households (young or old); of 'post-nuclear families', with a household consisting of one parent plus the child (following separation or divorce); households where adult children live together with middle-aged parents (especially due to housing difficulties);
- new poverties: found particularly in large cities in Italy, as well as in some other areas, differentiated according to causes (immigration, unemployment, etc.) and type of need, and which cause members of these families to express deep psychological and existential malaise which can sometimes be interpreted by others superficially and with preconceived ideas (e.g. 'neglectful parents', etc.);
- grandparents: to interpret their role in the economy and the management of the modern family and society, we need to abandon the traditional stereotypes which would have them be 'sweet little old ladies and shaky old men', and recognise some of the phenomena that are occurring, particularly in the Centre–North of Italy and the cities. There are many younger or more youthful grandparents, most of whom work or else do occasional jobs after retirement, and who travel and move about more. While adoring their grandchild, these grandparents maintain their economic and, where possible, physical independence; though willing to help out their own children, they also have their own interests and commitments which they want to pursue.

There are many other relevant phenomena and differences depending on whether we are talking about, for example, a young couple or a marriage that has lasted for some time; the North, the Centre or the South; the town, the country or the large city.

But focussing more closely on the problem and without making simplistic generalisations, we can identify (based on official statistical data), particularly in the Centre–North, a more-or-less typical profile for a family with a child attending the *nido*:

- higher level of parental education;
- parents are no longer very young, both generally have a job of a professional nature and both participate in the home with a high degree of collaboration and integration although there is still some differentiation;
- a period of consolidation before parenthood in which the couple establishes its relationship;
- the first child is often 'planned' and increasingly an only child. [*Editors' note*: for some time, Italy has had one of the lowest fertility rates in Europe, and indeed the world. In 2000, it had the second lowest rate in the then 15 member states of the European Union (Eurostat, 2003: 180).]

The arrival of the first child and parenthood causes yet more change, in the sense that this new family member not only changes the existing method of communication and lifestyle – because it attracts the focus onto him/herself, 'triangulating' (if we can use the term) the family – but also forces changes (and/or sacrifices) to their previous lives and relationships. The new-born child proposes and imposes a substantial modification of the family system and of its members. It is certainly not an easy matter and not everyone is successful.

Often, instead of improving the relationship of couples that have been experiencing a crisis (as we used to say), the advent of the child makes the crisis worse. We see couples who, at least in the first few years after their child is born, talk of their great loneliness and of their desire to meet others: because of loneliness, the need for interactive communication, a need to find out how to deal with a child who is so 'unknown', at least at the beginning, and for whom one wants the best and fears one's inability to provide the necessary care. Loneliness and insecurity can pervade not only the young couple we have tried to describe but many parents in general and many mothers in particular.

We will briefly look at how much easier it is today to combine being a mother with being a worker, but also at how much there still is to do to ensure that what has been achieved so far is not dispersed and wasted due to, among other things, the serious economic situation which causes women to return to the home. This is a cultural and political issue which we should be deeply concerned about because the *nido* has contributed much to this new image and quality of life that women enjoy, and these improvements may be put at risk if this slow but inexorable process of transformation should slow down even more, or worse, be interrupted. Here, all we need is to recall the extent to which work has given women a degree of power they have never had before, allowing them to experience motherhood and their relationship with their partners in ways that are innovative, both historically and culturally. They have experienced more self-realisation and fulfilment and felt more able to sustain a relationship of equality with other family members.

But at the same time, they have had to cope with strong and often conflicting demands, and with a deep sense of unease and feelings of guilt. They fear that as a result of their work, their children may be neglected, go adrift and be exposed to serious dangers. The people who work with these children cannot neglect these basic psychological aspects. The working woman needs to be reassured that in the *nido* we are able to satisfy quantitatively and qualitatively the needs of her child, and that the staff can be like her – but not too much like her, as she may then fear she is being substituted in her child's affections (a very big cultural, behavioural, and psychological issue to tackle).

Analysing and interpreting the phenomenology of families with a young child would be a huge and interesting exercise. However, we will simply invite everyone, including staff, administrators and politicians, to analyse the issue in depth, to give themselves tools to find data and experiences and to begin to understand what it means to be parents today. Or rather, what it means to be a father and to be a mother, which is different; to be the working father and the working mother of a young child; to be father, mother, man and woman in a society we have defined as the society of fragmentation, typified by the need for self-certification (i.e. where each person certifies his or her own authenticity) and the right to the greatest fulfilment.

There is a demand or a need to be understood in a holistic way, that is to be considered as a person as well as the parent of, so-and-so's father or so-and-so's mother. Being a parent today implies, in addition to a very high emotional investment, also a broader range of responsibilities, linked to a widespread awareness of educational issues and problems. It requires an environment of real socialisation, civil co-responsibility and social solidarity. What parents especially don't need is to be subjected to judgments and particularly pre-judgments. [*Translator's note*: a play on words, as in Italian the word *pre-judgment* actually means *prejudice*.]

In my view, there is no such thing as a good or bad parent, there are just different ways of being a parent, though we may not always be able to understand or interpret them. Because a parent asks every day what the child did at the *nido* and who s/he played with does not always guarantee that this person is a better parent than another who, in two years, may never have gone beyond asking if the child ate his/her meals and had a bowel movement. All that this allows us to conclude is that our relationship with the first parent is closer than that with the second, but no more than that. Our assessment cannot go beyond this because it does not have the tools to do so. On the other hand, we must remember that it is possible to be an excellent teacher and a terrible parent, or rather, that someone can just 'pass' as a parent of a one- or two-year-old child and be an excellent parent of the same child once the latter becomes an adolescent (due, for example, to changes in the same parent as a result of events that involve him/her at the personal level, such as his/her job or relationship with his/her partner). Parenthood is not a state of being but of becoming. The same, it should be added, is true for being an educator.

So we should avoid stereotypes and superficial, immediate judgements which risk undermining for good our relationship with that parent and therefore with that child. It is in fact doubly dangerous to linger on these 'pre-judgments', because often the quality of the contact with the parent and the image we have formed as a result, sometimes projects itself on the child in a 'sinister' way. We should avoid 'measuring the quality' of the parent on the basis of our expectations and of how we would like the parent to be, which is often how we would like to be ourselves as parents or how we would like our own parents to have been with us.

We stated earlier that on average, parents today have a broader cultural level than past parents. This has probably sharpened their sensibility to and knowledge of the skills needed to educate a child on the one hand, but on the other, it has made the parent more aware of his/her deficiencies in 'being with the child', or rather, in educating the child. This has given parents a 'predisposition' to dialogue and a 'need' for communicating and exchanging views with different people. In addition, the degree of social and human fragmentation and disintegration that characterise our existence have led to the emergence of another need, or rather to the quest for a new pleasure, that of getting together and being together as people, almost beyond the child.

To sum up, there is no such thing as *the* parent. There are parents, or rather, people who are also parents who should be credited with having an educational sensibility toward and concern about the child, albeit sometimes unexpressed or which we may be unable to see. We need to learn to see the parents' explicit and implicit needs and respond to them with new and effective answers.

The staff

At this point, as we are talking about the relationship between educators and parents, we cannot avoid talking about the staff, albeit briefly, and of the new (and old) phenomena that characterise them.

Educators, overwhelmingly women, often parents themselves and consequently subject to the issues we were referring to above, are of different ages, though mostly young, and hold a variety of educational qualifications. There has been an increase in the number of educators who are university students, who will eventually contribute to an increase in the number of 'dissatisfied' graduates. Often, in these cases, there is a rising sense of frustration among teachers due to a lack of job opportunities in middle and high schools, which forces them to find work at the *nido* level (sometimes even as auxiliary staff). All in all, *nido* educators experience a professional life which is one of the most composite, complex and interesting, but also loaded with ambiguities at different levels, including:

- *political-administrative ambiguity.* The definition of the *nido* as a service based on individual demand, making *nidi* similar, in this respect, to slaughter-houses and funeral services [*Added by CR when editing the book*: in Italy, to define a service in statute as being based on 'individual demand' means that it is conceptualised as being only for those who need it, as opposed to being defined as a social service, which is conceptualised as an investment for the whole of society. One consequence is that the cost is paid by users, which is therefore likely to be high and to discourage use of the service. By so conceptualising the *nido*, years of achievements and social progress have been undermined]; the issue of the professional status of *nidi* staff who are assumed not to need a very advanced level of education; a system that allows no substitute staff, so implying that staff absence is not viewed as a serious matter; the fact that staff may or may not have a professional development programme and that they may or may not participate in management councils: none of these have been helpful to *nidi* staff who are all too often left on their own by politicians, administrators, trade unions to define their professional profile, their professional typology and their professional ethics, for a complex profession that needs strong solidarity and large resources;

- *socio-cultural ambiguity*. Despite the humiliations and tribulations to which *nidi* have been subjected in the past, the role they have played in Italy at the socio-cultural level indicates a very positive overall balance sheet thanks to the impression they have made on social customs, culture, social service work and research. Often, however, *nidi* staff are not able to see and appreciate their socio-cultural contribution as they frequently work in isolated and individual situations, without the means to evaluate the quality and effectiveness of their work and guide it in the areas where research indicates there are important gaps, and without being encouraged to undertake their own research. The indications of what they achieve are often subtle and to be found in the children's progress, the affection they show, and/or from what the parents say. But the educator is not always able to grasp these signs and testimonies and, therefore, may not be aware of what they have achieved and of how their work is appreciated by the parents. Too seldom is the work of the *nido* connected with the broader community and with parents who do not use the service but whose needs are in many ways similar to those of the families whose children do attend the *nido*. The benefit of the *nido* – its cultural development – is all too often reserved for the few;

- *psychological–professional ambiguity*. The overlap between maternal and home-based work at times runs the risk that the boundaries between *nido* and home can become unclear, with professionalism negatively affected. Furthermore, the cultural activities pursued by some educators (as they are young) find no space or echo within the *nido*. *Nido* educators can thus feel that their professionalism is doubly stunted, i.e.

  - *with respect to the children*, since their education has taught them to use verbal language as the only language that can be used with children, when children, on the contrary, have the use of a great variety of non-verbal languages;

  - *with respect to the parents*, where the lack of basic professional training in this key aspect of their work becomes increasingly obvious, i.e. the low level of skills for dialogue and intercommunication not just with colleagues but particularly with parents, with whom collaboration is essential.

It is therefore necessary to reaffirm that the skills and knowledge of the staff member should be regarded as a process, not a fact. They become enriched through the collegial work carried out with the children, colleagues and parents; and members of staff become more qualified by means of participation processes. Indeed, I believe the following is a fundamental concept: the staff member is not only a 'manager' but also a beneficiary of participation and management. S/he is not 'the person who knows' addressing 'the people who don't know' (the parents) but a person who proposes, lets her/his skill as an educator and a person circulate through the system and compares it with the knowledge of the parents. The knowledge of the *nido*, therefore, is not the knowledge of the staff, nor that of the parents or of the children: it emerges from the osmosis of their different types of knowledge and, in turn, is shared and compared with that of the broader culture outside the *nido*.

The educator–parent (or rather, educators–parents) relationship is a highly dynamic relationship, which has to differentiate and modify itself according to each situation and its participants precisely because of the broad range of needs and possibilities of each individual. It therefore has to vary according to family profile, the socio-cultural context as well as the amount of time a child and her/his family spend at the *nido*. The kind and style of involvement displayed by a parent when the child first attends *nido* will be different from those displayed after months of attending. The interview we hold with a parent who is rarely at the *nido* will be structured and organised differently from that which we hold regularly with parents who take their child to the *nido* every morning.

But that's not enough, we also need the following:

(1) to reflect more and better on communication, to understand all the information we often receive, without necessarily being aware of it, from the person we talk to, whether adult or child, and to be able to control as much as possible all the messages that we in turn convey, through our gestures, smiles and looks;

(2) consequently, to understand that communication with families requires new contents, new tools and new methods:

(a) *new contents*, i.e. focussing not so much on the child being a child but on her/his advancement, processes and ways of tackling problems. The contents should not only make us feel satisfied but also troubled, surprised, and amazed by the constant discovery of the child's extraordinary abilities. These contents should exclude nothing and should not be restricted to what the parents want to hear about their child. At the end of a meeting, whether an individual or group meeting, these contents should help us understand children better and bring problems rather than certainties to the surface, focussing on processes rather than products, interpreted jointly by adults who, in addition to educating, are in turn being 'educated' by the child. These contents should help us interpret the essential contributions that the child makes (and can make, if we listen to him/her) to our educational project;

(b) *new tools*. Obviously, the contents and encounters we have defined above need different languages and instruments. Images and traces (photos, slides, films and, where possible, videos) should support (together with the children's products/marks), and even replace, verbal language wherever they are more effective. These images and traces should not be confined to meetings but also be displayed on the walls of the *nido* every day – not only for the parents but for the children themselves who can gain pleasure from seeing and recognising themselves in those images and traces, and whose value is acknowledged by the fact that adults have displayed them. There are also other tools, such as panels that gather together ordinary and extra-ordinary information [*Added by CR when editing the book:* I mean exhibiting on the walls projects and other work with the children], or duplicated standard forms filled in with necessary information (has the child eaten, slept and so on) that allow the parents to shift the focus of communication onto other topics if they wish to;

(c) *new methods*. It is essential to break old organisational patterns in order to identify new ways to meet together that can represent parents, staff and the children in different ways. There should be a 'spectrum of opportunities' to meet, relate and dialogue together in a way that is necessary but also pleasurable and enriching. Class meetings as traditionally conceived, where the staff member talks and is listened to, and scheduled to take place at preset times, can no longer be the *nido's* proposal to these new users, both parents and staff, who are so multi-media orientated and differentiated, as we have said so many times before. We cannot address them as parents by using methods which are so alien and abnormal in comparison to the broader cultural contexts in which they move as people.

What we particularly need to understand as members of staff is that the relationship with families provides enormous advantages in terms of the professional enrichment it can yield, the enhanced confidence and as a way of overcoming the loneliness, frustration and disorientation that sometimes make our job more difficult.

It seems obvious to me that this participation, this way of parents and educators being in the *nido* experience, substantially transforms the 'image' of the *nido* and the 'way of being' at the *nido*. Everything changes: the way spaces are structured, the way furniture is conceived, but particularly the way of being and doing things with children, which is enriched by the knowledge construction, reflection, and images produced within such a wide-ranging interactive communication. What particularly changes is the children's way of being at the *nido*, the feeling of security, pleasure and well-being, in addition to the greater and richer stimuli they receive. Participation (the sharing and co-responsibility of families in the 'construction' and 'management' of the *nido*) is vital for the child as well as for the *nido* itself because the child needs, almost physiologically, to live in a network of communications to relate to and benefit from. All this is fundamentally and vitally important.

We must not forget, however, that there is a degree of resistance to this sort of project being implemented:

(1) on the part of staff arising from:
    –   *lack of self-confidence*, at times derived from low self-esteem, and at other times from an awareness of the high professional level required by this sort of exercise. A high level of parent communication may lead the educator to close up, reducing exchanges which s/he perceives as a judgment on the part of the families. By contrast, a low level of parent communication, or one that stops at matters of daily routine, may lead the educator to give up trying to shift the dialogue to other topics;
    –   *difficulties with*, or a priori rejection of, working schedules that are not always convenient to one's personal life but which certainly make life easier for the families;
    –   *management behaviour* which fails to perceive sufficiently clearly the identity of the *nido* educator, for example comparing her to a primary school teacher or, more often, to a cleaning worker because being with young children is considered to be easy and not to require great effort or preparation – just common sense and being a woman.

(2) on the part of parents arising from:

- *'organisational' difficulties.* At times it can be difficult to find someone to leave the child with when they wish to participate at meetings, particularly when both parents wish to attend;
- *political-cultural attitudes.* In quite a number of cases we detect an underlying attitude of mistrust regarding the importance of participation, sometimes due to previous experiences or sometimes due to views passed on by others, but particularly due to a suspicion that it will not make any difference;
- *psychological difficulties.* It is not easy to share and publicise the fragments of one's own history, personal problems and beliefs which it is necessary to share for this kind of relationship to be effective. People are still not used to dialogue and sometimes fear the judgment of others.

(3) on the part of administrators and trade unions arising from:
- failure or resistance to understanding that theoretical concepts (such as decentralisation and participation) require practical action, and that it is not possible to act on one aspect or subject of the *nido* without involving and changing the other subjects. The *nido* is not separable: each action, whether performed or not, has repercussions on the whole *nido* as well as on other sectors of the municipal administration;
- distancing themselves from the *nido* and from issues related to it because of their complexities and the need for bold position-taking and decision-making;
- delay in understanding the great opportunity which the *nido* has represented and still more, represents today, i.e. a new way of making a political culture, and re-asserting the significance of the local authority.

These and other forms of resistance based on different reasons have to be overcome, acting with the utmost coherence and promptness. We need some basic choices to be made by administrators, trade unions and staff concerning the organisation and planning of the contents of participation and management, including:

- the greatest possible stability for educators;
- continuity of relationship between staff, the group of children and parents in the three-year period that children attend the *nido*;
- no introduction of new members and changes to the children's groups in the course of the entire school-year;

- recognised and dedicated times for developing the relationship with parents and for holding professional development sessions;
- meeting times that are convenient not only to staff but also to parents;
- tools to document, write, copy and display, some of which to be allocated to the *nido*, others to the administration offices;
- spaces to meet, to gather materials, and to keep archives for a group memory and a history of the *nido*.

Real participation

Given these conditions, it will be possible to interact and communicate with families in a new, real way, through:

- meetings with families who have applied for a place at the *nido* to discuss selection criteria (if there is excess demand);
- the June meeting with all the families of the children starting in September to visit the *nido*, and get to know the teachers and other parents, through an initial exchange of information;
- interviews conducted with sensitivity and discretion by the educators and preferably with both parents, at the *nido* or the family's home before the children start attending;
- interviews held a few days before children start attending to discuss and clarify matters, to inform parents and set their minds at rest, and agreeing a range of strategies and methods that will guide the behaviour of the adults (staff and parents) in the very first days of the child's attendance at the *nido*;
- parents staying at the *nido* during the initial settling-in period. This will have to be agreed, jointly managed and personalised for each child and family taking into account the needs of the three participants, i.e. the children, their families and the staff;
- the group or class meeting with a priority focus on the group profile, the proposals for pedagogical work, and the presentation of teaching methods (with images and small exhibits). The meeting will take place in the evening at the most convenient time for all the families, by joint prior agreement;
- the meeting between a group of parents and staff who are interested in discussing a particular topic (e.g. the father's role with an infant), which can be called by various members of staff or parents of children in any class group. The topic is analysed and tackled with everyone's contribution with a very close alternation of communica-

tion and listening. A variation is the 'in-depth study group', involving meeting over several evenings;

- the individual interview, at the request of parents or staff, to tackle specific topics relevant to the child and family concerned, or to provide an opportunity for a more substantial and closer dialogue on the development of the personality of that particular child;

- open meetings with 'experts', self-managed meetings and working sessions and so on; [*Added by CR when editing the book:* 'self-managed meetings' are meetings of parents who decide the theme and conduct the meeting, although the teacher is also invited. 'Working sessions' are working evenings where parents and teachers (but also grandparents, aunts and uncles, friends) work together on a project (often a piece of furnishing or an area in the *nido*) for which a need has been identified.]

- the 'workshops' in which we learn how to do things with, for example, colours, paper, puppets, shadow sheet and camera. The 'evenings in the kitchen' are another typical example of this, when the cook, together with new children and their parents, prepares the dishes that appear on the *nido* menu. Eating the dish together at the end is a moment of incredible exchange and communication;

- the parties for the whole *nido*, where everyone is invited and everyone actively participates, including children, parents, staff, grandparents and friends. The wider community is also involved in the planning and conduct of the event. Then there are other possibilities including the group party, a more intimate, personalised event based on the individual group of children and parents, when everyone brings something to eat or drink and a pleasant afternoon is spent together; or the grandparents' party, when grandparents and grandchildren have the *nido* all to themselves, playing together, where the youngest children can help their grandparents discover the *nido* and, in the end, even the most suspicious among them have to surrender;

- day-trips and country outings (where children, parents and staff spend a few days together at the seaside or in the hills, staying in hotels or hostels provided by local authorities), visits to the children's own homes, and days spent by the parents at the *nido* (by prior arrangement).

All in all, a real spectrum of opportunities and a 'web of relations' offered to *nido* users, grown-ups and children.

As far as the organisation is concerned, I would reiterate how organisation and planning is crucial for participation, too. This is precisely the goal of the management council, in which parents make up the majority. These councils promote and organise families' participation, establishing qualitatively and quantitatively significant relationships for those actively involved in the experience. The priority issues of council meetings should no longer be just fees or admissions, but the *nido* as a whole and as a system of communication. To be up to the task, the council needs to be able to structure and divide itself in such a way as to have exchanges with the broadest and most varied sections of the *nido* and its local community. It will therefore organise itself in working groups or committees (pedagogical committee, environmental committee, parties committee, and so on), organised either permanently or as an *ad hoc* response to particular needs, and will be coordinated by a secretariat made up of four or five members (staff and parents). [*Added by CR when editing the book:* management councils (*consiglio di gestione*) are made up of parents, teachers and citizens elected by other parents, teachers and citizens at public elections held every three years. The responsibility of councils is to promote participation by other families, assist teachers in decision making and realising projects, and develop relationships with the local area and with other *nidi* and *scuole dell'infanzia* in the city.]

These bodies and processes will need a great deal of respect and support, as well as the means to undertake investigations, for example into the user profile, how it changes from year to year, the needs, concerns and expectations of families, and their willingness to be involved. It will thus be possible to go on to identify the needs of the *nido*, of the children and the staff, the primary goals to pursue, and the ways and means and timeframes and people that will ensure that the decisions taken will result rapidly and efficiently in concrete action with the maximum pleasure and benefit for all concerned.

This way, the *nido* will be able to express its full potential without costing any more money, just an effort of the mind. It will also be able to be in dialogue with families whose children do not attend the *nido*. These families and children, who in some cases have not chosen the full *nido* option, may nevertheless benefit from some of the other opportunities offered by the *nido* such as festivals, working sessions, meetings with experts and all other initiatives to increase the involvement of families with the *nido*.

The *nido* could thus really become a strong cultural protagonist for all families and all citizens. It could open itself up to non-users on some occasions and interact with other local institutions, associations and groups, becoming emmeshed with its neighbourhood. It could contribute to the educational project and to the advancement of the culture not only of the *nido* but of childhood as a whole.

The great enemy which we must all fight is separation and isolation; the great value to be achieved is information and communication. A sort of communication, as we have said on many occasions, that is informative, formative and inclusive so that no-one is excluded from it and in which everyone is working together to find alternative solutions. A sort of communication that fully recognises and respects differences that are in turn regarded as nurturing the quality and quantity of communication. A sort of communication and a relationship (child–educator–parent–citizen) that are sought and enjoyed by their active participants, but whose primary beneficiary is always and above all else the child, who will be gaining the maximum advantage from this atmosphere of dialogue.

Chapter 2

Participation as communication (1984)

I think we can no longer talk about the *nido*, the family, social services and so on without 'historicising' these terms, i.e. without making any distinction in terms of time and space. '*Nido*' and 'family' mean different things depending on whether we are referring to the situation ten years ago or today, and if we are talking about the Centre, the North or the South of Italy. Both the families and the *nidi* are subjects–objects of change, in parallel with more general economic, cultural and political trends.

When thinking about and trying to interpret events and understand their causes, I think we should undertake studies that are not only longitudinal but also cross-cutting, in order to find relationships between facts and events, even the most seemingly unconnected ones. We would be making a serious mistake if, in order to understand an event and change our approach accordingly, we were to 'isolate' that event from the tight network of relations–connections in which it is situated, which it is influenced by and which, in turn, it influences. If we were to isolate the event from all that, we would be altering its very nature. We cannot talk about the *nido* and participation without setting both within the context of the organisation of spaces, timetables, pedagogical planning, staff working hours, professional development sessions, the ongoing political and cultural debate, and economic issues. More than a methodological proposition, this is a mindset, a different way of thinking from that which many of us are used to, as most of us are survivors from an education system where relations–connections were at best avoided, and at worst, actually forbidden. There was no relationship between what was happening outside school and what was going on inside, nor between what we were studying in history and the knowledge we were gaining in geography, and so on.

I think these clarifications are necessary. On the one hand, to respond to those who, on the basis of vague and superficial knowledge and considerations, would bundle everything together and judge from a generalised view of *nidi* in Italy. On the other hand, to introduce the concept of social management as an intense relationship and communication between the *nido* staff, the families of users and the management council.

Social management in the *nido* means the promotion and organisation of this relationship between families and staff, which is the objective starting point, but the relationship then needs to be consolidated through increasingly well-defined communication processes. Thus, communication becomes an item of the highest value, the end and the means, the strategy and the objective that involves staff, children, families, management council and the whole institution without distinction. To understand more fully the implications of this statement and its practical results, we need to analyse the subjects of communication, which include the following:

- *The family.* Starting from the assumption that it is risky to define any subject too strictly, there are a number of constant factors which appear to characterise families today. Families with a child under five are decreasing in number; the average age when men and women have their first child is increasing and children mostly remain only children. The average cultural level has increased, particularly women's, and women have emerged as the key protagonists of many of the changes that have occurred in the social and family context in recent years, although it is often women who have to pay the price for the contradictions that have gradually arisen.

  Of the many aspects we could mention, one of the most striking is the loneliness and isolation of many families with a young child. Loneliness, one of the most widespread diseases today, arises because having a young child often forces people to give up some of their old habits and friends. New parents don't know who to turn to to find out how to satisfy some of the needs of this young child who, at least in the early stages, is so 'unknown' (grandmothers are mostly not around and when they are they are not considered to have up-to-date knowledge, so the doctor or the next-door neighbour often become the only people available to provide advice and support). Furthermore, the birth of a child sometimes undermines the relationship between the couple. Parents, therefore, have a great desire to get together with others but in a new way.

- *The staff.* Mostly women and mothers, mostly belonging to a family such as the one described above. At the professional level, the problems of a very demanding job exacerbate the crisis of identity that teachers are experiencing today. Now more than ever before, teachers are aware that school and college do not generally provide adequate training for the work and that their real training begins after their formal education has ended. I believe that it is now absolutely necessary to have professional education as well as a job that is known and recognised, shared, public and participatory, and therefore significant.

- *The child.* Perhaps more than any other subject, the child feels the sense of insecurity and precariousness that characterises our current existence, and feels more than anyone else the need to be involved in a relationship, a supportive and communicative environment which, given his/her young age, is a vitally important factor of survival. [*Added by CR when editing the book:* I mean here physical survival first and foremost, but also the importance of good communication between the *nido* and the family, which is the only way to ensure a context that is aware of the child's identity, needs and wishes.] This means communication between adults, with adults, with peers, and with the spaces and furniture of the *nido*, in order to foster decisively the development of identity and self-confidence.

- *Management councils*, or more generally, participation. We have often talked about, and still do, the crisis in participation. The balance sheet of ten years of experience in participation and social management in the field of school education and elsewhere is certainly not very satisfactory. The causes of these disappointing results and the loss of faith in the process are manifold and varied. Not the least important among them are persistent and strong attacks on public administrations, the creeping conviction that participation processes cause sluggishness and overloading of the system, and the loss of faith in democratic institutions when it is discovered that they are by-passed or subverted by unaccountable groups working 'behind the scenes'. These elements are certainly important for understanding low levels of participation in *nidi*, wherever they occur. But they are insufficient.

There is probably something else, too, that is subtle but decisive. Too often, for example, the patterns of participation inside *nidi* follow slavishly those in *scuole dell'infanzia*, or worse, those set out in government decrees. Too often, internal imbalances among the management council participants (e.g. the overwhelming number of political representatives in relation to parent representatives, or the limited number of staff appointed to the council) have literally killed off any signs of development. I believe that in the *nido*, development and communication are almost physiological features and potentially present in every experience. However, to ensure that they do not fizzle out into a thousand rivulets or are not smothered at birth, they have to be animated with ideas and organised with tools and initiatives.

The strong and significant role of the management council in the *nido* seems to me to be to promote, foster and increase the participation and communication of the whole body of users, including parents, children, staff, citizens, administrators and politicians. This is why we do not accept the attitude of those who, when talking about participation in the *nido*, its quality and significance, are not aware that they are talking about the '*nido*' as a comprehensive and inclusive entity. We cannot analyse and criticise participation processes without analysing and criticising the overall performance of the *nido* as a whole. The family, the child, the staff member and social management acquire a value, a significance and a role that are quite different if we accept this founding principle as our starting point. Social management and participation are part of the educational process, they are an intrinsic feature of the culture and conduct of the *nido*.

The overall approach changes substantially if we see management – understood as social management – as a phenomenon that is seeping through the educational process, with the ability to sink deep into the soul and essence of school, not as some add-on or a worn-out ritual to conform to some formula or external requirement. Where social management permeates the *nido*, everything else structures itself accordingly:

- the architecture of the *nido* changes, as does the organisation of the spaces used by the children and adults, the furniture, the ways of communicating, and the verbal and written messages, which acquire a different role and significance;
- the timeframes change, particularly those of the staff and of the service;
- the meaning of professional education changes because professional development sessions have to re-establish the concept of participation within them.

There are no aspects, topics and sectors of participation, as opposed to aspects, topics and sectors of non-participation. In our view, the term 'participation' goes deep into and helps work out and reinterpret issues such as the professionalism of staff members, educational freedom, vocation in teaching, the role of the educator and the allocation of various rights and skills between the families and the professionals. In our opinion, however, its most important function is to redefine the concept of 'competence' which we often use in this context. [*Added by CR when editing the book:* 'educational freedom' above refers to the teacher's freedom to decide what is right to teach in a class and the ways in which she would like to teach. But very often the isolation of teachers has been legitimised in the name of 'educational freedom' – not sharing, being closed to dialogue with friends and colleagues. Along with the concept of 'teaching vocation', this has often led to a kind of basic sentiment for children ('I like children') being considered sufficient for teaching, avoiding any form of professional development. The motivation factor is certainly important, but the quality of the relationship with the child must be constructed through processes of professional development lasting across the teacher's entire working life.]

Competence and consensuality

'Competence' is a frequently recurring word. The generally accepted meaning of the term is the one that links it to the term 'professionalism'. We say: 'competence is the basis of professionalism', though we generally allude to a static quality that is acquired with an educational qualification once and for all. Some also claim that there can be 'difficulties with dialogue' within *nidi*, in cases where the *nido* becomes 'too competent' to be able to keep up the dialogue with and understand the needs of the families. This is almost equivalent to saying that a good *nido* would distance families from participation and dialogue.

The serious error, I believe, lies in the way the concept of competence is understood, and seeing it as antithetical to the term 'participation'. Competence is not a static term in this case, or a given. It is an approach, a willingness to work together, to have exchanges, to fine-tune our tools of knowledge acquisition; to be open to professionalism, cognitive progression, and to project design and planning. Competence is first and foremost an open process of professional development and self-development, of mutual enrichment, and a human willingness to work cooperatively and to take joint responsibility.

The participation project, as the project of communication that has gradually taken shape, also requires a precise definition of the following key factors: planning, organisation, focus and consensuality. These are necessary attributes that decisively influence the progress of social management. They should not be thought of as following any particular order of priority, as their highest form is achieved through their natural and permanent interaction.

The concept of 'consensuality' deserves to be elaborated further. We frequently talk about the majority and minority games that occur within councils, resulting in dangerous splits. But the life of the council and of participation and democracy within the *nido* cannot be a matter of minority or majority; it has to be one of common growth that occurs through the processes of common acquisition of knowledge and skills. There should be no solutions imposed by a majority, only solutions that emerge through a profitable dialogue of sharing and exchange, whose final result is the achievement of common development and construction.

Accordingly, the changed role of staff members in the *nido*, both educators and auxiliary workers, means that they are no longer just proposing the educational project or leading the social management but actually become beneficiaries of these experiences as well. The staff member should be the first to nurture the pleasure of participation, to draw meaning from meetings, and find the opportunity to qualify and enrich his/her professionalism through participation. Hence we cannot exclude part of the staff from social management and it is no longer viable to cater for social management time within the existing working hours.

To sum up, participation and management should be seen as a project that revolves around a broader educational project centred on communication. The project should have three main protagonists, i.e. the child, the family and the staff, whose destinies are closely linked. Our objective is their well-being, an overall well-being that involves everyone in an inter-connected way: if one of the parties is unwell, the well-being of the others is in jeopardy. This well-being is highly dependent on the quality of the communication between the parties, on the knowledge and awareness they have of their mutual needs and enjoyment, and the opportunities for encounter and gradual development that arise in an integrated system of communicative experiences. This system, while actively opposing any form of separation, guarantees the valuing and individuality of each person, formulating answers that fit individual needs for action and knowledge; and it avoids separation between family and institutional experience and the creation of hierarchies between individuals, functions and spaces, and any form of subordination between the *nido* and the family. This system also inhibits any possibility of separation between affective and cognitive aspects, and provides continuity between the children's problems and those of the families, the staff and society.

It will thus be necessary to find organisational approaches which, having communication as their goal, will sustain and give it value. To this extent, the class group will acquire a major role as the original and primary group for the encounters of children as well as adults. This is the basis for fostering families' communication not only with the educators but also with other parents.

Discovering aspects in common, the pleasure of talking and listening, finding that one actually knows more than one thought, that one is not a better or worse parent than others and that one is the active participant in a project: all these experiences should spark off the processes of growth and analysis which, by involving the local community and institutions, can make a real contribution to the consolidation of the culture of the *nido* and of the child, which is still so fragile in our country.

Chapter 3

Malaguzzi and the teachers (1996)

The year is 1996. Loris Malaguzzi, who in 1963 inspired the pedagogy of the first municipal school in Reggio Emilia and who would guide the experience from that moment on for nearly 30 years, had died two years previously. A sudden death, an enormous vacuum, arousing fear that we will lose the sense of the experience itself. I had worked with him side by side for 24 years. I had learned many things, but not how to do without him. They were hard months and years on a personal and on a professional level but we got through them thanks to our deep conviction that the knowledge, the things we had learned together in those years, was a living heritage, permanent research, an act of vitality expressed in the daily work done by each one of us. And the first, real authors of this continuity, of this vitality, were the teachers who had always been the first, fundamental inspirers and authors of Loris Malaguzzi's pedagogy and the Reggio experience.

These thoughts guided my decision when it came to preparing the paper for the conference held in Milan in February 1996. The title of the conference *Nostalgia del Futuro* (Nostalgia for the Future) was a concept dear to Malaguzzi to whom the conference was dedicated. The conference was organised by the Università Statale di Milano, and Professor Susanna Mantovani in particular both inspired and animated the conference. For many years, Susanna had not only been a convinced inspirer of our experience but above all a friend to Loris Malaguzzi. This friendship had been consolidated over the years, due in part to many shared experiences in the *Gruppo Nazionale Nidi* of which Loris was the president and Susanna vice-president. These were the reasons supporting Susanna's commitment in organising the conference, the first about Loris Malaguzzi following his death.

It was a very emotional and involving conference. There were speakers from Europe and the United States, all admirers of Loris and bound to him by sincere affection and admiration. I struggled to prepare my talk. Everything I wrote seemed banal or inadequate. But there was a need to talk about the role of the teachers in our experience and in schools in general; a need which had to do with intellectual honesty and gratitude but above all because on a

personal level I had learned so much from my dialogue with the teachers. In
fact I believe the profession of *pedagogista* can only be constructed through
constant exchange with teachers and then with children and their families.

I don't know how useful it may be for those who are listening, but
I wanted to say, first of all, how difficult it was for me to write this
speech. More than writing a speech, I had the impression of having to
reconstruct a piece of my life. I am sure that those who, like me, had
the great fortune of being able to share an experience with Professor
Malaguzzi for many years – and there are many of us – must feel unable
to do justice to the richness, the depth and the comprehensiveness of
his thought and, above all, of his shared experience. The 'partial' nature
of my speech is not so much a choice as a limitation – necessary and
understandable, but still not easy. Each time I am asked to write or talk
about Malaguzzi, I have the impression that I am leaving out something
important, that I will not be able to fully express the depth and breadth
of the experience we had whenever we confronted a problem with
Malaguzzi – even a modest problem.

So you might ask why am I telling you this, because one normally
doesn't – or perhaps shouldn't – talk about these things. Perhaps I should
not have written these things or said them, because they are so personal.
Yet I feel that I would not have been able to say or write anything
else, without having first made this declaration. I would not have managed to find the words to continue. Perhaps the emotion is too strong.
But the knowledge-building process (especially that which we had the
opportunity to share with Malaguzzi) is also an emotional process.

Now we can return to the topic of my speech: Malaguzzi and the
teachers, to which I would like to add a subtitle: 'Ariadne's thread'.
[*Editors' note*: in the classical myth, Ariadne, daughter of King Minos of
Crete, gave a thread to Theseus which enabled him to kill the Minotaur
(a bull–man to whom young Athenians were sacrificed each year) and
find his way back out of the labyrinth in which the Minotaur lived.] I
chose this mythological reference because it was the title that Malaguzzi
wanted to give to the book *The Hundred Languages of Children* [*Editors' note:*
Edwards, Gandini and Forman, 1993] when it was first going to be
published in the United States. 'Ariadne's Thread' is a metaphor for
the great and fundamental role played by the teacher – by teachers in
general and by the teachers in Reggio in particular; a metaphor for
the teacher's task of giving orientation, meaning and value to the experience of schools and children (a way out of the 'labyrinth'). Teachers
seen as those who hold the thread, who construct and constitute the

interweavings and connections, the web of relationships, to transform them into significant experiences of interaction and communication. It seemed to be difficult, however, to translate this title, to transfer it to the American culture, which is perhaps less familiar with the myth and thus with the metaphor, and this prevented the title of the book from emphasising the fundamental role that Malaguzzi attributed to the teacher, even though this idea becomes clear when reading many of the pages of the book written by Malaguzzi (and elsewhere as well).

The teacher's role is one of great protagonism and is inherently respected. This respect is related to the competence and intelligence with which the teacher is asked to carry out her role. The definition of the teacher's professional identity is thus not viewed in abstract terms, but in contexts, in relation to her colleagues, to the parents, and above all to the children, but also in relation to her own identity and her personal and educational background and experience.

Malaguzzi always asked us to start from the children in our attempt to reformulate an epistemology of both learning and teaching, and the roles of the teacher and learner in the educational process. He expressed his idea like this: 'We must give enormous credit to the potential and the power that children possess. We must be convinced that children, like us, have stronger powers than those we have been told about, powers which we all possess – us and children, stronger potential than we give them credit for. We must understand how, without even realising it, we make so little use of the energy potential within each of us.' Malaguzzi pointed out that the problem of school (and beyond) is above all related to a lack of awareness and the under-use of all the intelligences, abilities, skills and knowledge that we possess. The problem, then, is common to all of us – to children but also to adults, to teachers.

His criticism was that 'there is a sort of growing conviction, a tacit agreement which sanctions the idea that each adult figure in the school is perfectly free to live her individual personal life, without necessarily being mixed with, bound to, or in collaboration with her colleagues – leaving us with teachers who are unable to plan and work collectively.' For this reason, in Malaguzzi's words, we need to 'get out from under this big blanket of conformism and passivity, and re-discover the desire to think and plan and work together.' He also added that

Perhaps we are not fully aware of what *progettare* means, but we can be sure that if we take away the child's ability, possibility and joy in projecting and exploring, then the child dies. The child dies if we take away from him the joy of questioning, examining, and exploring. He dies if he does not sense that the adult is close enough to see how much strength, how much energy, how much intelligence, invention, capacity and creativity he possesses. The child wants to be seen, observed and applauded. [*Added by CR when editing the book*: these words of Malaguzzi and those quoted immediately above come from my notes of conversations with Malaguzzi.]

And when the child dies, the teacher dies as well, because the teacher's goal is the same as that of the children: to find meaning in her work and in her existence, to see value and significance in what she does, to escape from being indistinct and anonymous, to be able to see gratifying results from her work and her intelligence. The teacher cannot work without a sense of meaning, without being a protagonist. She cannot be merely an implementer – albeit intelligent – of projects and programmes decided and created by others for some 'other' child and for undefined contexts. The highest value and the deepest significance lie in this search for sense and meaning that are shared by adults and children (by teachers and students), though always in the full awareness of different identities and distinct roles.

In this marriage of intentions, in this common research (from which we derive the definition of adults and children as researchers), what is the role carried out by the teacher? How do we stay close to the child? Here lies one of the highest achievements of Malaguzzi's thought. The traditional relationship between theory and practice, which designates practice as consequent to theory, is redefined and, therefore, surpassed. Theory and practice are placed in a relationship of reciprocity, but one in which, to a certain extent, practice takes precedence over theory. Admitting this possible pre-eminence of action over logic could be upsetting, and could even lead to complete rejection, because we would seem to be renouncing rationality and the supremacy of theory, as well as our ability to predict.

Instead, we must consider that within an organisation (and the school is an organisation), logic becomes evident in our thought when we are able to create relations between actions that have already taken place. If, on the other hand, theoretical premises are assumed as conclusions, and if they 'reverberate' on the didactics, those who implement the educational project are not obliged to reflect, to think or to create. Excessive emphasis on the centrality of theory exempts teachers from being protagonists in the educational process, from pedagogical reflection and, indeed, from the overall responsibility of educating.

While we affirm the inseparability of theory and practice, we prefer an open theory which is nourished by practice made visible, contemplated, interpreted, and discussed using the documentation we produce. Documentation, then, does not mean a final report, a collection of documents, a portfolio that merely assists with memory, evaluation and archives: it is a procedure that sustains educational action (teaching) in the dialogue with the learning processes of the children. Documentation is a point of strength that makes the interweaving of actions of the adults and the children timely and visible, and improves the quality of communication and interaction. It is a process of reciprocal learning. Documentation makes it possible for teachers to sustain the children's learning, while at the same time the teacher learns (learns to teach) from the knowledge-building process of the children. For this reason, it is not enough just to observe, though the observation may be refined and aware. As we know that to observe means to interpret, we need to leave traces of our observation – interpretable traces.

So, to document means above all to leave traces, to create documents, written notes, observation charts, diaries and other narrative forms, but also recordings, photographs, slides and video, which are able to make visible the children's learning processes and ways of constructing knowledge (and thus also including the relational and emotional aspects), and these documents form the thematic nucleus for a competent observation. The documents we produce are partial findings, subjective interpretations which, in turn, must be re-interpreted and discussed with others, in particular among colleagues.

This creates one of the most important opportunities for professional training and growth, real training that derives from exchange, comparison of ideas, discussion and collegiality. It is here in these shared moments (which are not always easy because we are not accustomed to such constant discussion and putting ourselves on the line), that interpretive theories and hypotheses are generated which advance not only the knowledge of the group but also, if confirmed and supported, more general theories of reference (the relationship of theory to practice). And it is here, with this procedure, that the document and the event documented assume multiple meanings, creating the history and narration of the event as 'reasoned interpretation'. This is the origin of the slide documentaries, videos and books, as well as the written and photographic documentation that adorns the walls of our *nidi* and *scuole dell'infanzia*. These panels mounted on the walls become the focal point for intense daily communication, reflection, memory and interaction involving children, teachers and parents. They become real mirrors of our knowledge, in which we see our own ideas and images reflected, but in which we can also find other and different images with which to engage in dialogue.

This designates the school for young children as one of the most privileged places for the building of professional competence and knowledge that belongs not only to the teachers, but also to researchers, scholars and university professors. The school for young children is a place of enormous learning and great respect. Jerome Bruner said during one of his visit to our schools: 'I have the feeling, and I hope this won't embarrass my good friends, that when I am with the children at the Diana school or even for that matter at the Nido Arcobaleno with the very, very young children, that it is like a seminar at the graduate department of the university, with the same kind of respect, of exchange in talking about what you have just said, and about your former thinking.'

We are aware that the medium we choose for documenting the experience observed – in other words, for making it visible and 'sharable' – represents a partial perspective that can only be beneficial to the extent to which multiple documents of the same event are produced and/or multiple observers are involved using different media (for example, tape recordings, video and slides). Because this procedure enables discussion and the comparison of ideas, it permits us to analyse and to formulate hypotheses and predictions, and thus to consolidate our thinking. It is the basic support structure of our work. This visibility (documents and documentation as reasoned narrations) represents a fundamental support for the development of knowledge and the quality of relationships between the three protagonists of the educational experience: teachers, children and parents.

Documentation offers the teacher a unique opportunity to re-listen, re-see and re-visit ('re-cognition'), both individually and with others, the events and processes in which she was the co-protagonist, either directly or indirectly. This re-visiting gives us the opportunity to interpret the various documents produced, together with our colleagues, giving sense to the events that took place and thus creating common meanings and values. Moreover, as planning essentially involves making hypotheses and predicting the contexts, instruments, opportunities and relevance to the learning processes and to the desires of the children, then documentation is the heart, the uniqueness of each specific project. It is not always possible for us to document in such a comprehensive way, but when we can, documentation becomes a process of true creativity and growth for everyone involved. It is the true professional training of the teacher.

Documentation also offers children a valuable opportunity for re-visiting, reflection, interpretation and self-organisation of knowledge.

Documentation is a fundamental support for the self-evaluation and group evaluation of the theories and hypotheses of each child. It fosters the comparison and conflict of ideas, and thus argumentation in the philosophical sense. Documentation supports the memory, offering the child the opportunity to re-read her own process, to self-correct, to find confirmations and denials, and especially to make comparisons with the processes of the others. In the documentation, the child can see herself in a new light, comment on herself and hear others' comments – and this enables an important transformation in terms of the construction of knowledge and thus of identity.

Documentation provides an extraordinary opportunity for parents, as it gives them the possibility to know not only what their child is doing, but also the how and why, the meaning that the child gives to what he does, and the shared meanings with the other children. It is an opportunity for parents to see unknown aspects of their child, to see, in a certain sense, the 'invisible' child that parents are rarely able to see. But documentation also offers parents the value of comparison, discussion and exchange with other parents, and fosters growth in each parent's awareness of his or her own role and identity. Sharing the documentation means participation in a true act of democracy, sustaining the culture and visibility of childhood, both inside and outside the school: democratic participation, or 'participant democracy', that is a product of exchange and visibility. This is the same opportunity offered to us by the exhibition 'The Hundred Languages of Children' – an opportunity for exchange, reflection and discussion. This is one of the most extraordinary insights that emerged from Loris Malaguzzi's far-sightedness and visionary capacity.

So in this sense, the central position of documentation in the educational process of adults and children together takes us back to the primary role played by the educator (and with this term I mean both the teacher and the *atelierista*) in Malaguzzi's thought and work.

Malaguzzi never concealed the great expectations and hopes he had for the teachers. Those who knew him remember very well how he could also be exacting and demanding (though first of all with himself). But we also know that this was a tangible sign of the deep respect and gratitude he felt for teachers; respect for their intelligence, abilities and possibilities.

Malaguzzi always translated this respect into concrete gestures, shared battles, all-consuming passions and public manifestations, and all without compromising or renouncing his values. The fundamental role of the physical environment and of organisation in the educational system;

the right to permanent professional development, to collegiality, to participation; the importance of dialogue with the families: these were the great principles that Malaguzzi constantly sustained and asked us to sustain. The value of education, the will to overcome ambivalence (between education and instruction, between imagination and reality) and the awareness that teaching knowledge goes beyond pedagogical and psychological knowledge: these are the values that Malaguzzi always shared with the teachers, asking us to sustain them, act on them, and innovate them. Malaguzzi extended the same respect to the families and the children, about whom he was full of hope, faith and optimism. Full of the future.

I would like to conclude with an excerpt from a talk that Professor Malaguzzi gave to a foreign delegation visiting Reggio – one of the many, to which he always dedicated himself with great passion and commitment because, as he would say 'they are teachers'.

There is an extraordinary passage in the writings of Wittgenstein in which he recounts that he met a very young girl with whom he spoke extensively. One day, the girl approached him and said 'you know, I hope that . . .'. It was the first time that she had used the word 'hope' in their conversations, and Wittgenstein wrote that this experience troubled him for the rest of his life. Where lies the deep meaning of a child who says 'I hope . . .' for the first time? When is it that hope enters like a light into the life of a child, and why?

This is to say that the right to hope, and the right to the future, must always be the right of children and of adults, rights that all of us, the friends of Loris, are committed to defending together.

Chapter 4

Documentation and assessment

What is the relationship? (1995–8)

To fully understand the significance of this piece and the next ('Dialogues'), we need to go back to 1995, the year in which Howard Gardner proposed carrying out research together. At that time, Professor Howard Gardner was, among other things, the director of Project Zero, a research team at Harvard Graduate School of Education concerned with cognitive development and the process of learning. He was known throughout the world for the theory he had elaborated known as 'the theory of multiple intelligences', that is, a theory orienting research and schools towards considering the existence in children and adults of not one, but as its name says, several different intelligences (at least seven) (Gardner, 1985). It is a theory of great psychological, pedagogical and cultural importance which Malaguzzi and I came to know about thanks to a suggestion by Lella Gandini, who 'wove together' many of our relationships with eminent researchers and cultural figures in the United States. Gardner came to Reggio Emilia with his wife Ellen Winner to visit the municipal schools and illustrate his theory to Malaguzzi and an audience of educators from Reggio. A deep friendship was born of this encounter, based on mutual esteem and admiration which became richer with the passing years. Analogies and differences between the theories of the seven intelligences and the hundred languages made the dialogue enriching and inexhaustible.

This was probably one of the reasons persuading Howard Gardner to propose a common research project after Loris Malaguzzi's death. He left it to us, who were working in the Reggio schools at the time, and colleagues in Project Zero to define the subject. In order to do this Mara Krechevsky came to Reggio and after some meetings we agreed on a theme of great relevance for us (and for me in particular): the relationship between documentation and assessment/evaluation. In exploring this area of research, however, we realised that other themes were emerging, including individual learning and learning within and by learning groups and documentation of the documentor. More generally the centrality of the theme of documentation emerged. In this way a journey began which was of great interest for all the protagonists;

the Reggio schools (in particular the teachers and *pedagogistas* of the Diana and Villetta schools) and colleagues from Project Zero. The results of this research, which took place over three years, were published in a book titled *Making Learning Visible* (Giudici, Krechevsky and Rinaldi, 2001), where this paper and the next first appeared.

The book gathers together some of the most significant elements emerging from the research, among which I would like to mention:

- The value of documentation in process, i.e. during the process of learning-teaching enacted in the classroom. Documentation is therefore first and foremost an educational tool but also a great opportunity.
- The value of documentation as a tool for assessment/evaluation and self-assessment/self-valuation. This is why I was asked to write the piece which follows, where I think the advancement and enrichment deriving from the research itself can be felt. Certain considerations resulting from our dialogues go alongside the elements I have frequently used elsewhere to describe documentation.

'Dialogues' (*Dialoghi*) is in fact the title of the second piece, which describes the richness of the relationship with Project Zero, which was not easy but certainly gave results.

I hope it is also possible to see something of the strength of the contributions from Reggio teachers who, by documenting (i.e. acting through documentation), gave us not only their thoughts and reflections but also hypotheses and evidence which supported and backed up more general reflections. I underline this documentary value of the research because the topic currently seems to be of great interest, not only in my country but in many others. I feel that recognising documentation as a possible tool for assessment/evaluation gives us an extremely strong 'antibody' to a proliferation of assessment/evaluation tools which are more and more anonymous, decontextualised and only apparently objective and democratic.

The concept of documentation as a collection of documents used for demonstrating the truth of a fact or confirming a thesis is historically correlated to the birth and evolution of scientific thought and to a conceptualisation of knowledge as an objective and demonstrable entity. It is thus tied to a certain historical period and to profound reasons of a cultural, social and political nature that I will not examine here. Rather, I find it interesting to underscore how the concept of documentation, which has only recently moved into the scholastic environment, and more specifically into the pedagogical-didactic sphere, has undergone substantial modifications that partially alter its definition. In this context, documentation is interpreted and used for its value as a tool for recalling; that is, as a possibility for reflection.

The didactic itinerary and the learning path that take place in a school assume full meaning for the subjects involved (teachers and students) to the extent that these processes can be suitably recalled, re-examined, analysed and reconstructed. The educational path becomes concretely visible through in-depth documentation of the data related to the activities, making use of verbal, graphic and documentary instruments as well as the audiovisual technologies most commonly found in schools. I want to underscore one aspect in particular regarding the way documentation is used; that is, the materials are collected during the experience, but they are read and interpreted at the end. The reading and recalling of memory therefore takes place after the fact. The documents (video and audio recordings, written notes) are collected, sometimes catalogued, and brought back for rereading, revisiting and reconstruction of the experience. That which took place is reconstructed, interpreted and reinterpreted by means of the documents which testify to the salient moments of a path that was predefined by the teacher: the path that made it possible for the objectives of the experience to be achieved.

In short, according to this conceptual approach and didactic practice, the documents (the documented traces) are used after and not during the process. These documents (and the reflections and interpretations they elicit from teachers and children) do not intervene during the learning path and within the learning process in a way that would give meaning and direction to the process. Herein lies the substantial difference. In Reggio Emilia, where we have explored this methodology for many years, we place the emphasis on documentation as an integral part of the procedures aimed at fostering learning and for modifying the learning–teaching relationship. To clarify further what I mean, a number of assumptions should be stated that may initially seem far from the issue at hand but that – or so I hope – will aid in understanding that our choice and practice are neither random nor indifferent. In fact, I believe that documentation is a substantial part of the goal that has always characterised our experience: the search for meaning – to find the meaning of school, or rather, to construct the meaning of school, as a place that plays an active role in the children's search for meaning and our own search for meaning (and shared meanings). In this sense, among the first questions we should ask ourselves as teachers and educators are these: How can we help children find the meaning of what they do, what they encounter, what they experience? And how can we do this for ourselves? These are questions of meaning and the search for meaning (why? how? what?). I think these are the key questions that children constantly ask themselves, both at school and outside of school.

It is a very difficult search and a difficult task, especially for children who nowadays have so many spheres of reference in their daily lives: their family experience, television, the social places they frequent in addition to the family and school. It is a task that involves making connections, giving meaning to these events, to these fragments that are gathered over the course of many and varied experiences. Children carry out this search with tenacity and effort, sometimes making mistakes, but they do the searching on their own. We cannot live without meaning; that would preclude any sense of identity, any hope, any future. Children know this and initiate the search right from the beginning of their lives. They know it as young members of the human species, as individuals, as people. The search for the meaning of life and of the self in life is born with the child and is desired by the child. This is why we talk about a child who is competent and strong – a child who has the right to hope and the right to be valued, not a predefined child seen as fragile, needy, incapable. Ours is a different way of thinking and approaching the child, whom we view as an active subject with us to explore, to try day by day to understand something, to find a meaning, a piece of life.

For us, these meanings, these explanatory theories, are extremely important and powerful in revealing the ways in which children think, question and interpret reality and their own relationships with reality and with us.

Herein lies the genesis of the 'pedagogy of relationships and listening', one of the metaphors that distinguishes the pedagogy of Reggio Emilia.

For adults and children alike, understanding means being able to develop an interpretive 'theory', a narration that gives meaning to events and objects of the world. Our theories are provisional, offering a satisfactory explanation that can be continuously reworked; but they represent something more than simply an idea or a group of ideas. They must please us and convince us, be useful, and satisfy our intellectual, affective and aesthetic needs (the aesthetics of knowledge). In representing the world, our theories represent us.

Moreover, if possible, our theories must please and be attractive to others. Our theories need to be listened to by others. Expressing our theories to others makes it possible to transform a world not intrinsically ours into something shared. Sharing theories is a response to uncertainty.

Here, then, is the reason why any theorisation, from the simplest to the most refined, needs to be expressed, to be communicated, and thus to be listened to, in order to exist. It is here we recognise the values and foundations of the 'pedagogy of listening'.

The pedagogy of listening

How can we define the term listening?

Listening as sensitivity to the patterns that connect, to that which connects us to others; abandoning ourselves to the conviction that our understanding and our own being are but small parts of a broader, integrated knowledge that holds the universe together.

Listening, then, as a metaphor for having the openness and sensitivity to listen and be listened to – listening not just with our ears, but with all our senses (sight, touch, smell, taste, orientation).

Listening to the hundred, the thousand languages, symbols and codes we use to express ourselves and communicate, and with which life expresses itself and communicates to those who know how to listen. Listening as time, the time of listening, a time that is outside chronological time – a time full of silences, of long pauses, an interior time. Interior listening, listening to ourselves, as a pause, a suspension, as an element that generates listening to others but, in turn, is generated by the listening that others give us.

Behind the act of **listening** there is often a curiosity, a desire, a doubt, an interest; there is always an emotion. Listening is emotion; it is generated by emotions and stimulates emotions. The emotions of others influence us by means of processes that are strong, direct, not mediated, and intrinsic to the interactions between communicating subjects. Listening as welcoming and being open to differences, recognising the value of the other's point of view and interpretation.

Listening as an active verb that involves interpretation, giving meaning to the message and value to those who offer it. Listening that does not produce answers but formulates questions; listening that is generated by doubt, by uncertainty, which is not insecurity but, on the contrary, the security that every truth is such only if we are aware of its limits and its possible 'falsification'.

Listening is not easy. It requires a deep awareness and at the same time a suspension of our judgments and above all our prejudices; it requires openness to change. It demands that we have clearly in mind the value of the unknown and that we are able to overcome the sense of emptiness and precariousness that we experience whenever our certainties are questioned.

Listening that takes the individual out of anonymity, that legitimates us, gives us visibility, enriching both those who listen and those who produce the message (and children cannot bear to be anonymous).

Listening as the premise for any learning relationship – learning that is determined by the 'learning subject' and takes shape in his or her mind through action and reflection, that becomes knowledge and skill through representation and exchange. Listening, therefore, as 'a listening context', where one learns to listen and narrate, where individuals feel legitimated to represent their theories and offer their own interpretations of a particular question. In representing our theories, we 're-know' or 're-cognise' them, making it possible for our images and intuitions to take shape and evolve through action, emotion, expressiveness, and iconic and symbolic representations (the 'hundred languages'). Understanding and awareness are generated through sharing and dialogue.

We represent the world in our minds, and this representation is the fruit of our sensitivity to the way in which the world is interpreted in the minds and in the representations of others. It is here that our sensitivity to listening is highlighted; starting from this sensitivity, we form and communicate our representations of the world based not only on our response to events (self-construction), but also on that which we learn about the world from our communicative exchange with others.

The ability to shift (from one kind of intelligence to another, from one language to another) is not only a potential within the mind of each individual but also involves the tendency to shift across (to interact among) many minds. We enrich our knowledge and our subjectivity thanks to this predisposition to welcoming the representations and theories of others – that is, listening to others and being open to them.

This capacity for listening and reciprocal expectations, which enables communication and dialogue, is a quality of the mind and of the intelligence, particularly in the young child. It is a quality that demands to be understood and supported. In the metaphorical sense, in fact, children are the greatest listeners of all to the reality that surrounds them. They possess the time of listening, which is not only time *for* listening but a time that is rarefied, curious, suspended, generous – a time full of waiting and expectation. Children listen to life in all its shapes and colours, and they listen to others (adults and peers). They quickly perceive how the act of listening (observing, but also touching, smelling, tasting, searching) is essential for communication. Children are biologically predisposed to communicate, to exist in relation, to live in relation.

Listening, then, seems to be an innate predisposition that accompanies children from birth, allowing their process of acculturation to develop. The idea of an innate capacity for listening may seem paradoxical but, in effect, the process of acculturation must involve innate motivations and competencies. The newborn child comes into the world with a self that is joyous, expressive, and ready to experiment and explore, using objects and communicating with other people. Right from the beginning, children show a remarkable exuberance, creativity and inventiveness toward their surroundings, as well as an autonomous and coherent consciousness.

Very early in life, children demonstrate that they have a voice, but above all that they know how to listen and want to be listened to. Sociality is not taught to children: they are social beings. Our task is to support them and live their sociality with them; that is the social quality that our culture has produced. Young children are strongly attracted by the ways, the languages (and thus the codes) that our culture has produced, as well as by other people (children and adults).

It is a difficult path that requires efforts, energies, hard work and sometimes suffering, but it also offers wonder, amazement, joy, enthusiasm and passion. It is a path that takes time, time that children have and adults often do not have or do not want to have. This is what a school should be: first and foremost, a context of multiple listening. This context of multiple listening, involving the teachers but also the group of children and each child, all of whom can listen to others and listen to themselves, overturns the teaching–learning relationship. This overturning shifts the focus to learning; that is, to children's self-learning and the learning achieved by the group of children and adults together.

As children represent their mental images to others, they represent them to themselves, developing a more conscious vision (interior listening). Thus, moving from one language to another, from one field of experience to another, and reflecting on these shifts and those of others, children modify and enrich their theories and conceptual maps. But this is true if, and only if, children have the opportunity to make these shifts in a group context – that is, in and with others – and if they have the possibility to listen and be listened to, to express their differences and be receptive to the differences of others. The task of those who educate is not only to allow the differences to be expressed but to make it possible for them to be negotiated and nurtured through exchange and comparison of ideas. We are talking about differences between individuals but also differences between languages (verbal, graphic, plastic, musical, gestural, etc.), because it is the shifting from one language to another, as well as their reciprocal interaction, that enables the creation and consolidation of concepts and conceptual maps.

Not only does the individual child learn how to learn, but the group becomes conscious of itself as a 'teaching place', where the many languages are enriched, multiplied, refined and generated, but also collide, 'contaminate' and hybridise each other and are renewed.

The concept of 'scaffolding', which has characterised the role of the teacher, also assumes new and different methods and meanings. It is the context, the web of reciprocal expectations (more than the teachers themselves) that sustains the individual and group processes. In addition to offering support and cultural mediation (subject matter, instruments, etc.), teachers who know how to observe, document and interpret the processes that the children undergo autonomously will realise in this context their greatest potential to learn how to teach.

Documentation, therefore, is seen as visible listening, as the construction of traces (through notes, slides, videos, and so on) that not only testify to the children's learning paths and processes, but also make them possible because they are visible. For us this means making visible, and thus possible, the relationships that are the building blocks of knowledge.

Documentation

To ensure listening and being listened to is one of the primary tasks of documentation (producing traces/documents that testify to and make visible the ways of learning of the individuals and the group), as well as to ensure that the group and each individual child have the possibility to observe themselves from an external point of view while they are learning (both during and after the process).

A broad range of documentation (videos, tape recordings, written notes, and so on) produced and used in process (that is, during the experience) offers the following advantages:

- It makes visible (though in a partial way, and thus 'partisan') the nature of the learning processes and strategies used by each child, and makes the subjective and intersubjective processes a common patrimony.
- It enables reading, revisiting and assessment in time and in space, and these actions become an integral part of the knowledge-building process.

Documentation can modify learning from an epistemological point of view (enabling epistemological assessment and self-assessment, which become an integral part of the process in that they guide and orient the process itself). It seems to be essential for metacognitive processes and for the understanding of children and adults. In relation to recent studies that increasingly highlight the role of memory in the learning and identity-forming processes, we could hypothesise that significant reinforcement can be offered to the memory by the images (photographs and video), the voices and the notations. Likewise the reflexive aspect (fostered by the 're-cognition' that takes place through use of the findings) and the capacity for concentration and interpretation could benefit from this memory-enhancing material. This is only a supposition, but in my view it deserves to be confronted and discussed. In this movement, which I would define as a spiral as it weaves together the observation, the interpretation and the documentation, we can clearly see how none of these actions can actually be separated or removed from the others. Any separation would be artificial and merely for the sake of argument. Rather, I would talk about dominance in the adult's level of awareness and consequently of action. It is impossible, in fact, to document without observing and, obviously, interpreting.

By means of documenting, the thinking – or the interpretation – of the documenter thus becomes material, that is, tangible and capable of being interpreted. The notes, the recordings, the slides and photographs represent fragments of a memory that seems thereby to become 'objective'. While each fragment is imbued with the subjectivity of the documenter, it is offered to the interpretive subjectivity of others in order to be known or reknown, created and recreated, also as a collective knowledge-building event.

The result is knowledge that is bountiful and enriched by the contributions of many. In these fragments (images, words, signs and drawings) there is the past, that which took place, but there is also the future (or rather what else can happen if . . .).

We are looking at a new concept of didactics: participatory didactics, didactics as procedures and processes that can be communicated and shared. Visibility, legibility and shareability become supporting nuclei because they are the basis of communicative effectiveness and didactic effectiveness. Didactics thus becomes more similar to the science of communication than to the traditional pedagogical disciplines.

At this point, a particular aspect emerges that structures the teaching–learning relationship and that in this context is made more visible, more explicit. At the moment of documentation (observation and interpretation), the element of assessment enters the picture immediately, that is, in the context and during the time in which the experience (activity) takes place. It is not sufficient to make an abstract prediction that establishes what is significant – the elements of value necessary for learning to be achieved – before the documentation is actually carried out. It is necessary to interact with the action itself, with that which is revealed, defined and perceived as truly significant, as the experience unfolds. Any gap between the prediction and the event (between the inherent meanings and those which the child/children attribute in their action) should be grasped readily and rapidly. The adult's schema of expectation is not prescriptive but orientative. Doubt and uncertainty permeate the context; they are part of the 'documenter's context'. Herein lies true didactic freedom, of the child as well as the teacher. It lies in this space between the predictable and the unexpected, where the communicative relationship between the children's and teachers' learning processes is constructed. It is in this space that the questions, the dialogue, the comparison of ideas with colleagues are situated, where the meeting on 'what to do' takes place and the process of assessment (deciding what to 'give value to') is carried out.

The issue, then, is to consider the child as a context for himself or herself and for the others, and to consider the learning process as a process of construction of interactions between the 'subject being educated' and the 'objects of education' (seen as including knowledge as well as social-affective and axiological models of behaviour). This means that the object of education is seen not as an object but as a 'relational place'. With this term I underscore the way in which the teacher chooses and proposes the knowledge-building approach (assuming all due responsibility). It is a construction of relationships that are born of a reciprocal curiosity between the subject and the object. This curiosity is sparked by a question that stimulates the subject and the object to 'encounter each other', showing what the child knows (understood as theories and desires for knowledge) and the knowledge of the object in terms of its cultural identity. This identity is not limited to the elements that are immediately perceivable, but is also directed toward the cultural elaborations that have been produced around it, and above all those that *can* be produced in this new knowledge-seeking relationship. This re-knowing of the object is not only 'historical', that is, reproducing what is culturally known about the object (for example, what we know about a tree in its disciplinary interpretations: biology, architecture, poetry, and so on). It is also a living organism because it comes to life in the vitality, freshness and unpredictableness of this encounter, where the children can give new identity to the object, creating a relationship for the object and for themselves that is also metaphorical and poetic.

Documentation is this process, which is dialectic, based on affective bonds and also poetic; it not only accompanies the knowledge-building process but in a certain sense impregnates it.

Documentation not only lends itself to interpretation but is itself interpretation. It is a narrative form, both intrapersonal and interpersonal communication, because it offers those who document and those who read the documentation an opportunity for reflection and learning. The reader can be a colleague, a group of colleagues, a child, children, parents, anyone who has participated or wants to participate in this process. The documentation material is open, accessible, usable and therefore readable. In reality this is not always the case, and above all the process is neither automatic nor easy. Effective documentation requires extensive experience in documentary reading and writing.

Legibility

Documentation is thus a narrative form. Its force of attraction lies in the wealth of questions, doubts and reflections that underlie the collection of data and with which it is offered to others – colleagues and children. These 'writings', where different languages are interwoven (graphic, visual, iconic), need to have their own code, their own convention within the group that constructs and uses them – this in order to guarantee, even though partially, the effectiveness of communication. That is, these writings must be legible, effectively communicative for those who were not present in the context, but should also include the 'emergent elements' perceived by the documenter. They are three-dimensional writings, not aimed at giving the event objectivity but at expressing the meaning-making effort; that is, to give meaning, to render the significance that each author attributes to the documentation and the questions and problems he or she perceives within a certain event. These writings are not detached from the personal biographical characteristics of the author, and we are thus aware of their bias, but this is considered an element of quality.

The documenter looks at the events that have taken place with a personal view aimed at a deep understanding of them and, at the same time, seeks communicative clarity. This is possible (though it could seem paradoxical) by bringing into the documentation the sense of incompleteness and expectation that can arise when you try to offer others not what you know, but the boundaries of your knowledge; that is, your limits, which derive from the fact that the 'object' being narrated is a process and a path of research.

Assessment: a perspective that gives value

What we offer to the children's processes and procedures, and to those which the children and adults together put into action, is a perspective that gives value. Valuing means giving value to this context and implies that certain elements are assumed as values.

Here, I think, is the genesis of assessment, because it allows one to make explicit, visible and shareable the elements of value (indicators) applied by the documenter in producing the documentation. Assessment is an intrinsic part of documentation and therefore of the entire approach of what we call *progettazione* (*progettazione* is discussed in 'Note on terminologies' on page xi). In fact, this approach becomes something more than a prescribed and predefined procedure; it is a procedure that is nurtured by the elements of value that emerge from the process itself.

This makes the documentation particularly valuable to the children themselves, as they can encounter what they have done in the form of a narration, seeing the meaning that the teacher has drawn from their work. In the eyes of the children, this can demonstrate that what they do has value, has meaning. So they discover that they 'exist' and can emerge from anonymity and invisibility, seeing that what they say and do is important, is listened to and is appreciated: it is a value.

It is like having an interface with yourself and with whoever enters into this sort of hypertext. Here the text acts as vector, support and pretext of the children's personal mental space.

The teacher's competency

In this context, it is obvious that the role and competency of the teacher are qualified in a different way from how these elements are defined in an educational environment in which the teacher's job is simply to transmit disciplinary knowledge in the traditional way.

The task is not to find (and teach) a specific series of rules, or to present certain propositions organised into formulas that can be easily learned by others, or to teach a method that can be replicated without modifications.

The teacher's competency is defined in terms more of understandings than of pure knowledge. It indicates a familiarity with critical facts, so as to allow those who possess this familiarity to say what is important and to hypothesise what is suitable for each situation – that is, what is helpful for the learner in a particular situation.

So what is the secret? There is no secret, no key, if not that of constantly examining our understandings, knowledge and intuitions, and sharing and comparing them with those of our colleagues. It is not a transferable 'science', but rather an understanding, a sensitivity to knowledge. The action and the results of the action, in a situation where only the surface is visible, will be successful in part thanks to the success of the actors – children and teachers – all of whom are responsible, though at different levels, for the learning processes.

Proceeding by trial and error does not debase the didactic paths; indeed, it enriches them on the process level (that is, the process and our awareness of it), as well as on the ethical level.

There is also an element of improvisation, a sort of 'playing by ear', an ability to take stock of a situation, to know when to move and when to stay still, that no formula, no general recipe, can replace.

Certainly there are also risks, quite a few in fact: vagueness and superficiality can lead to mistaking a series of images or written notes for documentation which, without the awareness of what one is observing, only creates disorientation and a loss of meaning.

The issue that emerges clearly at this point is the education of the teachers. The teacher's general education must be broad-based and range over many areas of knowledge, not just psychology and pedagogy. A cultured teacher not only has a multidisciplinary background, but possesses the culture of research, of curiosity, of working in a group: the culture of project-based thinking. Above all, we need teachers who feel that they truly belong to and participate in this process, as teachers but most of all as people.

Loris Malaguzzi, architect of the pedagogical and philosophical thinking that permeates the Reggio experience, once said that we need a teacher who is sometimes the director, sometimes the set designer, sometimes the curtain and the backdrop, and sometimes the prompter. A teacher who is both sweet and stern, who is the electrician, who dispenses the paints and who is even the audience – the audience who watches, sometimes claps, sometimes remains silent, full of emotion, who sometimes judges with scepticism, and at other times applauds with enthusiasm.

Chapter 5

Dialogues

As I was reading the various chapters of this book prior to writing this conclusion, a number of aspects appeared to me to stand out so clearly that I was persuaded to share them with the reader.

The first concerns the learning processes of children and adults. For a long time now, Piagetian epistemological genetics has demonstrated that, from a very specific and abstract point of view, the logical structures of an adult are quite different from those of a child. According to this view, when an adult and a child are faced with the same problem, they will react and behave in very different ways. However, if we place adults and children in concrete situations which are different and yet require them both to make a cognitive effort that is commensurate with their respective potentials, it would seem as if the processes enacted do not differ so significantly.

In my view, this can be seen from much that has been written in this book. We notice, in fact, how, when faced with the need to reflect and to reformulate their existing knowledge, as happens when documentation is used, adults and children develop strategies which are often comparable. Essentially, these strategies involve a search for a theoretical, moral, and sometimes even physical 'stance' which allows the subjects to exercise greater control over the changes that are taking place; changes that refer to and sometimes undermine both the conceptual and the value systems that they have previously formulated. The nature of the relationship between the problem that arises and the person who has to resolve it is essentially analogous, just as the nature of the strategies that children and adults use for exploring, defining, hypothesising, and the emotional involvement, passion, sense of irony and fun they experience can be similar. A learning experience is therefore an 'educational endeavour', whether it involves adults, children or both.

The second aspect which I think can be gleaned from the book, concerns the work of the teachers. Thanks to our colleagues from Project Zero, their questions and the relentless way in which they delved into the everyday activities of our schools, it has become even more apparent to us that the teachers' 'practical' work is an 'interpretive theory' that integrates stories and micro-stories of research with real-life contexts. This ennobling of the teachers' practical work, which we have always believed in, has now acquired even greater value in being shared by our Project Zero colleagues.

This research project and this book demonstrate that, however one might look at it, the work of the teachers provided they are not left on their own, without rules or collegial support – not only produces daily experience and action, but can also become the object of critical reappraisal and theory building. In this way, practice is not only a necessary field of action for the success of the theory, but is an active part of the theory itself: it contains it, generates it and is generated by it.

A further aspect which deserves careful consideration is the way our dialogue with our Project Zero partners evolved. It was a complex process, at times made more difficult by linguistic and cultural differences. Yet, language, which started off as a barrier, turned out to be a sort of 'forum' that provided an opportunity to submit our own understandings to further scrutiny and clarification. A number of terms, in fact, seemed impossible to translate because the concepts they expressed were not easily transferable across the two experiences.

In Reggio, we use a language that originates from a micro-world which, despite its openness to dialogue and exchange, has had to and has sought to construct a language that is both generated by experience and generates experience. The fact that this language is highly visual and metaphorical has often made it extremely attractive to our Project Zero colleagues, but has also been the source of a few understandable suspicions.

First among these is the idea that we might be trying to skirt the issue, refusing, even if only momentarily, to de-contextualise it. Perhaps they were right. At times we were a little too vague, letting ourselves be perceived as enveloped in a kind of haziness that had much in common with vagueness. Occasionally, however, we perceived their persistent and punctilious questions as a sort of deviation which we felt could generate some possible philological and conceptual misrepresentations. We undoubtedly have a great love of metaphor; and this is primarily because children love and often make use of it. We see metaphor not as a rhetorical or stylistic device but as a genuine tool of cognition. As many other studies and investigations confirm, we have noticed that metaphors are particularly useful when new ideas are emerging from within groups of people (and, therefore, also groups of children), and the use of previous concepts and expressions is avoided on the grounds that they might be misleading. In this case, metaphorical language, precisely because it is more undefined, allusive and sometimes ambiguous, but at the same time open to new concepts, becomes the only tool available to the new understanding that is seeking to emerge and find an audience.

Perhaps it was due to the fact that we were trying to find new understandings in this research, and we ourselves were trying to understand, that metaphor (and, with it, examples) appeared to provide a supportive strategy. It seems to me that we were able to structure – though the reader will be a better judge of this – what Kenneth J. Gergen calls a 'transformational dialogue': a dialogue which is able to transform our relationship and, therefore, in a certain way, our professional and group identities. Instead of adopting a 'top-down' approach, with a prior definition of identical rules, ethics and practices for everyone involved, we managed to move into a sphere of action in which children and adults alike struggled successfully, it seems, with the problems of learning in a multiple and conflictual context. We thus compiled a sort of 'dictionary of experiences' which helped us to reflect, infer, hypothesise and understand.

For all this, I would like to thank Mara, Steve and Ben; for their heuristic skill, their ability to participate and enable us to participate in their philosophical thinking, knowledge and experience. I would particularly like to thank Howard Gardner, because during the joint meetings between the Project Zero and Reggio research teams he was able to confound our accumulated knowledge with a single question, forcing us to engage in healthy rethinking processes. Finally, I would like to thank our readers for their faith in us, and because by reading this book they enable our research to live on.

Chapter 6

The space of childhood (1998)

I wrote the following piece at the time when research carried out by Reggio Children in collaboration with the Domus Academy was being published. The research and the journey were unforgettable. They enabled those of us who participated to understand once again the richness of dialogue which from being interdisciplinary becomes intradisciplinary and in so doing favours metacognitive levels of reflection.

So what is Domus Academy and why the research? Domus Academy is a postgraduate training centre and research laboratory on design processes, situated in Milan. It is known throughout the world and is particularly interested in questions of research and of innovation. We contacted them formally in 1995 but our relations with them had started several years previously at a time when we felt the necessity not only of extending and deepening our knowledge of spatial environments, but of reconceptualising it, changing our ways of thinking about spaces.

The Reggio experience has always been very attentive to the subject of spaces and also, on a more general level, to environments in education. When I began working in the municipal schools in 1970, I was taken aback by the high level of awareness around the importance of quality in school spaces. In a national and international context in which the classroom was considered as an empty box which was both antiseptic and anonymous, and in which it was considered legitimate (and unfortunately still is) to create schools in basements and shop spaces, entering a Reggio school was first and foremost an emotional experience. One could feel them vibrating with life and though the thinking of Montessori, Freinet and Dewey could be recognised in them, it was apparent that the language of the spatial environment went beyond that, thanks to the attention paid to architecture and visual arts.

There was already a clear intuition of the relationship between the quality of space and the quality of the learning. The definition, so dear to Malaguzzi, of spaces as the 'third educator' gives a good indication of the levels of awareness that had already been achieved. In the same way, the impact of declarations by Malaguzzi on the rights of the child to a quality environment were also clearly visible. The right to an environment, to beauty, the right to contribute to the construction of this environment and this idea of beauty, a shared aesthetic: a right for everyone, teachers and adults in general, and which could only be expressed through a permanent process of research. Research on the one hand based on attentive and accurate observations of the child's and the adult's use of spaces and furnishings, and on the other attentive to what was being brought to light in studies concerning the way in which spaces and architecture in general are perceived.

I remember very distinctly one of the first (and for me fundamental) study groups in which I participated in 1972. The group was made up of *atelieristas* (at the time I think there were six and many of them had only recently been employed), some teachers and the architect Tullio Zini, a generous friend and great source of inspiration for the concept of environment and aesthetic of the environment which has been elaborated in Reggio Emilia. To structure our observations we used a system we developed ourselves in which we tried to connect time to space, that is to say, tried to connect the 'what' with the 'where' and the 'when'. This was in order to capture the real values being attributed to a certain space and the space's capacity for being suited to what was experienced there.

An example is the children's lunch. We began to reflect about lunch, about what it means in our culture, to think psychologically on the subject. But we were also very careful to take into consideration the observations made by teachers and the first photographic images which showed how the children behaved during lunch. In fact the images and notes which were taken highlighted how lunch for the children was first and foremost a moment for socialising and how they were capable of being independent if they were helped to value their own competencies. We also thought about the density of people in the dining area at that time, and we tried to understand how the space could be organised and insulated against noise to make the acoustics more bearable. And how could we make the space more personal, more welcoming? We needed smaller tables (with four places, six at the most), perhaps we could arrange some dividing panels which would dilute the visual 'noise' . . . and so we went on, with all the enjoyment and excitement of this 'brain storming' which was so involving.

As I said, this is an example. After this experience the *atelieristas* continued to design new furnishings, construct them and try them out. While in the meantime, relations became more intense with Tullio Zini and also with other architects who were given the job of designing new municipal schools, and with designers with whom furnishings could be re-invented. I defined this journey as 'permanent research', that is to say, research which, even though it poses certain objectives for itself, has as its primary aim superseding these same objectives with new questions.

So the journey has continued up to this day, up to the dialogue with Domus Academy. This is one of the most organic and structured pieces of research we have ever realised. On the one hand, in fact, it brought unification to knowledge we had accumulated over years and on the other it provided provocation for our knowledge with new questions, bringing it to crisis point and opening it up to new awareness.

I mentioned above that I wrote the piece which follows for the publication of the research conducted by Reggio and Domus, in a book titled *Children, spaces, relations – Metaproject for an environment for young children* (Ceppi and Zini, 1998). But the publication, and likewise my paper, should be considered not only as a result, a synthesis, but also as a starting point. Six years later much has advanced and changed vis-à-vis what is described and discussed in the book. Many other studies, publications and projects have been developed using it as a starting point. But still today, re-reading those pages and thinking back to that journey one can feel all the pleasure of standing before a real paradigmatic shift in describing and experiencing childhood spaces.

Not only schools, but all the spaces where children and adults live, are asking for great changes. They are in need of more meta-projects and ever new passions and enthusiasms.

Designing the space of a *nido* or *scuola dell'infanzia* – or perhaps we could just say designing a school – is a highly creative event not only in terms of pedagogy and architecture but more generally in social, cultural and political terms. This institution, in fact, can play a very special role in cultural development and real socio-political experimentation, to the extent that this moment (designing) and this place (the school) can be experienced not as a time and space for reproducing and transmitting established knowledge but as a place of true creativity.

Ours is a time of transition, and our generation is transient. Our task is to live a 'season of design' in which it is impossible to use the old pedagogical, architectural, ethical, social, and educational parameters and values, and in which it thus becomes essential to venture into the new and to lay plans for real futures. Though it is certainly a time of potential disorientation and confusion, of widespread uncertainties and contradictions, it is also an exciting time, rich in possibilities.

So much 'new' can be generated when we abandon the presumption that we possess incontrovertible truths or, on the other hand, that we are in the throes of a crisis and thus have no identity or values with which to confront the genetic mutations that are being produced and which pro-duce us. [*Added by CR when editing the book*: 'genetic mutations' is a metaphor for the profound transformation we are experiencing, a transformation which is changing the very essence, the very way of being of society and people, because it is transforming our way of entering into relationships and interacting and our concepts of space and time.] In this context, we will see ourselves not as 'mothers' or 'fathers' of the new, but as children in our own right who are generated by the new, provided we are able to seek out that which unites, and unites us, rather than that which divides us.

And thus, designing a school means, first and foremost, creating a space of life and of the future. This requires the shared research of pedagogy, architecture, sociology and anthropology, disciplines and fields of knowledge that are called upon to state their own epistemologies and to compare their languages and symbolic systems, in a new freedom born of the desire to dialogue and exchange ideas. This kind of research is also open to the contributions of the most advanced experimentation in the spheres of music, choreography, design, performance and fashion. Only by working in this way can we guarantee that the architectural project will be in itself research and therefore capable, day by day, of taking stock of its own outcomes, of the effectiveness of its language, of its capacity to dialogue with the process of 'becoming' which is the basis of true education. This means constructing a 'metaphor of knowledge' that both represents and suggests possible changes and actions.

In this, there is a clear contrast with everything that has guided the design and construction of much current school architecture at every level, in Italy but also throughout the world. This becomes evident if we look back on the history – or better, non-history – of the typical architecture of institutions for young children (non-history because there are so few worthy examples to cite, and thus no history). Many spaces for young children have been constructed in 'hand-me-down' buildings (former elementary schools, spaces initially designed for other purposes), and even in those spaces which have been the subject of an architectural project, the project was often developed in an *ad hoc* way and has been the result of random factors and a gross lack of awareness. For the most part, the idea has been to do or make a school, and only rarely to give a school meaning; that is, a place that has real meaning for a community and a society. [*Added by CR when editing the book:* I refer here to 'give a school meaning' because architecture is not the assembling of spaces, it involves a philosophy, a way of thinking about education, learning, the teaching/learning relationship, the role of action and doing in the construction of knowledge. The school building is a pedagogical project and, as such, must be the result of careful, in-depth dialogue between the pedagogical and architectural languages.]

Now is the time to create this symbiosis between architecture, pedagogy and the other disciplines in order to find better spaces, more appropriate spaces. We are not searching for an ideal space, but one that is capable of generating its own change, because an ideal space, an ideal pedagogy, an ideal child or human being do not exist. There is only a child, a human being, in relation with their own experiences, times and culture. The quality of the space can therefore be defined in terms of the quantity, quality and development of these relationships. Ensuring the existence and flow of this kind of quality is the primary task of relational pedagogy and architecture.

This relational element is substantiated in a way of thinking that is not primarily based on philosophical or scientific dogma but on the relationships that enable the child (and the person) to be a 'knowing individual', who therefore:

- makes distinctions, decides on limits and makes choices, all of which are essential building blocks of knowledge;
- is the protagonist in the act of cognition but also that of commentary, as learning must be accompanied by reflection and revisiting. What we have in mind, then, is an environment that becomes a sort of reflecting surface in which the protagonists of the learning experience can see the traces of their action, and which enables them to talk about how they are learning;
- experiences learning as practice, not so much to pursue an end but to change oneself, as the scientist and biological philosopher, Bateson, said. The essential condition of thinking in terms of relations is a working epistemology of action, which is first of all a way of acting. In educational practice, this becomes a way of working in 'laboratories', with the school conceptualised as one big laboratory, a 'workshop of learning and knowledge';
- expresses the aesthetic dimension as an essential quality of learning, knowing and relating. Pleasure, aesthetics and play are essential in any act of learning and knowledge-building. Learning must be pleasurable, appealing and fun. The aesthetic dimension thus becomes a pedagogical quality of the scholastic and educational space.

These are the reflections that have emerged over many years of experience and fruitful collaboration in research carried out in our *nidi* and *scuole dell'infanzia* focused on designing school spaces.

But what can this experience contribute to the search for a new epistemology of school architecture? We could begin with a series of fundamental premises.

Psycho-pedagogical and anthropological premises

The physical space can be defined as a language, which speaks according to precise cultural conceptions and deep biological roots:

- The language of space is very strong, and is a conditioning factor. Though its code is not always explicit and recognisable, we perceive and interpret it from a very early age.
- Like every other language, the physical space is therefore a constituent element of the formation of thought.
- The 'reading' of spatial language is multisensory and involves both the remote receptors (eye, ear and nose) and the immediate receptors for the surrounding environment (the skin, membranes and muscles).
- The relational qualities between the individual and his/her habitat are reciprocal, so that both the person and the environment are active and modify each other in turn.
- The perception of space is subjective and holistic (tactile, visual, olfactory and kinesthetic). It is modified throughout the various phases of life and is strongly linked to one's own culture: we not only speak different languages but also inhabit different sensory worlds. In the shared space, each of us makes a personal meaning of that space, creating an individual territory which is strongly affected by the variables of gender, age and, as we said, culture.
- Young children demonstrate an innate and extremely high level of perceptual sensitivity and competence – which is polysemous and holistic – in relation to the surrounding space. Their immediate receptors are much more active than they will be in later stages of life, and they show a great ability to analyse and distinguish reality using sensory receptors other than those of sight and hearing. For this reason, the utmost attention should be given to designing light and colours, as well as olfactory, auditory and tactile elements, all of which are extremely important in defining the sensory quality of a space.
- Considering the children's age and posture (babies spend a substantial amount of time seated or lying down, and for a certain period move only on all fours), greater importance should be given to surfaces that are normally treated as merely background elements, such as floors, ceilings and walls.
- We should make the maximum effort to be more aware of the

space and the objects we place there, knowing that the spaces in which children construct their identities and their personal stories are many, both real and virtual. Television, computers and other household appliances are now instruments of daily life, just as the coexistence of real, virtual and imaginary elements is an everyday phenomenon, to the extent of modifying – in a way that we might not even imagine – the definition of space and of the self that today's children are constructing.

The image of the child

It is important to underscore the determining role played by the definition of the identity, or image, of the child which has been developed within the pedagogical approach of *nidi* and *scoule dell'infanzia*. Many different images could be possible: highlighting what the child is and has, can be or can do, or on the contrary emphasising what the child is not and does not have, what he or she cannot be or do. The image of the child is above all a cultural (and therefore social and political) convention that makes it possible to recognise (or not) certain qualities and potentials in children, and to construe expectations and contexts that give value to such qualities and potentials or, on the contrary, negate them. What we believe about children thus becomes a determining factor in defining their social and ethical identity, their rights and the educational contexts offered to them.

One of the focal points of the Reggio Emilia philosophy, as Loris Malaguzzi wrote, is the image of a child who, right from the moment of birth, is so engaged in developing a relationship with the world and intent on experiencing the world that he develops a complex system of abilities, learning strategies and ways of organising relationships. This is:

- A child who is fully able to create personal maps for his own social, cognitive, affective and symbolic orientation.
- A competent, active, critical child; a child who is therefore 'challenging', because he produces change and dynamic movement in the systems in which he is involved, including the family, the society and the school. A producer of culture, values and rights, competent in living and learning.
- A child who is able to assemble and disassemble possible realities, to construct metaphors and creative paradoxes, to construct his own symbols and codes while learning to decode the established symbols and codes.

- A child who, very early on, is able to attribute meanings to events and who attempts to share meanings and stories of meaning.

Children's learning paths and processes thus pass through a relationship with the cultural and scholastic context which, as such, must be a 'formative environment', an ideal place for development which values these processes.

Children's competence and motivation can be either enhanced or inhibited depending on the awareness and motivational force of the surrounding context. Numerous studies have brought to light the importance of the adult's role in young children's development not only by means of direct and targeted actions but also indirectly, when the adults create educational contexts that enable children to utilise their own skills and competence. This is an important implication for the organisation of the physical spaces in a school for young children. If in fact – as Shaffer (1990) affirms – the 'innate programming' of each child establishes new objectives, then the pursuit of those objectives is a joint venture between the child and the adult who intervenes with indirect means which can also involve, as we said, the space, its confines, colours and objects, and so on.

These elements are not isolated but are part of a 'context of meaning', where objects engage in dialogue and are part of a shared problem or subject of investigation. The physical and psychological environments are defined reciprocally to give children the sense of security that derives from feeling welcome and valued, and at the same time guarantees the opportunity for developing all their relational potentials. Most of all, the *nidi* and *scuole dell'infanzia* are living spaces that are continuously characterised and modified by events and stories that are both individual and social.

Based on these considerations, we can move toward a reconceptualisation and reorganisation of school architecture, of the spaces and how they are connected, as well as their capacity to accept and support both the 'I' and the 'we', the small group and the large group, individual memory and collective memory. Our objective in doing this is to support: the possibility of acting and reflecting on one's action; the legibility of the space; the creation of transparency but also opacity (where and when the children are permitted to remove themselves from the adult gaze so that their privacy is respected); the capacity to stimulate curiosity, actions and gestures, manipulative and constructive skills; and finally to optimise the communicative effectiveness of the space.

The school as a system

It would be wrong, however, to overemphasise the protagonism and identity of the child *per se*, because the central focus is on the relationship between children and adults. The *nidi* and *scuole dell'infanzia* should be seen not as a single system but as a system of systems, a system of relationships and communication among children, teachers and parents.

In order to be truly considered relational, this kind of interaction must also extend to spatial relationships, with interconnecting classrooms that are also linked to the service areas (kitchen, dining area, bathrooms) and not separated by corridors or isolated walkways. There should be larger, more open spaces (like the common area or piazza) but also smaller, more confined spaces that foster the experience of working in small groups or individually. These choices of 'meaning' that foster the environment of relation–interaction also suggest the need for transparency on the inside (glass walls and windows that make it possible to orient yourself by sight and maintain the spatial relation) and towards the outside.

The pedagogical project must be interwoven with the architectural project in such a way as to support the processes that take place in this space, the processes of learning, teaching, sharing and understanding, on the part of all the protagonists: children, staff and parents.

The importance of the adult presence (staff and parents) means organising spaces and furnishings that facilitate and support the teachers' professional work and the staff-parent relations, including well-equipped meeting rooms, archives, libraries, greenhouses and work tools (such as computers, video-recorders and other equipment and materials that can assist the work of discussion and reflection on experiences involving children and parents); in other words, all that is essential for the daily work and sharing of the teachers and indispensable for supporting the parents' active involvement in the school.

The aim is thus to ensure that all three subjects – children, staff, parents – can inhabit the space effectively, but above all to guarantee their well-being as creators and users of the space and of what takes place there.

The school – *nido* or *scuola dell'infanzia* – is viewed as a 'living organism' that pulses, changes, transforms, grows and matures. This definition poses an issue that we would define as the processes of entropy, or the management of change. A living organism never remains the same, and a school for young children is never the same from one day to the next. So we must be able to ensure a continuity of identity within change, a memory of the past and 'memory' of the future.

The school that opens in the morning is different from the one left the previous afternoon precisely because of the many changes that take place during the day. When choosing materials, for example, we should carefully evaluate this question of modifications that leave traces and memories in the space and in the overall environment. The space and the furnishings in it have a right to age, and thus to show the marks of time. It would be distressing to have a space filled with 'sterile' materials that are impervious to time or wear, though obviously the necessary attention must be given to maintenance and hygiene. The idea is that we should avoid any choice or solution that would make a school building a sterile place rather than a living space.

This consideration of change refers to what takes place over longer periods of time – during the course of the year, the month – not only, as we have said, the day. The question lies in how many possibilities there are for the individual child and the group of children, the protagonists of the experience, to have a story, to leave traces, to see that their experiences are given value and meaning. It is the question of memory, narration and documentation as a right, and as that which embodies the vital quality of the educational environment.

The space of the *nidi* requires a number of specific considerations, though remaining within the overall educational project shared with the *scuola dell'infanzia*. The needs for safety (physical and psychological) and personalisation (i.e. a strategy that is as personalised as possible for each child) are clearer and more marked in the *nido* (for children from three months to three years old); the age of the children and their perceptive, cognitive and affective development require a high level of awareness in terms of the architecture. Careful attention is given to the organisation of the spaces (niches, more intimate spaces), to the surfaces (the materials used for floors, walls, ceilings), the perceptual aspects (sound, smell and touch, as well as light and colour), and to the furnishings and materials that can best respond to the needs for security and the desire for autonomy expressed by children of this age. The architecture of the *nido* must be respectful of the considerable differences among the individual children (in identity, rhythms, gender, habits), but must also satisfy the needs for discovery, novelty, morphogenesis and participation which are equally strong, though perhaps less evident, in children of this age when compared with older children.

I like to think of the environment of the *nido* as a sort of Japanese space – symbolic, metaphorical, soft, sensory, changeable, welcoming, appropriately sized, qualities which seem to characterise space according to Japanese tradition.

Most of all, though, both the *nido* and the *scuola dell'infanzia* (as well as other educational spaces), in order to be truly a place of production, learning, culture and socio-political experimentation, must be conceived and constructed as a place of action rather than just words, a true 'artisan workshop', which in our case is a clear cultural reference to the Italian Renaissance. It is through acting and doing that children are able to understand the path of their learning and the organisation of their experience, knowledge and the meaning of their relationships with others. Reflecting on one's actions helps to construct the differentiation which gives shape to the knowing subject, the known object and the tools of knowing.

Conclusions

The objective is thus to construct and organise spaces that enable children:

- To express their potential, abilities and curiosity;
- To explore and research alone and with others, both peers and adults;
- To perceive themselves as constructors of projects and of the overall educational project carried out in the school;
- To reinforce their identities, autonomy and security;
- To work and communicate with others;
- To know that their identities and privacy are respected.

The construction and organisation of the space should enable the teachers:

- To feel supported and integrated in their relationships with children and parents;
- To have appropriate spaces and furnishings to satisfy their need to meet with other adults, both colleagues and parents;
- To have their need for privacy recognised;
- To be supported in their processes of learning and professional development.

And finally, the space should ensure that parents can:

- Be listened to and informed;
- Meet with other parents and teachers in ways and times that foster real collaboration.

This space is process-oriented architecture, which fosters communication and is itself communication. It takes a form that is capable of sustaining the protecting interconnectedness – this system of systems – which is the *nido* and *scuola dell'infanzia*. It creates an environment that is pleasant to be in, that can be explored and experienced with all the senses, and inspires further advancements in learning: an environment that is empathetic, that grasps the meaning of, but also gives meaning to, the life of the people who inhabit it.

Chapter 7

Issues in educating today (1998)

It often happens that I re-read my talks after some time has passed and I feel a sense of unease: I would like to change them, add some things or eliminate others, correct words. What I mean is that I would like to adapt them to my current way of thinking, to what has changed in me. I feel they are inadequate.

But this does not happen when I read this talk. It was written in 1998 for a meeting with parents. We wanted to start off a journey of reflection on educating, involving parents from all our municipal schools, thirty-two schools then attended by about 2,500 children and their families. At that time I was director of the municipal schools and I was asked to write an introductory speech. With *pedagogista* colleagues in the coordinating team for schools, we decided that this speech of mine would be presented to an audience of parents and teachers drawn from all schools and then it would be distributed to each school where it could be the subject of reflection and discussion.

A journey was started which lasted an entire school year. Parents took part enthusiastically, revealing once again their high degree of competence not only for listening but for elaboration and discussion. Their conversations were recorded and transcribed and presented to all interested parents at a conference held at the end of the school year. The parents were extraordinary, active protagonists together with teachers.

In fact, in the Reggio experience the school-family relationship is practised not only as an individual relationship between parent and teacher, and certainly not as a relationship of subordination in which the teacher tells the parent what he or she should do, what is right or mistaken. Rather it is a common journey for building together – parents and teachers – values and ways of educating in contemporary society, inside and outside school.

As I mentioned before, I wrote this talk to encourage meeting and debate. Many things have changed in me and around me since 1998. In just a few years the world has changed profoundly, and after September 11 we live in a context filled with fear and a deep sense of loss of direction. And yet I find that some of the proposals, some of the questions in this talk, can still be useful to the reader as an opportunity for reflection around themes and choices which education still poses to us.

Every generation questions itself about what values and knowledge to transmit to the new generations, and how to transmit them, even though for centuries in our culture – as well as in others – the questions and answers were decided by the few, by an elite. And these few defined the values and place of education for all. The transmission of technical skills was basically simple, from father to son and from mother to daughter. With the advent of the industrial era, a different definition of the concept of State, and then a new conception of society, and the recognition of the rights of man and of citizens – all these developments created a new social order and a new concept of democracy. This is expressed in the right to work, to vote, and to school and universal education.

But it was only after the Second World War that this new social order began to make profound changes in Italy (in other countries it had already happened). New rights (and not only duties) and values emerged. But above all there were great transformations in the identity and definition of the role of the family, of women and men.

The new technologies and phenomena of globalisation have transformed – and will continue to transform – the identity of many of us as workers and as citizens, as mothers and fathers, and as children. The consumer society proposes and imposes new values, new relations between people and new concepts of time and space. It seems that there is no time for joy, for fear, for grief, for celebration. No time for individuals or for the group. Time selects the part of humanity that we want to live and transmit, which is more and more linked to the dimension of consumption and production.

I do not want to continue with an analysis that could become superficial and perhaps even tiresome. I would just like to introduce a possible series of questions for reflecting on the issue at hand: the family and its changes.

- The family has changed over the last few decades: how and what is different today?
- Why has the role of women in the society changed, and consequently the expectations on mothers?
- Has the awareness of the individuals that make up the family changed to the extent of creating a new definition and identity for the family?
- What has changed in the role of the father, who seems – some have said – to be increasingly 'maternal'?

- Who holds the authority? What is authority in the family of today? Authoritarian or authoritative? Or something else?
- How have the expectations of the society toward the family changed – if they have changed? And the rights of the family? And family policy?

Nuclear families, reconstructed families, complex family relations: all this is not enough (or maybe it is?) for understanding the growing expression of solitude and powerlessness on the part of many families. Families meaning mothers, fathers, grandparents, caregivers. It seems that more and more there is a sort of renunciation of educating and caring for children. Children are worried about but not attended to. More and more, other people and places are delegated (school, grandparents, sports) to do that which should be the task of the parents.

Or not? Could the opposite be true? That is, that the family is too alone and cut off, that there is too little cultural and economic help and support? There seems to be the absence of an educational project for the child.

Often we know what we would like for him or for her, but not who he or she really is and especially what he or she would like. Are we afraid of our children? Of those who are born and those only desired? Or is it because we want the best for them, and the best costs time and money? But what is the best? Who decides this? Based on what parameters?

This reasoning leads us to another possible and important subject for reflection: the relationship between childhood and society. What is childhood? Who defines it? How is it defined? What identities, what rights are given to childhood? Childhood, we know, is a cultural interpretation and construction. Every society, and every historical period, defines its own childhood, what is meant by, expected of and dedicated to childhood.

Now I think it is important in our reflections to look at what I believe is at the heart of defining the relationship between adult and child. The fundamental question (fundamental to our previous discussion and to the adult–child relationship) is the cultural and individual construction of the child that we make, what, in terms of our experience in Reggio, we call 'the image of the child'. Image as an interpretation, as a historical and cultural definition.

In substance, the child is defined by our way of looking at and seeing him. But since we see what we know, the image of the child is what we know and accept about children. This image will determine our way of relating with children, our way of forming our expectations for them and the world that we are able to build for them.

I think that all of you, by now, are familiar with the image of a competent child, on which our educational experience in Reggio is based. But competent in what? In relating with the world. Children do not know the world, but they have all the tools they need to know it and they want to know it. Within this relationship with the world, children come to know it and to know themselves.

I said a competent child. Competent because he has a body, a body that knows how to speak and listen, that gives him an identity and with which he identifies things. A body equipped with senses that can perceive the surrounding environment. A body that risks being increasingly estranged from cognitive processes if its cognitive potential is not recognised and enhanced. A body that is inseparable from the mind. Mind and body, it is increasingly clear, cannot be separated, but form a single unit with reciprocal qualification.

We learn with our mind and our body, just as with reason and emotion. A body that is also distinguished by sex. I am not referring only to genital organs, but also to the sexual identity that derives from being male or female. Children are male and female, girls and boys, and this is a profound difference. It is not the only one, of course, but certainly one of the most significant. For us it is both a limitation and a resource.

The ways of interpreting, of constructing relationships with the world are different between boys and girls. Also our own views and expectations of boys and girls are profoundly different. Girls, for example, seem to become autonomous earlier and to be able to find their own interests, even in moments of difficulty. And this is why some questions are raised for us on which we can reflect, on another important subject:

- How do we cultivate this difference? It seems that the society directs us toward an increasing non-difference between the sexes (fashion, languages, experiences).
- What kind of difference do we emphasise and how do we keep the differences in dialogue?
- How do we construct a difference without indifference? In the way of being a girl or a boy today, in part we construct the identity of the woman and man of the future, of the society of today and tomorrow.
- Are we moving, perhaps, toward a more 'feminine' future as some have affirmed? Or is it the contrary?

But to talk about children and sexuality, of the way in which they discover their sexual identities, also means talking about our own sexual identity, how we see ourselves as women and men, how in our society we have talked about, used, and abused sex and the sexual identity.

Educating is a difficult job because it means, above all, reflecting on and talking about ourselves, our taboos, silences, hypocrisies, fears, about our real feelings and emotions regarding children – our children – and ourselves. Certainly sex and the naked body have never before been so accessible to everyone; and, in a certain sense, never has it been so unknown, and I am not referring to information about sexual reproduction (how we are born, the sexual relationship, and so on).

Instead, I would ask you to reflect on sexual education, the sexual identity, on the identity of the whole person including body and sex. The body as a site of knowledge, pleasure, affection and desires. I would ask you to discuss how we can help children to accept their bodies, appreciate them, love them and respect them, just as we should love, appreciate and respect ourselves and others. A body that we must not be afraid of, but take care of and respect. A body that is a means of gaining knowledge. Learning by means of the body has been a common way of humankind and specifically of young humans. How can we support this without inhibiting it, protect it without denying freedom of expression?

This is the difficult task that awaits us. It is difficult because it means that we, too, are capable of freeing ourselves – thanks to the children – from the cultural 'glitter' that often surrounds our body and our sexual identity. And it means that what we transmit to children is not our fears, but our courage. A body that is familiar and loved is better and more protected and protectable. A known and recognised affectivity and sexuality is less easy to confuse with ambiguous caresses and attentions.

This is also a problem of limits, of rules, between that which is permitted and that which is not. It is a question of the rules: who establishes them, and how? Rules of the home, rules of the school. Should they be different? The same? What kind of consistency should we seek? What differences?

Rules are hard, for both the child and the educator (teacher and parent). They can be discussed, commented on, explained, agreed upon, overcome. But they are necessary, in my opinion. The problem of adults shirking the responsibility of progressively guiding children's growth cannot be resolved only by the school. It is a true educational project which only the dialogue between home and school can produce.

A kind of education that is not afraid of terms such as hard work and effort, concentration, mistakes, losing. And here is another focus point to be discussed. Hard work and efforts, the responsibility of educating and in educating: these are not just words having to do with school, but they are concepts and values on which we must all reflect. Are there responsibilities that belong exclusively to the family? And what do we mean by responsibility?

It is also interesting to reflect on the concepts of safety and risk: risk in growing, risk in educating. In order to grow, to become adults, children take risks. What do we want to risk with them and for them? What can and do we want to allow them to risk? I am talking about physical risks but also psychological ones.

The values of friendship, solidarity, respect for differences, dialogue, feelings, affection are some of the most important values for us as educators, especially because we work in institutions of childhood. These are values that can only be transmitted by living them. Experiencing friendship, respecting differences, engaging in dialogue and solidarity. Are we willing to do this? Are we willing to do this in a society that is so often governed by arrogance, isolation and separation? I ask you and also ask myself: certainly gradually and without ever leaving children and young people alone, but are we willing to educate in friendship, solidarity, affection, in a dialogue without hypocrisy and pretence (that is, 'do as I say and not as I do')?

It is true that childhood and adolescence are increasingly immersed in violence, sometimes victims of it, and sometimes practising it, and in many cases the two alternate. The risk for us is to feel prey to impotence, and thus to feel limited to a Utopia which is 'just there around the corner'. However, in my opinion, we cannot be nostalgic for the 'bunker-schools' or the rigid rules of the past, and we cannot establish with our children what we might call the 'culture of suspicion': the culture that encourages us to view the other as 'hostile', 'enemy', 'dangerous'; a culture that makes us view or interpret others and the world as hostile entities, always ready to abuse us, in both our physical and psychological identity.

Certainly we cannot ignore what we read and hear around us – in our own and other cultures – about the violence committed against children. But we need to raise our level of listening, our dialogue and attention toward children, to observe them and stay close to them, but not to scrutinise them, spy on them, impede them from maintaining their privacy, and above all not to inhibit their curiosity and joyous outlook on the world. What we need to offer them is a support that is strong, loving, firm and patient, that can help them grow toward the freedom of life.

We need to give them – and ourselves – more time to look inside ourselves, to dialogue with them and with others. Otherwise, I can see some enormous risks: the risk of growing up in an atmosphere of suspicion, in solitude, in aridness. To merely survive rather than to live. We can have values and feelings without knowing what to do with them or whom to give them to. This is a real waste of humanity.

There are reasons of the mind and reasons of the heart, which do not always coincide. What is important is to be able to recognise and know them, and to give shape and legitimacy to both. We are often afraid of these reasons of the heart, of these feelings. Feelings such as love, passion, fear, dread, joy, disappointment. But children are not afraid of these feelings. If we listen to these feelings, if we legitimate them, then children will talk about them, narrate them, share them, in order to give them a shape and accept them.

Emotions help children explore the world, and help them understand and create relations. Their emotions are intense and strong, and sometimes make adults afraid, so that we either evade the situation or downplay it with a smile. This is because we are unprepared to be open to emotions, and especially 'those' difficult emotions.

Marco says: 'Is pain and hurt the same thing? Are you talking about hurt? If you get mad, what kind of pain do you have? If you get mad because somebody hit you, there's pain there. If you get mad because your mommy yells at you, there's another kind of pain. When that happens to you, you go and hide.'

Valentina says: 'To disappoint means that somebody really doesn't do what they should do.'

Sara says: 'When I'm disappointed I go yellow and green. But for me it goes away in ten seconds. It's not fast like that for everybody, because everybody is different. If it goes away fast, then you can do more things and you have more fun.'

Laura says: 'Milo is in love with me, but I don't really love him. I'm in love with Samuele. I know it is crazy that I love somebody at my age, even X (the teacher) says it all the time like it was a joke and my mommy says it's not important because I'm still little, but I'm sorry, because for me it's very important.'

When you can talk about feelings (I repeat: anger, love, fear, trust, sadness, pain) then they aren't scary. We need to learn to have this kind of listening as well. The development of feelings, education in sensibility, enables us to reflect in a new and critical way, and to suspend acquired preconceptions. Feelings ask us to assume responsibility toward the feeling itself, which requires courage: the courage to admit it and describe it.

Recognising and talking about feelings brings out a part of our identity that is otherwise unknown, but is capable of exploding into forms that are not always educable. Recognising our feelings enables us to open ourselves to others and to understand the differences with others but also the feelings of others, the things that we have in common that make it possible for us to put ourselves into someone else's shoes.

Exchange, listening and sharing feelings and emotions is an essential part of our dialogue with children, who are so different from us, but really capable of understanding – especially when they are very young – the 'reasons of the heart'.

Chapter 8

Documentation and research (1999)

As I said in an earlier introduction, some themes and concepts recur. First because they are identifiers, i.e. truly identifying features of our experience. But it is perhaps also because they are more difficult to illustrate and probably more complex to understand. In fact to grasp their newness these concepts require a true change of paradigm on the part of the listener, but above all by those working in situations of pedagogical action.

One of these concepts is that of 'pedagogical research', or rather an understanding of the concept of research in defining the teaching–learning relationship as it takes place in everyday action. As I explain in the piece which follows, this is not an arrogant declaration but an attempt to do justice to the creativity and richness which happen each day when we try to understand and support the learning process of the child and teacher through pedagogical documentation.

It is no coincidence that this talk was prepared for an international symposium held in June 1999 in Reggio Emilia, entitled *Learning about learning*. At that time I was director of the municipal schools of Reggio, but I had decided to leave the position and dedicate more time to study and research. This was one of the reasons that I felt, or we felt, the need to promote a meeting which would highlight the rationale that lay behind this announcement: the importance of pedagogical research.

We were doing this at a time when school reforms were being discussed in Italy. More important, once again we were seeking educational legitimisation for *nidi* and *scoule dell'infanzia*, which were more often perceived and described as a service based on individual demand (see page 36) rather than as places of education. The more teacher development was being discussed at a national and international level without sufficiently emphasising the importance of group work and documentation, the more important this legitimisation became.

The presence of friends and colleagues coming from different parts of the world made the event as precious as it could be. Each one brought a contribution which was woven in with those by teachers, *pedagogistas* and *atelieristas* from the municipal schools in Reggio. These educators presented research projects carried out in the municipal schools on subjects considered to be of great interest at the time in national and international debate, like documentation and assessment, community participation, the town of Reggio Emilia, new technologies, ethics and morals, theatre, space and environment, music, special rights. The thesis they presented, through stories in words and images, proposes knowledge to be one form of action among others: just as there is no action without knowledge also there is no knowledge without action. Knowledge enters into the circuit of action in a permanent way and continually modifies it while at the same time undergoing modification. In this way the deep meaning of pedagogical research was made clear.

It gives me, and all of us from Reggio, great joy to be able to share with you this experience of life. Yes, an experience of life, because I see these days together not only as an opportunity for professional development, but above all a meeting between people who are searching for the meaning of teaching, of being teachers.

We will try to bring you in to our experiences, but in particular to the reasons and the motivations that compel us to live each day as a day that is unique, special, full of possibilities and the new. Knowing that each day is not a closed box, pre-packaged, something that has been prepared for you by others (schedules, planning), but rather a time that you construct with the others, children and colleagues – a search for meaning that only the children can help you to find – is the wonderful thing that we have found in our work and in which we would like you to share. It is what we call 'pedagogical research'.

And we believe that it is precisely documentation and research that provide the generative force which makes each day a special day. Now I would like to share with you some reflections that I hope will help you understand better. The first reflection I would like to offer you came to me from re-reading some of Maria Montessori's writings. Here is what Montessori wrote at the beginning of the twentieth century, the same century that we are now concluding:

- '[To start always] from the child . . . with the ability to welcome him as he is, freed of the thousand labels with which it is now presumed to identify him.'
- 'To shift the action of the school from teaching to learning, concretely and not just verbally, favouring the constructive and collaborative action of the children, and the presence of the teacher as a helper who is always available to them but never overpowering or

intrusive. . . . What children know how to do together today, they will know how to do alone tomorrow.'

- 'To construct, also together with the children, an educational environment for learning. . . . By setting up spaces, furnishings, materials, tools, projects, encounters, collaborative experiences, exchanging and comparing ideas.'

I asked myself and I would ask you: What more or different could we say to ourselves and to those who watch and listen to us with interest and curiosity? What more or different could we offer to each child and all the children that is not already contained in these words of Maria Montessori?

I know, following these words of Maria Montessori, much has been written, elaborated on, enriched and further defined. The context in which Maria Montessori worked was different, and her images were different as well. A wealth of research, carried out in various areas and also new fields of knowledge and learning, has made it possible for us to talk about 'scaffolding', about group learning, interdisciplinary approaches, expressivity and languages, and about reciprocity between learning and teaching. But I fear – and I would very much like to be wrong – that too little has actually changed in the way of doing and being school, in the daily life of the school, to the extent that the essence of Maria Montessori's words, in many situations (in Italy and throughout the world), remains unrealised. The causes are many, and come from a number of areas: political, cultural, trade unions, and so on.

One of these, however, seems to me to be a determining factor and one that is rarely taken into consideration. That is the fact that we have continued to talk about school, learning and teaching using only the verbal language, the spoken and written word. Generations of teachers have continued to undergo their initial preparation and in-service professional development without ever having reflected on the range of things we know about learning and on the relationship of learning with the context. And especially, foregoing any search for new ways, new languages, that could enable teachers to live, share, narrate and perform learning events.

These ways, these languages, this sort of 'contamination' between different languages could lead to new horizons (as has happened in other disciplines) and new leading roles, for the children and for the teachers. The teachers, for example, would be promoted from being simply practitioners to being the authors of pedagogical paths and processes. They would be able to contribute to overcoming, at least in the field of education, the arrogant idea of the continuing separation between theory and practice, culture and technique. Teachers would be able to stop seeing themselves, and being seen by others, as those who simply apply theories and decisions developed somewhere else.

The persistence of this idea (which means that teachers continue to be defined as 'practitioners') is an absurdity which must be overcome. It is the result of a misconceived, intellectualist and mistaken concept of research, of pedagogy and of education. Being able to reflect and discuss the ways in which children, and all human beings, learn (thus enriching the humanity of each individual and all of us) is a great possibility and necessity that the school up to now has not been able, or not wanted, to offer. It is time for change. The places where research on learning is carried out must be extended to the schools, and must enable both teachers and students to reflect in their daily lives on the ways they learn and build knowledge.

Yes, I am referring to documentation, in the way we have developed it in the Reggio experience: not as documents for the archives, or as panels hung on the walls, or as a series of nice photographs, but as a visible trace and a procedure that supports learning and teaching, making them reciprocal because they are visible and shareable. I think that this has been, and in the future could be even more, an important contribution of the Reggio experience to the field of pedagogy (but not only this field) at the national and international levels.

But I also believe that we have to go beyond. Documentation as visible listening, as the construction (by means of writing, slides, video, etc.) of traces that not only testify to the children's learning paths and processes, but that can actually make them possible because they are visible. A wealth of documentation (videos, tape recordings, written notes, etc.) developed and used during these processes is important because:

- It makes visible, at least partially, the nature of the learning processes and strategies used by each child. This means that the teacher, but above all the child and the children themselves, can reflect on the nature of their learning process as they are learning; that is, while they are building their knowledge. Not a documentation of products, but of processes, of mental paths.
- All this enables reading and interpretation, re-visiting and assessment in time and space. So this reading, reflecting, assessing and self-assessing become an integral part of the child's knowledge-building process.

For the teacher, being able to reflect on how the learning is proceeding means that she can base her teaching not on what she wants to teach, but on what the child wants to learn. And in this way she learns how to teach, and teacher and children search together for the best way to proceed.

In fact, what we document (and therefore bring into existence) is a sense of the search for meaning and for life that the children and adults make together. It is a moving and poetic sense, that only a poetic, metaphorical and analogical language can construct in its holistic fullness.

A second factor which I think has inhibited, even suffocated, the views about learning expressed by Montessori, but also by Dewey, Piaget, Vygotsky, Bruner and many others, is that the school has been denied access to the concept of research. We are well aware of what is meant by 'scientific research' and of the debate surrounding the so-called 'hard' and 'soft' sciences. But in Reggio we feel that the concept of research, or perhaps better, a new concept of research, more contemporary and alive, can emerge if we legitimate the use of this term to describe the cognitive tension that is created whenever authentic learning and knowledge-building processes take place. 'Research' used to describe the individual and common paths leading in the direction of new universes of possibility. Research as the emergence and revealing of an event. Research as art: research exists, as in art, within the search for the being, the essence, the meaning. These are the meanings that we attribute to the term 'research' (or we could also say 'researches' in the plural if that were possible in English), in the attempt to describe the vital force that can be common to adults and children inside and outside the school. We need to create a culture of research.

I am convinced that this 'attitude of research' is the only feasible existential and ethical approach in a cultural, social and political reality such as ours today, which is subject to changes, breakdowns and to hybridisations of races and cultures, which are positive as well as potentially risky. It is the value of research, but also the search for values.

Chapter 9

Continuity in children's services (1999)

The reason I thought of putting together the next two papers – *Continuity in Children's Services* and *Creativity as a Quality of Thought* – even though the themes they treat are so different, is not only their closeness in terms of time but also the fact that they were prepared for two conferences held in Italy, in Parma and Pistoia to be more precise. And it is exactly this element that I wanted to emphasise: the relationship between the Reggio experience and other Italian experiences. In fact I feel it is opportune to highlight two aspects of this relationship.

There is Reggio's essential (from essence as identity) belonging to the pedagogical and political history of services for early childhood in Italy. Reggio is one of many places which expresses the vitality, wealth and quality of Italian pedagogical research (especially in activist pedagogy in my country) and courageous investment by municipalities in services for early childhood.

But at the same time, Reggio, due in part to dialogue with many national and international situations and to certain structural choices in its pedagogy and politics, has cultivated and declared an identity which makes its differences obvious and appreciable. Among various elements of differentiation are: the *zerosei* (0 to 6 years) continuity project; the value attributed to creativity as a quality of human thinking also declared through the *atelier* and the figure of the *atelierista*; the value of the theory-practice relationship symbolised through working teams of teachers and *pedagogistas*; and the value of reflection as a formative element realised through pedagogical documentation. It was innovative to persevere in declaring aesthetics as an element of rights, part of children's rights, together with participation by families (among others) which was also defined as a right of the family but especially of the child and the teacher.

These elements were probably the reason for many people's interest, but they definitely grew from exchange and sharing with Italian colleagues and situations starting in the early 1960s. I remember car or train journeys with Malaguzzi and with colleagues (who soon became friends) to the most varied destinations in Italy, both north and south. Among the many places we visited and the many rich and generous realities we encountered, I particularly remember Pistoia and Parma for various reasons–some different, some similar.

Pistoia is a Tuscan city similar to Reggio for its size, political orientation and municipal school culture. We had dialogue with them on the theme of creativity and the *zerosei* (0–6) project, that is to say on the relationship between *nidi* and *scuole dell'infanzia*, relationships with the city, the role of the *pedagogista* and more generally on organisation. I believe it is due to this dialogue that we were able to construct our differences and therefore our courageous identities as well as our common passion for the themes of early childhood education.

Parma represents for me the richness of dialogue inside the same region, Emilia Romagna, thanks in part to important work by administrations and staff over the years. In 1972 I went to Parma for the first time with Loris Malaguzzi. They too were discussing a *regolamento* – regulatory measures – in the city for the organisation and consolidation of early childhood services and among central issues were those concerning continuity between *nidi* and *scuole dell'infanzia*. Reggio (as I have said before) had opted for the *zerosei* (0–6) project and placed a lot of emphasis on continuity. Parma opted instead for separating the two experiences and this choice was characterised by differentiating the two types of service, both in pedagogical and organisational orientation. So I was intrigued 30 years later when I was invited to take part in a seminar to reflect on this very subject of pedagogical continuity between *nidi* and *scuole dell'infanzia*, a subject which today in Italy has even more interest and urgency than before. In fact when *nidi* are separated from *scuole dell'infanzia*, they risk denial of their educational identity and being reduced to a mere solution for social needs and emergencies. At the same time *scuole dell'infanzia* risk losing the centrality of play and creativity in children's learning processes.

It is perhaps also for this reason that efforts in Pistoia to put creativity at the centre of recent processes of professional development take on a special value. The friendship between us and the reasons I have described here led me to accept Annalia Galardini's invitation to speak about creativity in Pistoia. In a subsequent meeting Vea Vecchi, an *atelierista*, presented her experiences in the Diana *scuola dell'infanzia*. I remember the meeting with great pleasure and gratitude: the kind you owe to someone who has sought to construct their identity together with you, through the differences.

My contribution is based on my experience of Reggio Emilia, where I have been working for many years and where a project has been developed to work with children from 0 to 6 years of age in *nidi* and *scuole dell'infanzia*. Briefly, the significance of the experience is due to a number of distinguishing characteristics, including the following: the same department of the commune, i.e. the Teaching, Education and Professional

Training Department, is responsible for the whole project; there is a single structure of pedagogical support and coordination; and all the services share the same values, epistemology, pedagogy and organisation (e.g. same opening hours, the same total number of working hours).

Why a '0 to 6' project? What considerations are behind it? What sort of continuities have been sought and are we still seeking to establish through this kind of choice? How topical is this sort of issue? Why is it still necessary to reaffirm the value and significance of this project?

Reflecting on a number of concepts and questions can help an understanding and discussion of our choice in Reggio and contribute to our reflection on this subject.

1 The concept of continuity

Why continuity? Whose continuity? The continuity of what? A continuity of thoughts and actions, which is therefore not identifiable with meetings – dialogues which characterise stages of development – however important they are. A continuity which cannot be summed up by interviews, however significant, between teachers from *nidi* and *scuole dell'infanzia* and with parents.

Continuity is a more complex and composite phenomenon than one based on just exchanges of information about what levels have been reached by the children. It makes reference to a quality which is intrinsic to living itself, to man, to his/her search for meaning, the meaning of his/her past, present and future. The continuity sought by the child has to do with being part of, and being engaged in, a project; a 'life project' where the various parties to the project and the places of his/her education (family, *nido, scuola dell'infanzia*, and social context) know each other and dialogue with each other from their different identities, to help his/her search for identity and meaning. Continuity, above all, as a right of the child and an internal quality of the *nido*, involving dialogue within the *nido* and with the outside world; all this in space and time.

2 The concept of change – although at first sight it may appear in contradiction to the concept of continuity

Is change a value? What change? What change are we talking about? I would suggest as important the sort of change which defines the life of man, the kind of change that generates and is generated by discontinuity as a generative factor; a biological fact and a cultural value that is inescapable; change as a transition from one 'state', that of being, to another, that of being able to be; the change which we effect and are affected by; the change that affects the child and which the child does not want to and cannot relinquish. Though change may not be easy and can sometimes be painful, it is vital. Vital in relation to life, because life is change, and the first few years of life are a period of great transformation.

We talk about the right to change: change is both a right and a value. It is a quality of life and of living which requires awareness to give oneself direction. What is necessary is to give meaning to change and accompany change. Children ask that of us, too; that we accompany their changes and their search for new identities, their search for the meaning of growth and for identity within change, their search for the meaning of change. It is a matter of seeing, reading, interpreting change through the eyes of other children and adults in order to understand it, appraise it and appreciate it.

3 Our image of the child and of childhood

These images are carried within ourselves. They are acquired through the system of representations which every social group develops in the course of its history. They are the expectations directed to the child by his/her social context. It is through these representations and images that every society and individual relates to children.

In my view, our age, this turn of the century, and our cultural area of the world is characterised by a deep discrepancy between what is described in the psycho-pedagogical literature and experienced in some situations, and what is actually done and experienced in most daily life. Much has been said and written about the competent child (who has the ability to learn, love, be moved, and live), the child who has a wealth of potentials, the powerful child in relation to what s/he is and can be right from birth. In practice, however, very little has been done that takes this image seriously.

4 The concept of learning

Much has been said about the individual's construction of knowledge, its timeframes and methods, and about the construction of identity. But in practice, the way we act and relate to the child reveals a complete denial of these possibilities.

Many pedagogical approaches, policies and institutions dealing with childhood are inspired and legitimated by the idea of a fragile and weak child. And the younger the child (especially children under three years), the more legitimate it seems to be to deny the many qualities which identify him/her.

A rupture has developed between the first two to three years of life and the second three. The differences between these age groups, though important in characterising them, have been assumed to be to the total disadvantage of the younger child, resulting in a real erosion and distortion of his/her rights. We are witnessing a real social, cultural and political negation of the young child in his/her public identity as the bearer of citizens' rights. The identity of childhood is thus being hidden.

Perhaps this is the only way in which people can justify arguments about treating *nidi* differently. Their costs – which are undeniably high – are never seen as social investments but always just as expenses. This is why issues like the different pay for educators in *nidi* and *scuole dell'infanzia*, or the recent decisions regarding professional education (university education required only for teachers in *scuole dell'infanzia*) no longer surprise anyone. It is also the only way to explain (but not justify) the attitude of teachers in *scuole dell'infanzia* who reject comparison and exchanges with *nidi*; it is their fear of being dragged downward.

The ever-increasing risk of standardisation of *scuole dell'infanzia* and the attempt to make them increasingly like compulsory elementary schools give rise to a completely distorted approach to the relationship between *nidi* and *scuole dell'infanzia*. The paucity of *nidi* across this country and often, sadly, their low visibility and the low recognition accorded to them (in the social and cultural sphere) risks increasing their separation from *scuole dell'infanzia*, with the risk of isolating the *nido* from every other part of the educational system.

The research that has taken place in the *nido*, showing its qualities and value, has been to little avail. In the image of the public and the national government, too often the *nido* appears as a place of 'care-taking' and of 'social assistance'; an expensive place that does not educate.

There are, therefore, many reasons, of a political, economic and cultural nature, which hinder the real development of the concept of continuity across the 0 to 6 age group. What seems obvious, however, is the need to break out of the vicious circle into which the *nido* has fallen and to start afresh not only from an economic and employment perspective, but from the image of the child, the child's rights, the child's ways of learning, of building knowledge and identity in a context that is supportive and welcoming, so as to identify the educational qualities of these institutions.

What is needed, therefore, is to reflect starting from the child and the strategies that are most likely to allow his/her possibilities to really express themselves. Then, but only then, can we start to negotiate and tackle economic issues (costs), trade union issues (staff conditions) and the needs arising from social organisation (families' working hours, etc.), to find flexible solutions that are compatible with the needs and rights of other subjects (teachers, parents). Only by proceeding in this way will we be able to talk about continuity, or rather, to reflect on the concept of continuity and agree a new meaning for this term.

Continuity meant, first and foremost, as long-term *progettualità*, a long timeframe that may sustain not only the search for meaning but also the differences and similarities between the changing identities (those of the children and those of the institution). [*Added by CR when editing the book*: dialogue between *nidi* and *scuole dell'infanzia* will only be possible in so far as they are able to express what differentiates them as well as what they share. So they share listening to children, care of the environment, the value of dialogue and participation. But their strategies and forms of organisation are different. For example, the way I organise an environment for a six-month-old baby is different from the one I organise for a four-year-old child: but both are inspired by a high level of attention to creating a context which is able to encourage processes of learning and interaction in children and between children.]

Continuity meant not in the sense of standardisation but as a coherent and coordinated development of the educational process. This should imply no erosion of methods and means but, on the contrary, should involve a search for different strategies and contexts, aiming toward a common goal (i.e. allowing each and every child as well as each and every adult (teachers and parents) to share common meanings, giving rise to *nidi* and *scuole dell'infanzia* that are not a preparation for life but *are* life), and values constructed together. These are not places where teachers try to pass on information but where teachers and children try reciprocally to understand each other.

This may eventually guarantee identifying the proper differences and the necessary similarities between the two institutions, in a relationship of mutual esteem and respect. This relationship comes from sharing meaning, knowledge and development, and the processes that make it possible for them to be achieved, i.e. the process of educating, the role of early childhood institutions, and the meaning of teaching in relation to learning. In other words, it means making the theories of reference explicit and making them the object of reflection, discussion, comparison and exchange.

These assumptions and goals have enabled my city of Reggio Emilia to organise and follow common education processes which allow dialogue to take place with differences as the starting point. Conscious differences that are discussed and ready to be redefined through exchange and change. *Nidi* and *scuole dell'infanzia* can thereby derive great mutual advantage not only in terms of dialogue but also in terms of identity and awareness.

Continuity as a *progettualità* with a broad scope and a long timescale (six years) of possibilities is important not only for the child, both for his/her processes and development, but also for teacher education (which should focus on the 0 to 6 childhood project), the relationship with the families (six year programmes influence the development of the parenting experience), and the social, cultural and political impact of this experience. The *nido* is presented as a place that is not unique but is of primary importance in developing the 'image of childhood'. A strong image of childhood and of the school of childhood means a stronger contractual position. [*Added by CR when editing the book:* what I mean by 'stronger contractual position' is that stronger bargaining power for children derives from recognising childhood and children as social subjects, subjects bearing rights and who, as such, cannot be ignored and offended.]

Continuity here means continuity of values, i.e.:

- *Value of professional education* as self-education;
- *Value of education* as children, teachers and parents constructing knowledge and identity together, implying the value of subjectivity through the recognition of the individual paths and processes of memories, documents and traces;
- *Value of participation and collegiality* as comparison, exchange and negotiation;
- *Value of the context* in terms of space, timeframes and materials.

Continuity in Reggio has been translated into an organisation which pays the utmost respect to differences, allowing the distinctive qualities of every institution to express themselves. But at the same time, our organisation fosters dialogue and communication at all levels through: the co-presence of teachers (more than one teacher working with the same group at the same time); collegial professional education sessions; sessions for parent participation; and through the training provided by formal meetings between institutions.

5 The transition stage between the *nido* and the *scuola dell'infanzia*

We set out from the belief that children – and others – ask us and wish to make forecasts that support their understanding and structuring of the event of transition. Often, what is defined as the egocentrism of the child (but also of the adult) is actually a phenomenon of *disorientation*. We have to help them and ourselves to foresee the rules, roles, and expectations that permeate the context.

Accordingly, in the last year of the *nido* (but also of the *scuola dell'infanzia*) we make a more intense effort to develop forecast frameworks for the children, the parents and the teachers. It is important for all three subjects, albeit taking into account their different concerns, to be able to master the transition period through understanding, through feeling expected and welcomed, through feeling that one's individual identity is recognised (acknowledging the fear – particularly by parents – of anonymity), through feeling that one is being listened to (in one's hopes, desires and anxieties); in short, to feel respected and welcomed.

It is in this sense that a number of initiatives acquire value and meaning; initiatives such as visits to the *scuola dell'infanzia* for the parents and children, who can spend a whole morning there as a group; class meetings with the teachers of the *scuola dell'infanzia* to explore together expectations (and continuities); and providing basic information and reassurances (including information material, pamphlets, and small publications where the five-year-olds themselves talk to the children about to start at the *scuola dell'infanzia* about their experiences through words, drawings and photographs).

Further opportunities are provided through a sort of 'identity card' of the *scuola dell'infanzia* and the class, with the names of their future friends and the teachers; and by an invitation to the children about to start the *scuola dell'infanzia* to gather their memories of how they spent their summer, which means collecting personal stories and narratives. This little 'holiday diary' will stay with the child during his/her first days at school and might help to smooth the transition between one context and another.

All this material is delivered to the families in June during a meeting with the new children, their families and teachers, arranged specifically for this purpose: having an ice-cream or a cup of tea is a good pretext to get together as a group and define together its physical makeup, the identities which form the group and the path it intends to follow. In August we hold individual interviews and another meeting of everyone together which takes place a few days before school starts, when parents and teachers try to make forecasts and identify strategies. In addition, there are interviews with individual families and meetings between the teachers at the *nido* and the *scuola dell'infanzia*, which we try to arrange at the *nido* in order to give greater value to the documentation materials from the *nido* – individual and group traces, which are a testimony of the child's experiences.

These meetings have to be approached with an understanding that one is not going to describe who the child is, even less evaluate the child through a 'final assessment', but rather to *narrate* his/her experiences in that particular context – the *nido* – through documents that speak of the child and on his/her behalf. It is a conversation aimed at giving the colleague in the *scuola dell'infanzia* – who uses the same languages as the *nido* worker and, most of all, shares values and meanings in those areas I mentioned earlier – guidance in how best to create a welcoming environment. The history and the traces of the child's work are collected in albums, some of which are individual notebooks and others group documents.

Last but not least, in developing continuity, there are professional development sessions and meetings for the teachers from the *nidi* and *scuole dell'infanzia*, held both separately and together, to prepare 'the event', the move from one institution to another, including the farewell and the welcome party to which the teachers are mutually invited.

There are many more things happening well into the autumn when, after an initial period of settling in, the teachers have an opportunity to meet again for further exchanges, to make suggestions and to give advice. A great many actions, a great many thoughts, but only one goal: making the child and his/her family authors of their own story, open to change, thankful for the past, but full of 'nostalgia for the future'.

Creativity as a quality of thought (2000)

I believe that some of the most important questions we have to ask ourselves as teachers, but also as educators in general and as adults, are these:

- How can we help children to find the meaning of what they do and what they experience?
- How can we respond to their search for the meaning of things, the meaning of life itself?
- How can we respond to their constant questions, their 'whys' and 'hows', their search for that which we like to think of as not only the meaning of things but the meaning of life itself, a search that begins from the moment of birth, from the child's first, silent 'why' to that which, for us, is the meaning of life?

These are central questions.

It is a difficult search, especially for today's children, who have so many different points of reference in their daily lives: the experience of the family, television, the places of socialisation. Young children make enormous efforts to put together all these often disconnected fragments, which they encounter not just over a lifetime but even in the span of a single day. And in these efforts, children are sometimes left alone, by their families and also by schools. But they continue their search just the same, stubbornly, tirelessly, making mistakes, and often doing it alone, but they persevere. Quitting would mean precluding any possibilities or any hopes, precluding the possibility not only of having a past but also of giving oneself a future. And children do this right from the beginning of their lives.

This search for life and for the self is born with the child, and this is why we talk about a child who is competent and strong, engaged in this search toward life, toward others, toward the relations between the self and life. A child, therefore, who is no longer considered to be fragile, suffering, incapable; a child who asks us to look at her with different eyes in order to empower her right to learn and to know, to find the meaning of life and of her own life, alone and with others. Ours is a different idea and attitude toward the young child, who we see as active and who, along with us, searches every day to understand something, to draw out a meaning, to grasp a piece of life.

The enormous problem is to understand the meaning of that which we are constructing, the why of things, to search for reasons and answers. And this is not tied to a specific age – I believe that it is a quality of human life. To have a different understanding of reality does not mean having different rights. Yet it appears often to be the case that a kind of hierarchy is imposed, which creates levels of understanding and then relates these to the recognition of rights. Very often the theories and understandings expressed by the child are defined as 'misunderstand-ings' or 'naïve theories', and as such not deserving to be listened to or of respect. This places the child on an inferior level, defines him as 'imperfect', his contribution not considered significant.

By contrast, we know very well what it means to feel that you are the child's travelling companion in this search for meaning. The meanings that children produce, the explanatory theories they develop in an attempt to give answers are of the utmost importance. They strongly reveal the ways in which children perceive, question, and interpret reality and their relationships with it.

These theories, these explanations that children produce, are wonder-fully sweet: 'It's raining because the man on TV said it was going to rain'; or 'It's raining because Jesus is crying'. But these statements must abso-lutely not be taken as 'misunderstandings', a term often used in peda-gogical culture, that is, something that must be corrected. Rather, they should be viewed as something much more important. The genesis of the young child's desire to ask herself questions is very early in life. This gives greater significance to the child's stopping to study a flower for ten minutes, her enchantment with rain on a window, and her various won-derings, her 'whys'. For when a child asks the question 'why', this is also the most generative moment.

From a very young age, children seek to produce interpretive theories, to give answers. Some may say these theories are ingenuous and naïve, but this is of little importance: the important thing is not only to give value to but, above all, to understand what lies behind these questions and theories, and what lies behind them is something truly extraordinary.

There is the intention to produce questions and search for answers, which is one of the most extraordinary aspects of creativity.

The competent child is one who has an adult who views her as such: the level of expectations is a determining factor. I believe, for example, that for us in Reggio Emilia, it has been vital to get away from the idea of 'objective observation', that is, to eliminate objectivity in favour of the subject, but especially the possibility of looking at the child with love, with complicity. [*Added by CR when editing the book:* I use 'complicity' here to mean a sort of alliance or solidarity which makes children and adults feel as if they are together, linked by a common desire for understanding and knowing, and able to struggle and rejoice together.] This complicit view can also lead to the realisation that what underlies the children's observations are the many 'whys', their attempts to explain to themselves why a flower is like it is, why mommy says 'flower' and what a flower is. But in a flower there is the meaning of life, and in the relationship with a flower there is the search for the meaning of life.

This is why I would like to reflect for a moment on what we call, though we do not claim this is original, the 'pedagogy of relationships and listening', which originates precisely from the idea that children are the most avid seekers of meaning and significance, and that they produce interpretive theories. This idea is not only the genesis of this pedagogy of relationships and listening, but also the possible genesis of a 'relational creativity'. For adults and children alike, as I said before, understanding means elaborating an interpretation, what we call an 'interpretive theory', that is a theory that gives meaning to the things and events of the world, a theory in the sense of a satisfactory explanation. We take the term 'theory', which usually has such serious connotations, and instead make it an everyday right, and we recognise this right in the child who we define as 'competent'.

Can a three- or four-month-old child develop theories? I like to think so, because I feel that this conviction can lead to a different approach and, in particular, to these concepts of listening and relational creativity. A theory, therefore, is viewed as a satisfactory explanation, though also provisional. It is something more than simply an idea or a group of ideas; it must be pleasing and convincing, useful and capable of satisfying our intellectual, affective, and also aesthetic needs. That is, it must give us the sense of a wholeness that generates a sense of beauty and satisfaction.

In certain ways, a theory, if possible, must be pleasing to others, too, and it needs to be listened to by others. This makes it possible to transform a world that is intrinsically personal into something shared: my knowledge and my identity are also constructed by the other. Sharing theories is a response to uncertainty and solitude. Here is an example. A three-year-old said: 'The sea is born from the mother wave.' The child has conceptualised and is developing the idea that everything has an origin. Putting together all the elements in her possession in a creative way, the child formulates a satisfactory explanation and, while she is conceptualising it, she shares it with others. Or to take other examples:

- 'The weather is born from the storm.' Here the child makes an association, and waits only to be listened to and not rejected. Her capacity is to create composite representations with unusual languages and combinations.
- 'The wind is born from the air and has the shape to bang thing': statements such as this one give dignity to the term 'competent child'.
- 'But when someone dies, do they go into the belly of death and then get born again?' This is what the search for meaning and the formulation of theories means: here the child has put together all the elements she has at hand, and perhaps also her own anxieties.

The word 'listening', not only in the physical sense but also in the metaphorical sense, thus becomes no longer just a word but an essential approach to life. Here is what we mean by listening: listening is an attitude that requires the courage to abandon yourself to the conviction that our being is just a small part of a broader knowledge; listening is a metaphor for openness to others, sensitivity to listen and be listened to, with all your senses. It is a word that should not be aimed only at children but also toward others. In particular, listening means giving yourself and others the time for listening. Behind each act of listening there is desire, emotion, openness to differences, to different values and points of view. We therefore have to listen and give value to the differences, the points of view of others, whether man, woman or child, and especially to remember that behind each act of listening there is creativity and interpretation on both parts. Listening therefore means giving value to the other; it does not matter whether you agree. Learning how to listen is a difficult undertaking; you have to open yourself to others, and we all need this. Competent listening creates a deep opening and predisposition toward change.

Listening is a premise of every learning relationship. Of course learning is an individual act, but we also know that learning is taken to a higher plane when there is the possibility to act and reflect on the learning itself. Representing our learning process and being able to share with others becomes indispensable for that reflexiveness which generates knowledge. In this way, images and intentions are recognised by the subject; they take shape and evolve through action, emotion, expressiveness and iconic and symbolic representations. This is the generative basis of languages, learning and creativity.

The concept expressed before about the sea and the mother wave was probably expressed in answer to a question and within a specific context, and this idea could become even more wonderful and powerful if the child were asked to represent her idea graphically. More explicitly: let's take the example of a drawing made by Federica (three years, two months old) and see how the child resolves the problem of representing a running horse (see Figure 10.1).

Federica knows that horses have four legs; she turns the piece of paper over and draws the other two legs on the reverse side (see Figure 10.2).

She has managed to bring together multiple languages and has learned to encode them: this is expressivity, creativity. A similar solution was reached by a five-year-old girl, who took the piece of paper and set it against the window, then traced from the other side.

We are looking at extremely creative moments at both the cognitive and expressive levels; the two girls have searched for three-dimensionality in a two-dimensional medium.

What clearly emerges here is a particular image of the child and of the teacher, as well as a culture of listening. On one hand, there are

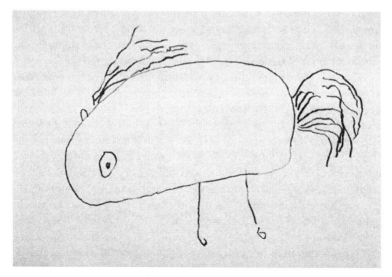

Figure 10.1

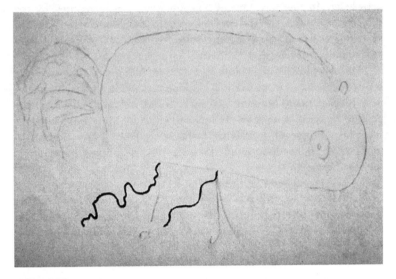

Figure 10.2

schools that do not listen in this sense because they have a curriculum to follow and they try to correct 'mistakes' immediately, to provide quick solutions to a problem and not give children the time to find their own solutions. On the other hand, there are schools that believe it is right and proper to listen more attentively and propose other opportunities where these girls could continue to pursue their own research, so that they are advancing on the cognitive as well as the communicative level.

What is extraordinary in the human mind is not only our capacity to move from one language to another, from one 'intelligence' to another; but also that we are capable of reciprocal listening that makes communication and dialogue possible. Children are the most extraordinary listeners of all; they encode and decode, interpreting data with incredible creativity: children 'listen' to life in all its facets, listen to others with generosity, quickly perceive how the act of listening is an essential act of communication. Children are biologically predisposed to communicate and establish relationships: this is why we must always give them plentiful opportunities to represent their mental images and to be able to represent them to others.

Thus, moving from one language to another, from one field of experience to another, children can grow in the idea that others are indispensable for their own identity and existence. This is a fundamental concept of values that we can choose to follow or not. We realise not only that the other becomes indispensable for our identity, for our understanding, for communication and listening, but also that learning together generates pleasure in the group, that the group becomes the place of learning. We thus create what we call a 'competent audience', subjects capable of listening, of listening reciprocally and becoming sensitive to the ideas of others to enrich their own ideas and to generate group ideas. This, then, is the revolution that we have to put into place: to develop children's natural sensitivity toward appreciating and developing the ideas of another, sharing them together.

This is why we consider the learning process to be a creative process. By creativity, I mean the ability to construct new connections between thoughts and objects that bring about innovation and change, taking known elements and creating new connections. Here is an example (see Figures 10.3, 10.4 and 10.5). A three-year-old child is playing with a piece of wire. First he makes a bracelet and then, on the back of the chair, the wire becomes a horseman riding his steed, and finally it is transformed into the horse's ear.

As we know, human beings are equipped with two forms of thinking: convergent thinking, which tends toward repetition, and divergent thinking, which tends toward the reorganisation of elements.

Divergent thinking is the type we see in the previous example. It is the

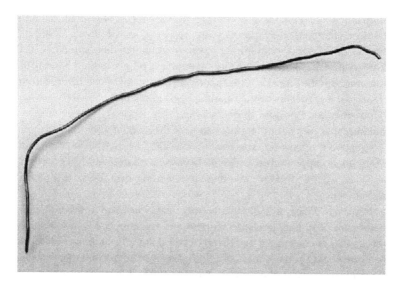

Figure 10.3

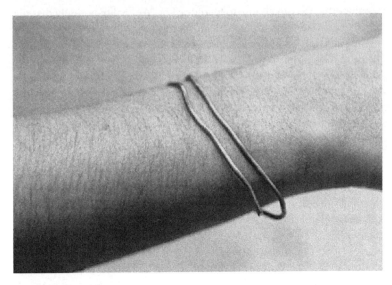

Figure 10.4

combination of unusual elements that young children put into place very easily because they do not have a particular theoretical background or fixed relationships. Why, instead, is it so hard for us adults to use divergent thinking? First of all, because convergent thinking is convenient, but also because changing your mind often represents a loss of power. Children, on the other hand, search for power by changing their minds, in the honesty that they have toward ideas and toward others, in their honesty of listening. But they quickly understand that having ideas that diverge from those of their teachers or their parents and expressing them at the wrong moment is not a positive thing. So when this happens, it is not creative thinking that dies but the legitimisation of the creativity of thinking.

Creative thinking can also lead to solitude. Creativity is relational; it needs to be approved in order to become a shared asset. Too often, however, we are afraid of this creativity, even our own, because it makes us 'different'.

In play, as Piaget noted, children take reality in hand in order to take possession of it; they freely decompose and recompose it, consolidating this quality of convergent and divergent thinking. Through play, children confront reality and accept it, develop creative thinking and escape from a reality that is too often oppressive. It is here that some of our most serious mistakes take root.

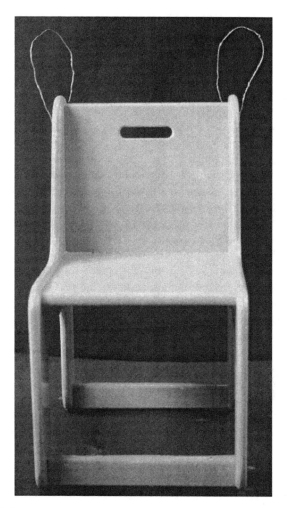

Figure 10.5

The dimension of play (with words, playing tricks, and so on) is thus an essential element of the human being. If we take this dimension away from children and from adults, we remove a possibility for learning, we break up the dual play-learning relationship. The creative process, instead, needs to be recognised and legitimated by others.

Creativity is not just the quality of thinking of each individual but is also an interactive, relational and social project. It requires a context that allows it to exist, to be expressed, to become visible. In schools, creativity should have the opportunity to be expressed in every place and in every moment. What we hope for is creative learning and creative teachers, not simply a 'creativity hour'. This is why the *atelier* must support and ensure all the creative processes that can take place anywhere in the school, at home and in the society. We should remember that there is no creativity in the child if there is no creativity in the adult: the competent and creative child exists if there is a competent and creative adult.

Think of our relationship with art: art has too often been separated from life and, like creativity, it has not been recognised as an everyday right, as a quality of life. The disciplinary development of the sciences has provided many benefits; but it has also led to problems such as the over-specialisation and compartmentalisation of knowledge. In general, our social system also adheres to this logic of separation and fragmentation. We are too often taught to separate that which is connected, to divide rather than bring together the disciplines, to eliminate all that which can lead to disorder. For this reason, it is absolutely indispensable to reconsider our relationship with art as an essential dimension of human thinking. The art of daily life and the creativity of daily life should be the right of all. Art, then, as a part of our lives, of our efforts to learn and to know.

I conclude, in homage to Gianni Rodari who inspired this presentation, with a quote from his book *Grammatica della Fantasia* (The Grammar of Fantasy): 'Every possible use of words should be made available to every single person – this seems to me to be a good motto with a democratic sound. Not because everyone should be an artist but because no one should be a slave.'

Chapter 11

The construction of the educational project

An interview with Carlina Rinaldi by Lella Gandini and Judith Kaminsky (2000)

I remember well the moment when Lella Gandini and Judith Kaminsky asked me to give this interview. To be more precise, they asked me to organise into the form of an interview the contents which inspired many of the talks I had given to study groups visiting the municipal schools of Reggio. 'Study group' is a term we use to define groups of people (teachers, researchers, politicians, administrators) who ask to visit our schools and become familiar with our experience. They come from all parts of the world (New Zealand, China, Australia, North and South America, Europe). For the most part they live in contexts which are sensitive and attentive to problems in education; but sometimes the contrary is true and coming to Reggio opens up their hearts to what is possible.

Between 1994 and 2004, 112 study groups have visited Reggio Emilia, about 14,000 people from 79 countries. The groups are made up of about 100 to 150 people (but sometimes more) who usually come from the same country. The visitors have different identities: for example differences can be noted between approaches in countries of Latin origin and those of Anglo-Saxon origin. But all of them have a desire to get to know and explore more deeply the elements characterising the experience of Reggio, i.e. what makes Reggio . . . Reggio!

And so by following their questions we have learned to build our stories, those speaking of our identity and in a certain sense of our differences. We have heard about their cultures and experiences; but at the same time, we have become more aware of our own identity and the historical reasons determining it. Thanks to the groups, we began to appreciate the courage of inconvenient and difficult choices, we felt pleasure and pride in belonging to a community project which was not only our experience but the city itself.

I have often been invited to take part in a group of speakers invited to present the experience. For this reason I had prepared different notes over the years which I used to construct my talks. So when Lella Gandini and Judith Kaminsky asked me to make this interview together we went through the notes I had gathered in over a decade. For the most part the questions in the interview reflect questions which we had been asked; but there are also declarations, statements that we wished to make even though they were not explicitly requested. An example of this is the question on the image of the child which for us was and is fundamental but which has rarely been asked.

So reading the interview you can encounter some of the elements which appear to define the identity of the Reggio experience as I have perceived it: the image of the child and childhood; the concept of education and learning; the child-teacher relationship; the relationship between children; the relationship with families and the city; and the fundamental role which documentation has assumed in developing the quality of pedagogy in the municipal schools in Reggio. These are also recurring themes in other work collected here in this book because our dialogue with other experiences has been based on these elements.

It may be possible in this interview to perceive the profound influence the writings of Loris Malaguzzi and many other authors have had on me, from Piaget and Vygotsky to Gardner, Bruner and Hawkins. My reading of Bateson, Morin and the socio-constructivists, starting with the Italians Donata Fabbri and Alberto Munari, were especially important. I have recently been fascinated in reading authors defined as postmodern and also books by Umberto Eco and Italo Calvino, and I have always read Gianni Rodari, whom I had the honour of meeting and spending time with, together with Loris Malaguzzi. To all of these, to the others I have not quoted and to colleagues I have known in all these years, my deepest thanks. Please let me thank also Amelia Gambetti who has always been my friend and working companion, Paola Riccò and Emanuela Vercalli, because thanks to them I was able to effectively synthesise all the questions that have been asked of us and collaborate on the *progettazione* of study groups which represent as closely as possible our desire to dialogue with visitors' questions.

But my introduction to this chapter would not be complete without clarifying the fundamental role played by interpreters who have followed each other down the years; starting with Leslie Morrow, who had the courage to accept the challenge posed by language that we use here in Reggio. A language which has been specialised, becoming a kind of 'local' idiom, constructed over the years through our interpretations of codes and languages which are typical of pedagogy in Italy and elsewhere. It was necessary to translate without betrayal, make what was local global without losing its identity. Leslie and her colleagues have done this successfully. My thanks, our thanks, go out to them.

From all your work in Reggio Emilia, has a particular idea of children and childhood emerged as a reference for your research and practice?

Everyone (you, us, each parent . . .) has his or her own image of the child. Consequently, we have our own educational theories that are developed based on personal experience as well as constructed or acquired as part of our society and culture. Whether we are aware of it or not, we cannot live without theories. There are many images of the child, and many images of childhood. We need only think of psychoanalysis or the various branches of psychology and sociology. Though these theories are quite different, they tend to have one recurring aspect in common: the deterministic identification of the child as a weak subject, a person with needs rather than rights.

These positions have probably gained widespread approval because they work well for certain images of motherhood, women, and the family, images that are more 'convenient' and accommodating. They are certainly easier to manage than the image that is part of our theory, which views children as strong, powerful and rich in potential and resources, right from the moment of birth. In this sense, we share the values and meaning of the constructivist and social constructivist approaches. We see a child who is driven by the enormous energy potential of a hundred billion neurons, by the strength of wanting to grow and taking the job of growing seriously, by the incredible curiosity that makes children search for the reasons for everything. A child who knows how to wait and who has high expectations. A child who wants to show that he or she knows things and knows how to do things, and who has all the strength and potential that comes from children's ability to wonder and to be amazed. A child who is powerful from the moment of birth because he is open to the world and capable of constructing his own knowledge. A child who is seen in his wholeness, who possesses his own directions and the desire for knowledge and for life. A competent child!

Competent in relating and interacting, with a deep respect for others and accepting of conflict and error. A child who is competent in constructing, in constructing himself while he constructs his world and is, in turn, constructed by the world. Competent in constructing theories to interpret reality and in formulating hypotheses and metaphors as possibilities for understanding reality.

A child who has his own values and is adept at building relationships of solidarity. A child who is always open to that which is new and different. A possessor and builder of futures, not only because children are the future, but because they constantly re-interpret reality and continuously give it new meanings.

The child as a possessor and constructor of rights, who demands to be respected and valued for his own identity, uniqueness and difference. To think of a child as a possessor of rights means not only recognising the rights that the society gives to children, but also creating a context of 'listening' in the fullest sense. This means that we must recognise and accept the uniqueness and subjectivity of each individual (and thus each child), as well as create spaces that are self-generative, i.e. spaces where each child can create and construct new rights. [*Added by CR when editing the book:* a society which 're-cognises' (re-knows, re-understands) its childhood adds not just a social subject but modifies itself because in recognising children's rights it recognises new rights for everyone.]

In terms of education, this type of theory requires us to respect the subjectivity of the learner, a point which is extremely important not only from a pedagogical point of view but also in terms of values, social policy and culture. It also means that, as educators, we assume an enormous responsibility.

This image of the child that you describe is truly fascinating.

Yes, it is. And the results of recent biological and neuroscientific research also lend insight and support to our philosophy, as they give us guidance in the attempt to respond to an essential question: how is knowledge constructed? How do we learn?

Making a connection with these disciplines provides us with some extremely important and thought-provoking information, such as:

- The human brain is extremely plastic.
- In the first seven to eight years of life, there is a surplus of neurons that allows practically infinite possibilities for development.
- Genetic information is not sufficient for establishing the connections between these billions of neurons, so that many connections take place in the interaction with the external environment.

From this we can infer:

- The uniqueness of the human brain and of each individual.
- The importance of the opportunities provided (i.e. the quality of the context), and therefore the synergetic reciprocity and the natural solidarity between the individual and his surrounding environment.

Such findings have wide-ranging significance. They confirm the need for education which is ecological in the truest sense of the word; and they clearly underline the dangers of not using the human brain to its full capacity, with the consequent waste of humanity caused by the lack of educational contexts that are commensurate with children's enormous potential.

So the result is a different conception of education and learning . . .

That's right. Learning does not take place by means of transmission or reproduction. It is a process of construction, in which each individual constructs for himself the reasons, the 'whys', the meanings of things, others, nature, events, reality and life. The learning process is certainly individual, but because the reasons, explanations, interpretations and meanings of others are indispensable for our knowledge building, it is also a process of relations – a process of social construction. We thus consider knowledge to be a process of construction by the individual in relation with others, a true act of co-construction.

The timing and styles of learning are individual, and cannot be stand-ardised with those of others, but we need others in order to realise ourselves.

Certain fundamental consequences arise here on both the theoretical and practical level. First of all, there is a complete shift as regards school, education and society as a whole, which could again be expressed in a series of important questions:

- What is the relationship between social knowledge and individual knowledge?
- What is the relationship between adult and child? Between an adult who has some knowledge – and by knowledge we mean an inter-pretation of reality that is constantly evolving – and a child who wants to possess that knowledge, but in his or her own way, his or her own time, and above all in order to recreate and modify it. This leads to another question:
- What is the relationship between teaching and learning?

So what is the role of the teacher in this relationship with children?

The teacher is not removed from her role as an adult, but instead revises it in an attempt to become a co-creator, rather than merely a transmitter, of knowledge and culture. As teachers, we have to carry out this role in the full awareness of our vulnerability, and this means accepting doubts and mistakes as well as allowing for surprise and curiosity, all of which are necessary for true acts of knowledge and creation. This requires a 'powerful' teacher, the only kind of teacher suitable for our equally 'powerful' child. School thus becomes a place of research, where the children, along with the teachers, are the primary researchers.

If we believe that children possess their own theories, interpretations and questions, and are co-protagonists in the knowledge-building processes, then the most important verbs in educational practice are no longer 'to talk', 'to explain' or 'to transmit' – but 'to listen'. Listening means being open to others and what they have to say, listening to the hundred (and more) languages, with all our senses. To listen is an active verb, because it means not just recording a message but also interpreting it, and this message acquires meaning at the moment at which the listener receives it and evaluates it. To listen is also a reciprocal verb. Listening legitimises the other person, because communication is one of the fundamental means of giving form to thought. The communicative act that takes place through listening produces meanings and reciprocal modifications that enrich all the participants in this type of exchange.

The task of the teacher is to create a context in which children's curiosity, theories and research are legitimated and listened to, a context in which children feel comfortable and confident, motivated and respected in their existential and cognitive paths and processes. A context in which well-being is the dominant trait, a context of listening at many levels, full of emotion and excitement. The role of the teacher (and the group of teachers) also involves constant hypothesising on the possible developments of the educational project, and this is closely linked to the other aspects that characterise the teacher's work: listening, observation, documentation and interpretation.

The metaphor that might best represent our image of the school is that of a construction site, or a permanent laboratory, in which children's and teachers' research processes are strongly intertwined and constantly evolving. Here, teachers build an awareness of knowledge and the processes of its construction through a progressive understanding of the structure and skills being developed by each child and the group of children, as well as of their individual and group identities. The question of 'knowledge of knowledge' leads to another fundamental point of our philosophy: one of the primary tasks of the teacher, and thus of the school, is to help the child and the group of children learn how to learn, fostering their natural predisposition toward relationships and the consequent co-construction of knowledge.

So, going back to the question about the relationship between teaching and learning in our philosophy, I would say that our long-term experience and in-depth analysis has shown us that teaching and learning are absolutely complementary, and in this sense we feel close to Vygotsky, Bruner and the socio-constructionist theorists. This complementary relationship is effectively summarised by an imperative often repeated by Professor Malaguzzi: 'never teach a child something that he can learn on his own.'

And in this context, what kind of relationship is established among the children themselves?

The role and importance of peers and working in small groups is clear. It is a reciprocal relationship that creates a strong sense of solidarity and fosters organisational and self-organisational dynamics from which differences can emerge, and these differences in turn generate extremely significant acts of negotiation and exchange.

The relationships between children become a context in which the co-construction of theories, interpretations and understandings of reality can take place. The small group work becomes a source of cohesion, a space in which thoughts take shape, are expressed and compared with others' different interpretations; new thoughts are generated; meanings are negotiated; and 'the hundred languages' can emerge. The relationships between children offer opportunities to lend and borrow ideas, whether the teacher is directly present or not, and for cognitive conflict, imitation and generosity. In this context, children experience the pleasure of being given back pieces of their own knowledge, enriched and elaborated on by the contribution of the others through this system of communication and exchange.

In this way, both individual and group thought grows and advances. Controversy and the conflict of ideas play a fundamental role in this system, bringing out the significant aspects of individual thought and at the same time giving new meaning to the knowledge-building process. This is because knowledge develops much more within a context of diversity rather than in one of homogeneity, and also because in situations of conflicting interpretations, the need to argue your own point of view is the catalyst for the fundamental process of metacognition (knowledge of knowledge), providing an opportunity for 're-knowing' your knowledge in a different light, enriched by the new and different opinions offered by others.

These are very complex questions, accompanied by equally complex psychological dynamics. The composition of the group, including age and gender (mixed or single sex), the number in the group, its spatial location, the interest in and proximity of the topic at hand, are all elements that structure the exchange process. To understand the child is a long and difficult job that we can only learn by working along with children, and this also means understanding ourselves in a new and different way. Listening to children is difficult, and interpreting what we observe in a comprehensive way is even more difficult, just as it is not easy for teachers to work in a condition of constant interaction and discussion with others. It requires a great sense of balance as well as openness toward others.

The change required in the role of the teacher also involves offering children a consistent and authentic image of adult life, because children want adults to have faith in them, and this can only happen when the adults have faith in themselves. Children need to be appreciated and to live within an educational context that encourages research, because the school is by definition a place for learning and the creation of knowledge. The school must be a place where the symbolic and value systems of the culture and the society are experienced, interpreted, created and recreated by children and adults together. Only in this way does a school really become a place where true culture is produced: the culture of knowledge.

In your work, observation has a fundamental role.

Our theoretical assumption is that there is no objective point of view that can make observation neutral. Point of view is always subjective, and observation is always partial. But this is a strength, not a limitation. As Fabbri (1990) and Munari (1993) affirm, we are sometimes frightened by subjectivity because it means assuming responsibility. So our search for objectivity is often driven by the fear of taking on responsibility. There is no adult point of view, then, which is objective with respect to the child. Instead, we have a world of multiple interacting subjects who construct reality starting from different points of view, because observing means not so much perceiving reality as constructing reality (just as educating means sharing meanings). Observation is thus not an individual action but a reciprocal relationship: an action, a relationship, a process that makes us aware of what is taking place.

To observe means above all to choose, and thus it is indispensable to delimit the fields of observation. Deciding what to observe is primarily the responsibility of the observer, but it is even better when the choice is shared collectively. In any case, the motivation behind an observation must be clear. Observation is not only a process, but is in itself an interpretation. What we observe is a possible clue that will confirm or refute our theories and hypotheses.

In your view, how should teachers observe?

The question of tools of observation takes us immediately to documentation; that is, documenting events by means of photographs, slides, video, written notes, recordings. If observing also means interpreting, then the medium we choose for documenting is certainly not irrelevant to the quality of the overall observation. The same sequence of actions or the same process filmed with a video camera or photographed or recorded and transcribed will be seen differently even when documented by the same person. This does not remove any of the value of documentation, but rather means that we need more documentation, as many testimonies as possible.

All the documentary fragments – videos, slides, transcribed tape recordings – become the basis for attempting to interpret the children's processes and to understand the meaning that children attribute to these processes, their personal elaboration of symbols and symbolic systems. Like metaphorical detectives, we follow the children's footprints, the directions they take and in which they lead us. In this way, the project being carried out (and documented) incorporates the substance of the thoughts, theories, and desires of children.

This is only possible through an in-depth reading and equally in-depth interpretation of the various documentary materials. This reading and interpretation takes on much greater value when it is made collectively, in the fertile terrain of dialogue and exchange. The more interpreters there are, the higher the probability of representing a sufficiently rich and varied network of possibilities. Not only do children benefit from this process, but also the teachers who take part in it, not just as suppliers of interpretations and meanings and organisers of learning contexts, but as beneficiaries of the process themselves. The moment in which we begin to comment on the documentary materials and collectively construct our interpretive hypotheses is always exciting. Discussing, offering your own ideas, taking advantage of others' ideas and constructing together with the same dynamics as those of the children is a wonderful opportunity for our own thinking and growth.

The interpretations we make on our observation and documentation are extremely important not only for the teachers and for their work with the children, but also for the parents. Documentation viewed in this way can foster the growth and quality of the processes of family participation, giving it new and different meanings. Through the documentation, parents can have a direct look, with real and tangible examples, at the enormous wealth of their children's potential, which is made visible. To give visibility to children's potential requires that this potential is experienced and expressed. In this process, the parents are stimulated to participate in their children's education not only to satisfy their curiosity about what their child is doing at school but also to try to understand the 'why'; in other words, to discover the children's knowledge-building processes and the meaning that the children themselves give to what they do. All this means giving everyone involved the opportunity to construct and share the act – and above all the values – of educating.

Documentation (like observation) thus deeply involves questions of values. It offers a true experience of democracy because democracy also means exchange, and this exchange is made possible by the visibility and the recognition of differences and subjectivity. When differences and subjectivities are in dialogue, they become educational values that are not only declared but also lived.

Documentation, or all the materials produced during observation, is also an important instrument for the children. Through procedures that are analogous to those of the adults, children can see themselves in a new light, and revisit and reinterpret their own experiences of the events in which they were the direct protagonists. This kind of process produces new cognitive dynamics, a new and different vision of oneself and one's actions in relation to others, and this is true for children as well as adults. To experience a process and see it reproduced (that is, see ourselves reproduced) in the documentation – and thus in the thought – of another person, creates that sort of disorientation that opens the way to amazement, doubt and the desire to know more and to know ourselves better.

Along with observation and documentation, you use another term: 're-cognition'. [*Translator's note*: the term '*ricognizione*' in Italian means 'recognition', 'reconnaissance' or 'acknowledgement', but in Reggio it is used in the hyphenated form '*ri-cognizione*' to give it the new or further meaning of 'to know something again' or 'to be aware of what we know' through re-reading, discussing and comparing our ideas with others. I have used this same non-standard form in English – 're-cognition' – because I feel it is the only way to express this concept in a single word.]

Yes, this is a fundamental term in our philosophy. As we have said, we believe that children are competent, that they have their own knowledge and theories on any subject that may arise as an element of research. Each child has his or her own 'baggage' of hypotheses on the possible sense and meaning of things. These hypotheses derive from children's personal experiences, and they want to communicate them to others, adults as well as other children.

Children love discussion and conflict, they know how to listen to the ideas of others and if they want, to make these ideas their own. They have no qualms about changing their minds, and are always ready to venture the new and the unknown. These convictions require us to make use of a special kind of listening, which involves children working in groups (mostly in small groups) to share their thoughts on the problem being discussed or to produce hypotheses and interpretations on the various themes involved in the project underway.

Re-cognition, then, does not mean simply 'gathering' thoughts, but the enrichment of one's own knowledge through the knowledge of the others. When you share something you know, you do not simply transfer this knowledge to the others, but you re-elaborate it at the moment in which you evoke it and reorganise it so as to be communicated. In this way, it is no longer the same knowledge as before. When the context is changed, the organisation of the thought changes, as does the knowledge. Re-cognition accompanies the learning process step by step, drawing meaning from these exchanges with others and from the continuity of the process over time. It is through these processes of re-cognition that both children and adults find personal and cultural enrichment, and for teachers it is also an important source of professional enrichment.

Re-cognition is basically an attempt to re-visit and re-understand what has taken place by highlighting previously constructed relations, developing and challenging them, and consequently producing new ones. Re-cognition is thus an important concept for both children and teachers, not only for the reflections that we make based on an analysis of the children's theories and work, but also as a methodological procedure that teachers working together need to adopt. Thus, re-cognition is seen as a search for awareness of our own knowledge and how it is structured, and as a method of continuous and permanent professional development.

In Reggio Emilia, you prefer to use the term 'project' rather than 'curriculum'. Could you explain this in more depth?

If we consider that:

(a) Learning does not proceed in a linear way, determined and deterministic, by progressive and predictable stages, but rather is constructed through contemporaneous advances, standstills and 'retreats' that take many directions;

(b) The construction of knowledge is a group process. Each individual is nurtured by the hypotheses and theories of others, and by conflicts with others, and advances by co-constructing pieces of knowledge with others through a process of confirmation and disagreement. Above all, conflict and disturbance force us to constantly revise our interpretive models and theories on reality, and this is true for both children and adults;

(c) Children produce their own theories, important theories by which they are inspired. They have their own values and meanings, as well as their own timing which both has and provides meaning, and which directs the course of their learning processes. This timing must be understood, respected and supported.

As a result, the term 'curriculum' (along with the corresponding terms 'curriculum planning' or 'lesson planning') is unsuitable for representing the complex and multiple strategies that are necessary for sustaining children's knowledge-building processes. We should stop for a moment to contemplate this important word strategy. A strategy, like a plan, means predicting and implementing a sequence of coordinated operations. But differently from planning, strategy is not based exclusively on the initial hypotheses, so that the subsequent decisions and choices are made in relation to the development of the work and of the objectives themselves. Strategies are constructed and de-constructed. Strategies benefit from adversity, chance and error. Strategy involves the ability to take action into the realm of uncertainty, on the part of both protagonists of the process – adults and children – and requires listening, flexibility and curiosity. Strategy is characteristic of the way children proceed, as well as of any authentic act of knowledge-building and creativity.

This is why we prefer to use the terms 'project' and *progettazione* to define this complex situation, to describe the multiple levels of action, which are definite and indefinite at the same time, carried out in the dialogue between children and adults.

The word 'project' evokes the idea of a dynamic process, an itinerary. It is sensitive to the rhythms of communication and incorporates the significance and timing of children's investigation and research. The duration of a project can thus be short, medium or long, continuous or discontinuous, with pauses, suspensions and restarts.

The statement of a hypothesis on how the project might proceed is valid only to the extent that it is seen precisely as a hypothesis and not as a 'must', as one of a thousand hypotheses on the direction that might be taken. Above all, making hypotheses is a way to increase the expect-ations, excitement and the possibilities for being and interacting, for welcoming the unexpected as a fundamental resource. A greater ability to predict will help us to know how to better observe and interpret that which happens among children. In this sense, the links with the concepts of observation, documentation and re-cognition become strong and meaningful.

Progettazione is also a way of thinking, a strategy for creating relations and bringing in the element of chance, by which we mean 'the space of the others'; i.e. that undefined space of the self that is completed by the thoughts of others within the relational process.

In a school based on relationships and interaction, which legitimates research as a permanent attitude and way of working of both children and adults, what meaning is assumed by the term 'professional development'?

This term, like many others, must be redefined to distinguish it from old stereotypes that derive from a pedagogy and practice dating back to courses of study which attempted to pour ideas into teachers, to shape them, so that they could, in turn, pour ideas into children to shape them according to pre-arranged objectives and methods. In this way, every-thing was clear-cut, consistent, predictable and pre-packaged. The results were guaranteed – or at least it was thought so. But this method had nothing to do with research, reflection, observation, documentation, doubt, uncertainty or true education. And nothing to do with the child.

The term 'professional development' does not fully convey the com-plexity of this process, which could be defined as a 'daily existential dimension', an attitude that deeply marks our personal and professional identities. We view professional development above all as change, research and renewal, as an indispensable vehicle for strengthening the quality of our interaction with children. Professional development is a right of each individual teacher and of all those who work in the school. It is also the right of the children to have a competent teacher who can enter into a relationship of reciprocal listening, who can change and renew herself dynamically with the utmost attention to the changes that take place in the reality in which the children live. We have said that professional development is the right of the entire staff of the school, and this group becomes a new subject, a unit which has its own needs and rights, such as the right to think, plan, work and interpret together in a collegial way.

This collegial dimension is not merely the sum of individual thoughts, nor is it a play of minority and majority thinking. Instead, it is a new way of thinking and building together. Each teacher, therefore, has individual rights and also rights pertaining to the group. The staff's most important right in terms of practical and organisational issues is to be able to work in a collegial way with children, colleagues and parents.

What are the conditions for working in this way?

In our view, professional development as both an individual and group right implies the following:

- *Daily working conditions.* These conditions must enable the practice of listening, observing, doing research and documentation, all of which are essential for the development of the child and the group of children. This is a matter of organisation, but I believe it is also an ethical issue. In terms of the environment, the space must be rational and well thought-out but also welcoming, a space where teachers and other staff can move, act and work well with children. It means a child/adult ratio which allows meaningful relationships to be established between adults and children and among the children, in a continuum of complete stories rather than single episodes. It requires two teachers to be present together with the same group of children on a long-term basis, and this means over the course of the day, the week, the year, and even over several years. Two teachers working together are needed in every class in order to observe from different points of view the processes involved in children's learning, to document and interpret those processes, and to use their findings as clues for how to plan for possible developments of the project. These are essential elements of the role of the teacher, and the co-presence of teachers, in which they plan together and share ideas and decision-making, is an absolutely essential condition for working.

  The daily life at schools is qualified and constantly re-qualified by the teachers' observations, interpretations and evaluations, constantly changing thanks to the actions and reflections of the children and teachers together. This is the best guarantee we can give, not only to the teachers, but also to the children and their families.
- *Time and space.* Listening, observing and documenting are essential but not sufficient for our work. If we do not interpret events, we cannot share the meanings and significance of that which takes place. Interpreting is fundamental for advancing the work and

growth processes of children and teachers. For this reason, a time and place must be set aside daily and also weekly in which the teachers' interpretations, hypotheses and doubts can be discussed and expanded with their other colleagues in the school.

Every week the school staff meets to dialogue and discuss their hypotheses on the work in progress in each class by viewing the documentation together. Given that the group is formally gathered together, a wider range of issues is also addressed which are connected to the general running of the school and the system of schools. There is thus time set aside within the work schedule for these meetings (2½ hours per week). The meetings are held in the afternoon, after 4 p.m. when most of the children have gone home. The staff choose a suitable meeting place for fostering exchange and study together, and according to the equipment needed (e.g. audio-visual materials). The only requirement is that of interaction, as this time is designed for being together: with a co-teacher, with all the school colleagues, with personnel of other schools, and the primary feature is communication.

- *Parent participation.* Meetings with parents represent another important form of professional development, provided that they do not involve formulaic rituals, merely descriptive language, or worse yet, the language of assessment, and that they are collective rather than individual. With the aid of the documentation, the processes, theories and intelligences of the children are shown and shared. So the abilities of all the children, and not just the performance of one particular son or daughter, are made visible, commented on and interpreted together. Comparing different cultural or subjective points of view, listening to different opinions and reaching a common consensus: this is all part of the teacher's professionalism which is enriched and re-defined in this dialogue with parents.

What are the skills that this type of professional development gives the teachers?

First of all we must think of the preschool teacher as a person who is part of contemporary culture, who is able to question and to analyse this culture with a critical eye. A person who loves to read, who has interests such as cinema or theatre and is happy to remember, discuss and critically examine such experiences. In short, an intellectually curious person who rejects a passive approach to knowledge and prefers to construct knowledge together with others rather than simply to 'consume' it. To consider the teacher as such is both a premise and an objective.

Professional development can be organised in such a way that it brings together men and women from all walks of life who are looking for new meaning and new values both within and beyond the conventional boundaries.

They can be interdisciplinary encounters with scientists, architects, film or theatre directors, musicians, poets, and so on, who share with us not only their specific knowledge, but also their works, their learning processes, the sense and meaning of their chosen work. It is up to us to interpret and adapt this information to our own needs.

All this becomes meaningful and adds to our professional competence if we are able to put it into practice. Our task is to facilitate an analogous involvement of the child in the surrounding culture, while respecting his own personal strategies, his own ways, his own timetable. Children are competent in this regard. We must support the child's 'journey' by building a network based on the continuous intertwining of the fields of knowledge and the fields of experience.

What we mean by the 'fields of knowledge' is the cultural symbol systems through which a child is introduced to the organised and historically established knowledge to which the school is related. It is through the application, interpretation and revisiting of these symbol systems that children can grow, understand and actively experience the arts, the sciences and life in general. The different symbol systems define contexts of experience, or fields of experience, into which children venture with their own strategies, desires, timing, questions and curiosity. Children need time to meditate and to experiment on their own, but above all with their peers.

The teachers are asked to abandon the set programme, the prescribed curriculum and the usual obligatory courses, and to join efforts with the children. The teachers must, therefore, have in mind a clear map of the cultural symbol systems and how these systems are constantly expressed and transformed. At the same time, though, teachers must never lose sight of the procedures, the paths, the particular ways in which children organise their behaviour and ideas in order to appropriate a piece of the world and of life. And here we also experience joy, excitement and growth along with the children.

I would now like to make a final consideration. There are many human, cultural and theoretical encounters with and through which we have woven together our experience in Reggio Emilia. We have had many exchanges of ideas, thoughts and suggestions, enabling us to build the sense of research and change which is characteristic of our experience. So we would like to extend our gratitude to all.

Chapter 12

Teachers as researchers

Formation and professional development in a school of education (2001)

I made this presentation at a conference in St Louis in the United States. The conference was organised by Reggio Children and an association called the St Louis Reggio Collaborative, which was created by a group of school teachers and directors and university teachers that decided, some years ago, to develop a system of schools in that city inspired by the experience of Reggio Emilia. They have since created an important experience, thanks also to the support of Amelia Gambetti.

Among the many initiatives they have organised, in 2001 the Reggio Collaborative in St Louis decided to dedicate a three-day conference to the topic of teachers as researchers. This topic is very important to us in Reggio and especially for me. So I accepted with great pleasure the invitation to attend this event and, preparing the speech, had the opportunity to go deeper and understand more this concept of the teacher as researcher. Later that same year, I went back to St Louis as a visiting professor at Webster University, at the invitation of Professor Brenda Fyfe.

Why should we talk about personal and professional development, or 'formation', at the conclusion of our work here? [*Translator's note*: in Italian, we use the word *formazione*, or formation in English, for professional development as well as the more general formation of the person.] I think it's quite clear: because talking about documentation and research, or better, documentation as an essential element of didactic and pedagogical research, means talking about personal and professional development and education. In fact, personal and professional development, like education, should not be seen as static or unchangeable qualities, achieved once and for all, but rather as a process, an ongoing path that we follow from birth throughout our lives, now more than ever. Personal and professional development and education are something we construct ourselves in relation with others, based on values that are chosen, shared and constructed together. It means living and living ourselves in a permanent state of research.

And here, 'values' is an important word. For the term 'education' is strongly correlated with the term 'values', where 'to educate' also means – and for certain aspects primarily means – to educate the intrinsic values of each individual and each culture, in order to make these values extrinsic, visible, conscious and shareable.

But what is a value?

The term has many meanings, just as the terms 'education', 'formation' and 'subjectivity' are contextual concepts – that is, they can only be defined in relation to the cultural, political and historical context. One consideration is that the term 'value' seems to come not from the philosophical sphere but from the economic and cultural sphere. A possible definition could be: 'Values are the ideals that a person aspires to in his or her life', which act as a point of reference in our judgments and conduct, and according to which we conform (or not) in our relations with the social group of reference (community, society, culture).

Values define cultures and are one of the fundamental elements of societies; every community shares values. Values are therefore related and correlated to the culture that holds them: they determine the culture and are determined by it. Values are not universal, nor are they eternal. It is we, as people, who choose our values, confirm them and sustain them. But it is also societies, and their public places, that create values, prioritize them, highlight and transmit them.

For us in Reggio the school is one of these places, a place where values are transmitted, discussed and created. This is one of the biggest responsibilities that schools have, and that all of us have, and we must be aware of this responsibility. The younger the child, the more the school and its teachers must be aware of this most important task and feel a deep sense of responsibility.

But what values are we talking about?

We said before that each society, each community, constantly defines its own values. On the basis of our experience in the municipal schools of Reggio, we can mention some of the values that have been the building blocks and guiding elements of this experience. The first is the value of subjectivity, which we view in terms of wholeness and integrity (holistic value). I have chosen the term 'subjectivity' among a number of possible ones (such as 'person' and 'individual') because I think it more clearly highlights the relational and reflexive aspects involved in the construction of the individual subject. Each subject, then, is a construction, both self-constructed and socially constructed within a context and a culture.

Recent studies on the brain have clearly demonstrated the uniqueness and unrepeatability of each individual and of his or her construction as a subject. We know much about how the individual is defined in relation to the environmental context, and the strong influence of social interactions on the destiny of each of us (particularly in the early years of life). Therefore, it is necessary to be receptive to this subjectivity, to recognise and support it.

Hence the reasons for many of our methodological choices, such as: observation and documentation, working in small groups, the organisation of the space, the use of *ateliers*, and so on. In all these choices, we attempt to allow the subjectivity of each child and each teacher to emerge in relation to his or her relationships with others. And here I would like, once again, to underline the importance of this value of subjectivity in the way that we have described it. The relationship between subjectivity *and* intersubjectivity, in my opinion, is fundamental not only on the cognitive (and psycho-pedagogical) level, but also on the political and cultural level. I believe that this issue is vitally important for the future of humanity itself: the relationship between the individual and others, between Self and Other, is a key issue for our futures.

To choose whether our individual construction is independent from others or exists with others and through others, means resolving not only the old Piaget–Vygotsky debate, but also the one between different images of the human being and humanity, between societies oriented toward the individual in competition and societies based on the individual constructed with others, who seeks out others. It is a political and economic choice that can influence the entire educational system but also the social system. In these passages, we can clearly see how the sciences, and above all pedagogy, are not neutral but are partisan. And as you know, ours is a pedagogy of partisanship – that is, it holds certain values.

This value of subjectivity, with its implication of the uniqueness and unrepeatability of each individual, is strongly connected with the value of difference. Differences in sex, race, culture and religion. Differences because we are individuals, because we are all, in fact, different.

The globalisation which is fostered by our extraordinary communication systems (such as television and the internet) has the potential to create a widespread phenomenon of standardisation and encourage the construction of cultural stereotypes. Within this context, the greatest damage that the school can do is to *not* attempt to break down these normalising schemas, instead encouraging a 'culture of normality', feeding the need for 'normality' – that is, for norms or standards – which we see so much of nowadays. We need our differences – though there is a risk that we run, also in Italy, which derives from any kind of fundamentalism, where differences become factors that divide, separate and isolate.

In our lives, somewhat instinctively and without educational input, we begin to recognise otherness. But very early in life (particularly in relation to certain others who are 'more other', more outside), we tend to develop a concept of certain 'others' who are less valued; that is, who are worth less than we are, and their difference is seen as something negative and therefore to be eliminated, negated or rejected.

In order to educate ourselves, we must try to understand differences rather than wanting to cancel them. This means approaching each individual in terms of his or her background and personal story, and with great sensitivity. It means 'listening' to the differences (what we refer to as 'the pedagogy of listening') but also listening to and accepting the changes that take place within us, which are generated by our relationships, or better, by our interactions with others. It means letting go of any truths that we consider to be absolute, being open to doubt and giving value to negotiation as a strategy of the possible. All of this means – or more precisely, can mean – greater possibilities for us to change, but without making us feel displaced or that we have lost something.

In this definition of the value of differences, we find a richer and more contemporary definition of the value of participation – or, participation as a value. In our educational experience, participation – that is, feeling a part and having a sense of belonging – is not limited just to the families (though this process is absolutely fundamental), but it is a value and a quality of the school as a whole. And this means providing for spaces, languages and, more generally, organisational methods and strategies that make this kind of participation possible – something that we constantly work toward in our experience. Yet though the educational and pedagogical aims must be explicit and clear, at the same time, participation requires a certain sense of indefiniteness and ample spaces of possibility.

These reflections lead to another value that is part of our experience, and that is, the value of democracy, which is intrinsic to the concept of participation: participation of the families, but also of the children and teachers in the school project. This extremely important issue deserves at least a brief mention, because we must not forget how closely the school is connected to the society in which it is situated. There is the recurring question of whether the school is limited to transmitting culture or can be, as we in Reggio aspire to, a place where culture is constructed and democracy is lived. School and democracy, a theme that was dear to

Dewey, is an important commitment for all of us: school as a place of democracy, in which we can all live democracy.

Finally, among the many values involved, I would like to mention one that may be seen as debatable to consider as such, but which I feel is fundamental for us, and in a certain sense a founding principle of our experience: the value of learning. Learning is and can be a value if we are aware that learning – which is pursued by each individual in times and ways that cannot be programmed – is a 'relational place' that makes us reflect on the meaning of education itself and search for new paths in educating and personal and professional development.

In educational practice, this means being open to the complex, con-flictual and unpredictable nature of human learning, wherever it takes place, both inside and outside the institutional contexts that are directly involved in education. The entire educational system today – with a lot of hard work, contradictions and many risks – is involved in this process of evolution from a school of teaching to a school of learning. Learning is the emergence of that which was not there before. It is a search for the self as well as for the other and others that surround each individual.

Those who participate in an educational process, in fact bring their own growth and development into play, and do this on the basis of their own expectations and their own plans. There is a constant relational reciprocity between those who educate and those who are educated, between those who teach and those who learn. There is participation, passion, compassion, emotion. There is aesthetics; there is change. In this sense, I would also like to mention the value of play, of fun, of emotions, of feelings, which we recognise as essential elements of any authentic cognitive and educational process. Learning thus becomes a value because of its force in creating a synthesis of the individual and his or her context, in an affective relationship between those who learn and that which is being learned, a relationship filled with emotion, curiosity and humour. For each of us, the cognitive act becomes a creative act, which involves the assumption of responsibility as well as autonomy, an act of freedom. Knowledge – or better, subjective understanding – becomes an individual responsibility and needs a sense of optimism and future in order to be realised to the fullest.

So what, then, do we mean by professional development? It is simply learning: our job is to learn why we are teachers. It means keeping our distance from an overriding sense of balance, from that which has already been decided or is considered to be certain. It means staying close to the interweaving of objects and thoughts, of doing and reflect-ing, theory and practice, emotions and knowledge. Perhaps the only way is to constantly search for – without ever finding – a balance between rules and limitations (some of which are obviously indispensable) and the real emotion and passion of learning.

So, I have described some of the values that inspire and orient daily life in the schools in Reggio and some other places in the world. But these values are very distant from those which prevail around us nowadays: individualism, egoism, career, success, money, and so on – values that are not easy to oppose, and will not be so in the future. This is why schools, starting from those for the youngest children, must first of all be places of education towards values and in values. This kind of school requires us to be courageous and consistent; it requires passion and emotion, reason and feeling, commitment and hard work. But it can also give us so much; most of all, the deep sense of what it means to be a teacher.

Chapter 13

The organisation, the method

A conversation with Carlina Rinaldi by Ettore Borghi (1998)

When Ettore Borghi phoned me for this interview I felt great emotion and confusion. There were various reasons for this, the first of which was the deep tie of affection and esteem connecting me to the interviewer. Ettore Borghi was in fact not only one of my city's most sensitive and attentive councillors, he was also a philosopher and historian of genuine profundity and generosity.

Before knowing him as the city councillor responsible for education and culture, I had learned to appreciate him as a teacher of philosophy in the classics lycée in my city. Few teachers have been so well loved and respected by students and recognised by colleagues as a cultural and moral point of reference. When he began his term as councillor, I had been a *pedagogista* in the municipal schools for several years and I was impressed with the attitude which he assumed from the first: a high degree of listening and respect towards our experience and its protagonists. His dialogue with Malaguzzi was particularly rich and interesting (this was the early eighties) and our discussions on pedagogical, philosophical and cultural issues were fascinating.

His ability as a historian and his curiosity about the journey of the municipal schools as, in the first place, cultural and political, before being pedagogical, emerged loudly and clearly. In this way the relationship between the city and its schools became increasingly close and well informed. This was why many years later, in 1998, Ettore Borghi was asked to edit the first book on the history of Reggio's municipal schools. The protagonists from those years were the first to ask him: administrators, teachers and parents who felt that they wanted to declare, in a historical document, the values which had inspired the inception of the experience and guided their choices and passions.

In a commission created specially for the occasion it was decided to interview representatives of the different categories which had 'constructed' the history of the Reggio experience: educators, parents, administrators, other citizens. These interviews were not only to be 'a journey through memories' but a search *for* meanings and *inside* meanings which had been constructed during that long journey. This then was why I felt such varying and conflicting emotions when Professor Borghi telephoned me.

The fear of remembering, of abandoning myself to memories which were so sweet and cruel, was quickly eliminated by my growing pleasure in a conversation which offered me the possibility of re-conceptualising thoughts and journeys in life and work. The questions were precise and unusual; the conversation was recorded and would later be transcribed. When I re-read the transcription I was impressed by the quality of the text; there was very little which needed correcting or modifying.

This is proof of the reciprocity which featured in the conversation, and it is probably the fact that the interview was well-conducted which made it worthy of being included in the book *Una storia presente*, published by Istoreco, an important Reggio institution dedicated to historical studies. The book was wanted and supported by the Friends of Reggio Children Association, which is a project gathering together all those people in the city who have not only experienced the Reggio schools, but who consider these schools to be one of the liveliest expressions of the city's identity.

Great efforts were required to produce the book. The combined commitment of women councillors who have been protagonists in the experience like Loretta Giaroni, Eletta Bertani, Ione Bartoli and Sandra Piccinini and of teachers, auxiliary staff, *pedagogistas* and parents has given the city and each one of us one of the most beautiful stories a community can write: the story of an ideal and a utopia which has never been entirely completed and so is open to the contribution of each one of us.

Carlina, I would like to ask you about the events of an experience you are very familiar with, having been directly involved in it yourself. I would like to organise our discussion around the history of what used to be called 'nursery schools'. To be more precise, I'm referring to the past shortages of these schools and to a conceptual flaw which was translated into a serious act of negligence: I am referring to a conception of these services for children under six years that was based on social welfare and which meant that for decades they were left to the arbitrary whims of private philanthropy and made to depend on the Ministry of Internal Affairs, which neglected them. Did the municipal schools of Reggio Emilia already have a clear identity as schools, as educational places in the full sense of the word, at the time when you started to work there or did it emerge gradually? And, beyond this, what was the substance of this identity?

I think I can say that it was already clear at the time. I say this especially in light of a number of reflections I had the opportunity to share with Loris Malaguzzi himself, and also being mindful of some analyses I was able to listen to precisely about the importance attached to the term 'municipal schools of early childhood' [*Translator's note*: this is a literal translation of '*scuole comunali **dell'**infanzia*' – emphasis in the original – to render the genitive sense, although we usually translate the term as 'municipal early childhood institutions/preschools'.] The term stressed this idea of 'school' as an educational place and a place of 'education' by virtue of being process-based – a theme which we might pick up again later – that is, education as a process which applies not only to the children but also to the adults: the teachers and the parents. To see 'education' as a permanent process meant being open to a concept of school that was unusual for the time (I am referring to the early seventies). Particularly this famous term 'of early childhood', which was the result of lengthy discussions which underlined its importance, showed that some concepts were very clear from the very beginning.

I say this because Loris Malaguzzi discussed the term 'of early childhood' on different occasions with Bruno Ciari, Giorgio Bini and others. [*Editors' note*: Ciari and Bini were leading educational thinkers and practitioners in the 1960s and 1970s. Ciari introduced Freinet's educational philosophy into Italy and played a leading role in developing municipal schools of early childhood in Bologna.] The alternatives discussed were 'school of (early) childhood' and 'school for (early) childhood', and the clear conclusion was that the schools were *of* early childhood; that is, the rightful protagonist and subject of the school (these terms came later, around 1975/76, but I think the concept was already there at the time) is the child. But – as I learned very soon to say and perhaps to understand only some time later – the child in relation: to his story/history, his family, his cultural context and, consequently, to other stories/histories that school would provide the opportunity to encounter and construct. Thus the protagonist, the rightful subject is the child, but not separated from the historical–cultural context, indeed the child is the rightful subject–protagonist–citizen. This is the value of that term *of*, which seems to me to have been the intended purpose at the time.

The other term is 'childhood'. This was also intended as a statement, a statement of what I like to define today – I certainly learned it then but developed it over time – as a social category, which does not exist if it is not declared as such, in the sense that every culture, every historical time translates its *own* childhood, and forgets not so much its childhood but its image of childhood to which it grants its treatment, civil and judicial, and in terms of status and well-being.

I came into the system at the time when the 1972 regulations were being drawn up, which was a point at which Loris Malaguzzi, but also other participants at the time, were having to define and choose terms more than once. [*Editors' note*: this refers to the regulations for its municipal schools drawn up by the municipality of Reggio Emilia, as the result of a lengthy dialogue between teachers, parents and other citizens.] I was able to take part in the discussions and I think I can therefore say that, at least in the early 1970s, this concept of school, of education as a 'participatory' public event, as an ongoing process, a place in which culture is not only transmitted but produced (and not only the culture of childhood but that of human beings) was already clear. I can also surmise – this is perhaps something about which I am less certain, though I have a strong sense of it – that in the 1960s, when it all began, the years when the first municipal school was opened, the concept of school as a rightful place of childhood was already present. Related to this, it is no coincidence that Loris Malaguzzi loved to recall the genesis of the Reggio experience: the preschool in Villa Cella, and the declaration which is still inscribed on the school as the place where peace-building is achieved by educating the new generations. [*Editors' note*: the Villa Cella was the first *scuola dell'infanzia* in the Reggio area, built through the hard work and solidarity of women and a small village of farmers and workers. It was opened in 1947. Malaguzzi described it as 'the beginning of our entire experience', although the first municipal school in Reggio was not opened until 1963.]

For over a century, the lack of recognition – cultural and political – of the educational importance of the first few years of life led to an underestimation of the problem of personnel and its cultural and professional education. The state did not introduce specific regulations for the basic education of nursery school teachers and relegated them to a lower level of education than primary school teachers. Would it be wrong to suppose that the network of municipal schools in Reggio Emilia offered an in-house training system for its personnel, making up for what the national teacher training system was unable to offer? And, if so, who were the subjects and what were the factors that contributed to this undertaking? It doesn't seem to me that this only involved exchanging a few pedagogical ideas.

I agree wholeheartedly with what you suggest. I think that this idea of being an educational and formative place not only for the children but also and especially for the staff was very much and very clearly there when I started in Reggio. I think Loris Malaguzzi was strongly committed to the importance of professional education for the staff. This came to him from his knowledge of the most advanced experiences in this field, such as those of the Montessori or Agazzi schools, from pedagogical literature that is still important both in Italy and abroad (I am thinking, for example, of Piaget, Dewey, Bruner), but also from his own experience as a teacher and psychologist. Therefore, when I started, it was very clear that this was one of the defining features of the schools, that would enable them to be places where things are tried out.

I think it was a kind of professional development that had its origin in research and a process-based approach – process-based approach as the ability to keep up with the times and with current culture, not only past culture – as being integral to the idea of the school, its very identity, and these had to be guaranteed precisely by the professional development of the staff. And I think the origins of this were found in the cultural value which at the time (I am talking about the 1960s/70s) tended to be given globally to these ongoing professional development processes, which lay outside the more traditional idea of school for which teacher education was a one-off training experience tied to the school curriculum. Being aware of one's own knowledge, but especially having the ability to think about one's knowledge, and to think about how to make the child and the young person party to the construction of this knowledge – which means being concerned about a possible cultural construction of their way of thinking, of thinking about oneself as apprentices, to think of oneself as a thinking being – did not, I think, form part of the discussions at the time. Or if it did, it did not form part of the mainstream practices of the time.

I think I should underline two things in particular. First, the conviction – that derives from what you might call the eclectic professional development that Malaguzzi had – that the teacher's professional development is a cultural education, which is certainly rooted in an awareness of the past, but also in a contemporary reality and as such, therefore, has to have a two-track approach. One is related to the great cultural debate concerning the human being, being a human being, being a citizen; the other concerns the child and pedagogy, and pedagogical research. But at this point we have another intervening issue, the idea that this holistic approach could be enhanced significantly through the figure of the *atelierista*, a permanent provocation, almost to signal the daily desire to break with a particular history of pedagogy, not the activist pedagogy that we were talking about.

Then there was also the idea to have meetings not only on matters that were strictly of a pedagogical nature but to look at a broader spectrum of issues. I think we still have posters and other material of all the initiatives that were undertaken (from the '*maggio pedagogico*', a series of meetings with people from the world of culture, psychology and pedagogy for the benefit of teachers and parents, to meetings with parents in the sixties, and so on) with eminent people from the world of contemporary culture, from theatre to history, ethology, ethnology, art, and so on. All these disciplines had to interact with the teacher, whose task was to renew, above all, her curiosity in relation to the child and the child's processes: the child, not as a static subject, but as a subject who is constantly undergoing modification and evolution. The word 'research', in this sense, leaves – or rather, demands to come out of – the scientific laboratories, thus ceasing to be a privilege of the few (in universities and other designated places) to become the stance, the attitude with which teachers approach the sense and meaning of life.

Clearly, the contribution of school to the child's search for sense and meaning, has not only to satisfy questions, but most of all nurture pleasure. But the search for sense and meaning applies to the professional development of the teacher, particularly the teacher of the young child and the young person. To take up a reflection that has been made several times, I find that the great strength of the work experienced as a collaborative exercise consists in the search for a common sense and meaning of school, for a common sense and meaning of school in society, which, I think, those who look at us from the outside, find extraordinary. Only a week ago in Sweden, people were commenting again on the extraordinary nature of our teachers as people who are constantly seeking to understand why things are done, why they should be done, why they should be proposed to the children, and as people who are trying to convey to the children this search for sense and meaning.

Thank you. As you were speaking, I was reminded that at the time when your schools were extending their interest into psychology, ethology and the other subjects you mentioned, the same was happening in Italian 'high' culture, which up until that time had been closed to all this research and experience, and was therefore left behind and had to catch up in all the fields of the human sciences. And not only with regard to the quality of the research and publications, but also to the identity, the cultural profile of teachers, as we used to say 'of every rank and level'. I don't know if you agree.

I think the link you make is extremely important. Perhaps somewhere in your research this will have to be accounted for. Right from the start in this history, there was – and this is actually one of the most extraordinary things I personally recognise in Loris Malaguzzi – a systemic vision, an ability to cry out, to put together, to mix all the questions that are so topical now. I think we can find traces and signs of these from the very origins of this story. I don't know if I'm making up a lovely fairytale from my own story, but in all honesty, I think things were as I've described them in this experience. I remember we used to do courses to talk about stars and astronomy (these were such unusual relations!) and it wasn't so that we could explain stars to the children, but so that the teachers could feel and grasp, together with the children, the joy, the surprise, the wonder of it, as qualities which childhood demands. I repeat, mine might be a romantic and poetic narration, but I like this idea . . . and I like to convey it to others!

While I was working with the Villa Gaida nido, founded by the municipality in 1912, I discovered that the salary of the cleaners and cooks was little more than a third of the teachers'. [Editors' note: For a fuller discussion of the origins and significance of the Villa Gaida, see page 178.] I won't go into the issue that, at the time, raising teachers' pay was very necessary, not least in order to counteract the common phenomenon of qualified staff leaving to work in primary schools. But I'm thinking of the symbolic significance of that pay differential, which obviously implied a clear undervaluing of the role of those who, to all intents and purposes, were regarded as servants. By contrast, could you explain what the function of the auxiliary staff is now in the experience of municipal schools?

Sure. I'd ask you though, before we go on to this question, to let me go back to a thought I touched on earlier: a quality which I recognise Loris Malaguzzi had, and, I think, all of us who worked with him have (but I want to acknowledge him as the first to have it), which is the ability to listen, in a wider sense, something I've also tried to write about. Loris Malaguzzi was very curious and was able to listen to us and the teachers very carefully. You may be familiar with the strategy of the teachers' diaries, which was quite important and well-known at the time. The teachers were invited to write not only what was happening, but one or more episodes and sentences by the children that they found striking. In my opinion, these are the first indications of what later became known as documentation, the ability to leave traces upon which to reflect, to think about, but also a practice that gives a voice to those who are the real protagonists, and gives even more meaning to the words 'research', 'pedagogical reflection' and 'pedagogical researchers'. We should think about looking in more detail at the documentation system, such as was developed in an original way in Reggio and which arose, I think, yet again, not from an ideology but from an extremely original approach of listening and thus made people more aware of their own knowledge and their own thoughts.

The teachers knew this and it is something that allows me to say that Loris Malaguzzi was someone who had a great ability to work in a group, a great ability to listen and to give a voice to the different protagonists. I think, therefore, that this approach was really a forerunner of group work. Recently, we were recalling with some of the teachers, let's call them 'mature' teachers, the extent to which these meetings, this fact of asking questions, inviting people to reflect, and his attitude of listening helped us to understand what we had been doing. Hence the origin of documentation, as I was saying, but also the origin of group work and then of working with the children . . .

Yes, also because it wasn't necessary for these participants to have any special pedigrees or particular qualifications; what mattered was humanity . . .

Absolutely. It was the aspect of humanity, yet it was also perhaps a syllogism, a simple but, to my mind, a very effective syllogism: if school is a place of education, *all* the places within school, *all* the people there are educational, they are 'educating'. Therefore, just as there are no first class and second class spaces – in this sense the architecture made for visible kitchens, it did away with corridors and under stairs spaces and placed everything on the same level, in a real sense, but also in a very metaphorical sense – so, too, there were no first class and second class staff. Consequently, the cooks and the auxiliary staff had a specific role to fulfil 'in the interest of the users'. But, at the same time, it showed an awareness of group action and therefore offered a greater degree of participation not only in the work of others but also in understanding the meaning of one's own work.

I remember in-house professional development sessions on pedagogical theories held together with auxiliary staff. I also remember having discussions on why it was not a good thing to destroy a building for cleaning purposes and how to maintain and preserve it, not as a rule imposed from outside, but I'd say as an experience of shared meaning. I remember particularly the precious insights that these people gave us, perhaps from their ability (based on the different backgrounds they had) to listen to children with different eyes and from a different angle, and in different spaces with extremely high levels of intimacy, because these were people who shared with the children situations like going to the bathroom.

So, the body was something you couldn't ignore.

This was yet another level of interaction, there wasn't the mind and the body – that was something new then, in the 1970s – but all was part of the same identity: the value of the person, the value of the school, therefore the value of all the protagonists of the school. I think the *nidi* helped us tremendously in this. Indeed, we shouldn't forget that in the early seventies (1970–71 to be precise) the first *nido* was opened. This was, above all, an event with a strongly political and cultural dimension, even for our city, which already had a tradition in the field of education.

It was also an extraordinary opportunity to reflect once again on our pedagogical (and obviously cultural) project. The young child, the image of the young child, came bursting in, posing new questions and providing important opportunities for reflection. Our pedagogical culture had, bravely, to allow itself to be revisited. The (few) certainties acquired during previous years regarding organisation – that is, timeframes, spaces and roles in the *scuole dell'infanzia* – were transformed into doubts and questions when we considered *nidi*. There was no 'history' of *nidi* behind us, but rather we faced hostility and suspicion: the young child should have been at home with the mother, this was still the dominant image of the time. But it was precisely due to the *nidi* that we were able to see the great potentials of the child in full, and a role for the teachers, and in some respects, the auxiliary staff which was different but highly significant. This was how the 'Zero-to-Six Project' was born, one of the few in Italy to provide pedagogical and institutional continuity between the *nido* and the *scuola dell'infanzia*.

But, above all, we had a great opportunity to reflect deeply also on the professional profiles of the staff. Hence the importance of the declaration made at the time – which is perhaps not appreciated so much today – that *all* staff (teachers, cooks, auxiliary staff) had to do the same number of working hours, the same number of hours for professional development, with the opportunity, or rather the right and the duty to take part in, in-house professional development sessions for all the staff, as well as in specific training sessions. This gave rise to a very particular form of training, a forerunner of things to come, that our cooks and our auxiliary staff did (I think we can still find the relevant details today), which had and still has its own specific focus, on the best way of rearranging things and tidying up, not only for the significance which children (and we, together with them) attribute to space, but also for what hygiene can represent for achieving quality and well-being in *nidi* and *scuole dell'infanzia*. Therefore I think this declaration, which was so strong that it appeared on the regulations, was altogether clear.

Subsequently, our task was to continue, together with auxiliary staff and cooks, to find and update the meanings. The great thing, but also the difficult and sometimes painful thing, was that no achievement was ever taken for granted, never! And the participation by the families was to be yet another chapter in which the key process – with respect to certain values – was to understand what strategies could be adopted to ensure that these things would be declared as values.

We are gradually painting a picture of a complex universe of adults, performing as actors within the system of relations to which the children belong. Did the hiring of men only serve the symbolic purpose of breaking the 'maternal' stereotype?

Yes, I agree with your emphasis on seeing the children as 'actors'. I think the introduction of men, at times, did have the role of breaking the maternal stereotype, but it was also a recognition of the right of the child to have beside him or her, during such an important time and in such an important space, protagonists with a different identity, like the male identity. Therefore – I'd like to put this more clearly – first of all it's a question of recognising children's right to have a male figure beside them at school, where they spend such long periods of time and at such an important age for constructing their identity. This is important not only for boys, but certainly for girls as well, and, for some aspects, especially for the girls who are often relegated to a 'women only' school environment. Obviously this was also a provocation in relation to the idea of a school that was defined as 'maternal', and which had to act as a substitute for the family to such a great extent. [*Editors' note:* 'nursery schools' in Italy have, until recently, commonly been called *scuola materna*.] Furthermore, to go back to something we have already discussed, it was also the studies on psychology that were raising the problem of the construction of identity. Those were years in which the debate on women's identity, and consequently on the identity of both men and women, was becoming ever stronger. So, somewhat provocatively, but also very obviously I think, early childhood institutions were becoming aware of this gender gap.

The problem was that we were going against a cultural stereotype which still persists today, or rather, which we still have to reckon with. There are only a few, indeed very few, men working in schools. Many of the current reasons for this are still the same as they were then, and they are the same in almost every culture. I mean to say that in Europe, not to such an excessive degree as elsewhere but still significantly so, we can see the difficulties in getting men working in schools, particularly in schools for young children, as being linked to an image of the child that is poor, fragile and heavily based on the child's strong need for a 'maternal' female figure. Today, we see a strong transformation in the definition of the paternal identity; culturally, the father who takes care of his child is much more accepted. However, as far as the *scuola dell'infanzia* is concerned, we still haven't seen this change, even less so in the *nido*.

This probably has also to do with the social image of these schools and is also connected with the low salary and the fact that it is not proportionate with the commitment required, seeing as the staff in these services are the ones who work the longest number of hours and have the lowest salaries. In the end, in a culture where the important salary is the man's, where it's the men who are the major breadwinners in the family, the people who accept this work because they see a sense in it, a cultural sense, are rare. So, in Reggio Emilia – but also in Italy, generally, and in the parts of the world where I've had the opportunity of talking about this – we haven't had such a significant number of male figures as we might have expected in light of recognised pedagogical principles. Therefore, it was an extremely important statement and the problem is still a topical one nowadays . . .

At least in terms of its symbolic value, it remains significant!

. . . it also remains significant in terms of its real value, because in the cases where we've been able to observe teachers working in pairs, there is a positive value when the pair is not all male or all female; and the children are very sensitive to this.

The universe of adults is getting richer: we have the atelierista *but also the principle of at least two teachers working together with a group of children – which might be called the principle of co-presence.*

I'd like to underscore the extremely innovative element of the teachers' co-presence, in addition to the presence of the *atelierista*, as we'll see later. The co-presence of the two teachers, though they share a common professional position, relied wholly on the difference between them, and I think was permeated by the idea of different points of view, dialogue and exchange as an essential quality of education and educators, who develop their sensibility toward the child and his or her identity thanks to a very high level exercise which they are invited to undertake, which they are encouraged to undertake, and which they are forced to undertake with their colleague. I think this is where the profound sense of collective work originates – today we could talk about 'working in a group' – and in a way which very much anticipated future developments precisely because of this systemic conception and this idea of the relativity of the image of the child, so that the value of difference is introduced precisely through the introduction of the co-presence of the two teachers with different perspectives. This is something which still hasn't been developed and accepted in Italian schools, also because there is a lot of confusion between didactic freedom and individualism. I think that behind this didactic freedom there is also all the loneliness and the abuses – inflicted and suffered – of the single teacher.

This is a pair which proposes dialogue with the outside and opens dialogue with the other professional figure, the *atelierista*, who brings in an intended and calculated difference. The metaphor of the hundred languages is represented by the *atelierista's* professional education, with a background which is geared toward visual languages. The theory of the hundred languages was already emerging in the 1970s and the *atelier* – it may not have been so clear at the beginning – asserted its identity primarily as the place of the hundred languages: the graphic, pictorial, sculptural, plastic, mathematical, poetic languages and much more; including the languages that arise from a dialogue with different disciplines and cultural worlds, as we were to understand better later on. Therefore, this figure who brings in a different experience, who wants to push differences to the utmost, encourages a pedagogical approach which will tend to focus increasingly on children's subjectivities and consequently offer a plethora of opportunities that is as wide-ranging as possible. Therefore, I now like to say (and, thankfully, I am not the only one) that the whole school should be a great *atelier*, where doing, reflecting, action, sensory perception together with the virtual, and the local together with the global, can find their expression in a school that is now transformed into a great laboratory of research and reflection.

However, as we were saying, then the other colleagues, the auxiliary staff, too, become interactive participants in the dialogue with a pair of teachers who are seeking the other person's point of view. But nothing came easy: it was a hard process, we also had to deal with the everyday problems and contradictions. There are also those who went under, in the sense that they weren't able to stand the dialogue: there have been and still are tensions, because learning to negotiate, adopting the other person's point of view is a difficult art and can never be taken for granted, but here it was pushed to the utmost levels, and was even applied to architecture – yet again – (which avoided, as we were saying before, corridors, real and metaphorical barriers of all kinds, though providing specifically designated areas) and even to the participation process. This means starting from pairs, from co-presence (exalting the value of exchange, of difference as change), and moving to participation, as the other, highest expression of the value of dialogue, such as we've experienced it.

I haven't talked much about this so far, but I'd like this interview to be permeated with the sense of, and be sensitive to, the difficulties which all this represented. It was always an uphill climb. It is a story of hard work but also of satisfaction, joy, where we – at least, as far as I was concerned – never, ever lost track of the sense of what we were doing.

I see you've introduced the theme of participation, and I'd like to link up to this subject. So far we've looked at the people on the 'inside' and professionals. But we haven't exhausted the subject. There is, in fact, participation, which has worked and continues to exist today, but in the state school system participation has always struggled and is now melting away. There was a basic difference then.

I can talk to you about this using some reflections I happened to make recently, which is not, therefore, how we saw the issue at the time. Recently I was talking to Paola Cagliari [*Editors' note*: a *pedagogista* in Reggio Emilia] about this subject and we both emphasised that, even at that time, the idea of participation was not and could not be relegated only to participation by the families. This is because the school, in itself, is a 'participatory' place, a place of participation by the children, the teachers and the families in an educational project that is based on, and hinges on values which have to find expression in daily action.

One of the things that arouses people's curiosity most is the way we've managed to maintain our dialogue with the families and the community during all these years. This story, too, hasn't been easy or simple; at times we had misunderstandings, clashes and differences, some of which were then resolved and others which weren't. I think that centring on the child, the image of the child and education as the main focus of our attention is one of the values to which people, including families, are responsive.

[*Added by CR when editing the book*: what I want to emphasise is that dialogue with families, participation by the town, has always character-ised the identity of the experience – participation in the sense of being part of a project, being a protagonist together with other protagonists. It has not been easy, there have been extremely difficult moments, but it has been a marvellous training ground for democracy. Learning the value of divergence (differing opinions), of the construction of consent (agreement), of negotiation was a long, complex exercise which is not finished. But it allowed all the protagonists (parents, teachers, adminis-trators, politicians, other citizens) to understand that the concept of participation is not only a fundamental strategy of politics; it is also a way of being, of thinking of oneself in relation to others and the world. It is therefore a fundamental educational value and form of educational activity that the child can appreciate from a very young age.]

Yet another final proof, if one should be needed, came from our Washington experience, therefore a foreign experience. I refer to Washington, where a nursery school has been established that is in dialogue with Reggio in what is a 'black' ghetto – and unfortunately the term 'ghetto' still has a meaning there. When this school opened, six or seven years ago, 'white' people were advised not to go to these areas, especially at certain times of the day. Amelia Gambetti [*Editors' note*: a Reggio educator working most of the time in the United States], who coordinated the school for a number of years, had quite a few difficulties in being accepted at the beginning since she was white. But the parents took their children to the school, they felt that the school respected them and, above all, respected their children, valued their children, and they responded with extraordinarily high levels of attendance and sensitivity. It seems to me that in Reggio, as in Washington, the fact that you are able to discuss the issues of education today (what 'educating' means), of parenthood, of one's own contradictions, and also to search for the sense and meaning of being a child, of going to school, of being a parent, I think that all this contributes to parents continuing to find meaning in these schools.

We did note, unfortunately, after the introduction of the 'delegated decrees' [*Editors' note*: Italian regulations concerning social management in compulsory schools and family participation], when the results were not good, that excessive bureaucratisation drove out commitment to participation. So, too, did a fear of conflict. One thing I've noticed is that a trait in our culture, I'm not sure whether to say in the Reggio Emilia culture or in Italian culture, is to accept conflict as part of dialogue. They say that a person from Reggio Emilia (maybe an Italian) begins to have a dialogue when an American or a Swede stops. Here, then, you hit upon some very important cultural issues: the way you deal with and develop ideas about conflict, error and forgiveness; and how you accept declared differences and don't make them the seed of enmity. This is a trait that belongs to our culture in Reggio Emilia, it is perhaps, too, a trait in Italian culture, and it is a trait that is enhanced particularly by our kind of school.

What I can say to you is that this interest on the part of the parents in the education of their children and this willingness to connect back and forth from their child to the school has been sustained over the years. Not all the parents, not all the time, not the same everywhere, but it is a phenomenon that has always stayed with us.

It's important because in this way the logic of handing over to the 'specialist' does not prevail and the legitimacy is established of the principle that, to some extent, everyone is a specialist, and the parents are specialists . . .

Precisely: they are participants who bring with them a particular point of view as well as values. Then, obviously, the school has to recognise its own identity and know up to what point to negotiate.

I'd like to start once more from the school in Villa Gaida. This was an isolated episode which did not have a follow up, since the war and fascism prevented it from becoming a starting point for setting up a network of schools. This was a real pity, since to the administrators of the time and the then director, Giuseppe Soglia, the mainly educational function of the so-called 'asili' (nurseries) was clear. These reflections lead me to ask you about the importance of setting up a network-based organisation of institutions, starting from the common links between the municipal schools of Reggio Emilia themselves, and later with similar experiences in other municipalities. I'm inclined to think that even the rightly acclaimed example of the Diana school [Editors' note: a scuola dell'infanzia in Reggio, described by the American magazine Newsweek in 1991 as the best nursery in the world] would not have had the same history if it had remained in 'splendid isolation'.

I totally agree with this statement. On the question of the network, there is a wonderful comment by Jerome Bruner on the Reggio Emilia experience, where he says that the most exceptional thing of all is that it has lasted for so long and is, above all, the cultural expression of a city, the municipal schools being the 'normal' public services of a city that has generated them and sees in them a reflection of itself. Because I'm convinced that the great political importance and the real and symbolic value of these institutions is to be found not only in the fact that they are a service, but, as we were saying earlier, as a statement of the place where the local culture develops its own image of children and childhood; I think this is crucial. Not only this, of course, but I think a community has to have places where it can develop its image of the child, its image of childhood. Therefore the cultural and political value of this is very high.

But being a network also means being inside a system where you gain identity through your dialogue with others. This is why we experienced the recognition of the Diana school with joy but also a certain degree of embarrassment and difficulty, not so much for Diana itself, but because we had to explain to a lot of people that the real value was not so much in the Diana school itself. The real value was in a school which is symbolic of, and represents, a network of more than thirty schools for children from zero to six years old. I think it would also be interesting to know why the mass media and others wanted and continue to want to put the emphasis on the school as an 'experimental' kind of school. Howard Gardner said that one of Dewey's successes was that he also created his own school – but it was only one school and it lasted for four years. We have thirty schools here and they've had the courage to keep going, from generation to generation of citizens of the same city, and also to generate dialogue and reciprocal exchanges with other municipal experiences not only in Italy but also abroad, and to be themselves generated by this dialogue, by having dialogue and exchange as an integral part of themselves.

Opening new schools with new forms of management, as there is now the possibility of doing (cooperative-run *nidi* and this kind of thing), is important and possible precisely because they are within a network system. Each school is a network and the schools form a network with each other, and this system has created a strong culture of exchange and change. Even the delegations from other places, the people who come to meet with us, represent an extremely important opportunity for professional development, because the view of others, the questions that other people ask about us are extremely important for creating knowledge and stimulating self-reflection. A network of this kind helps us to achieve levels of awareness and responsibility and an ethical position which are difficult to maintain.

Therefore, going back to the statement made earlier, the importance of being perceived as schools that operate within a network should be underlined, and this network is extending. I think it would be extremely interesting to see the map of this phenomenon, extended worldwide. Those who are part of it already feel tied to something which is symbolic, something more than a geographical reality. There is this new cultural geography of people who share, who accept the fact of sharing values, which goes beyond geographical borders and creates a network of people who share common understandings and common ideals. And this, I think, is because our schools in Reggio were conceptualised as a network, not only because the first *scuola dell'infanzia* and then the second started to hold joint professional development activities, putting together the experience of one school and the next and then that of the *nidi*, but also because the first national and international conferences in Reggio were themselves a statement of the willingness to be a network. Also

Loris Malaguzzi went to Switzerland to get to know the Piagetian school, and there were other paths that we followed. We shouldn't forget that the *Gruppo Nazionale Nidi Infanzia* (the National Group for Nurseries) was established in Reggio Emilia, and that ever since the early 1970s we used to travel around Italy, participating in conferences and building relations based on the Reggio Emilia experience. We formed friendships with some cities that still hold fast today, with Pistoia for instance.

A network means a system, therefore a degree of centralisation and of functional hierarchy: hence the role of the central administration office and of the pedagogical team (of pedagogistas) in these links and in planning.

There are some unforgettable passages by Malaguzzi on the value of organisation – organisation as a value – which make it seem incredible that it should be defined as the Cinderella of schools, misunderstood as far as its structuring value is concerned. In organisation, every element is inspired by a value; organisation expresses a value and is not an end in itself; it finds its own reasoning and constantly seeks a *raison d'etre*, to the point of questioning itself. The organisation of the day, for example, which we set out in such a detailed way, is not meant to take freedom away but to give freedom, as a sharing of meanings and gestures, to render the meaning of gestures.

[*Added by CR when editing the book*: by talking about the 'meaning of gestures', I want to indicate the importance of agreeing on the meaning of everyday activities with the children. For example, laying the table with the children means understanding that you are not only organising the table in a functional way but organising a meeting or encounter because eating a meal together is an important moment for socialising, conversation and friendship. In the same way, it is important to agree that tidying up an area is a fundamental condition for being a community.]

Here, too, there is a search for equilibrium between social organisation and family organisation, as well as a school organisation which is able to acknowledge and attribute value, for instance, to the moment of encounter, to the symbolic passage between the family and the school. Therefore organisation here means a structure which gives value; that is, there is no point talking about the value of dialogue between home and school if you are not able to make this act and react in everyday life. Hence, the attention we pay to the moment when the children come into the school in the morning and when they leave, hence the effort, once again, when we organise the timetable of the staff and the spaces of the school, to seek timeframes and ways which can recognise the right of the child to be well-loved and well-cared for in the morning, to be well-parted from within the family, but at the same time, respecting the auxiliary staff who have to do the cleaning, trying, as I was saying earlier, to organise not times but values from which times can be derived and shared.

There was recently a Swedish delegation who couldn't believe that there wasn't a principal in every school. Quite honestly, I have to say that in each school, there is, at the most, a leading figure, recognised *de facto* as such. But the important thing is that each figure is recognised for his or her value, including his or her pedagogical value, rather than for his or her role. Then we see that there may be the person who has an extraordinary skill for working out schedules or keeping the cash-box, and it is good that they should have those defined tasks, just as it is good that there should be a person who has the task of planning weekly professional development sessions or keeping the records, all based on the value which the individual person can bring.

This leads us to the pedagogical team [*Editors' note*: the group of *pedagogistas* working in the municipal schools], which has a crucial role. It is a sort of metaphorical 'place' which fosters dialogue between schools and within the schools themselves, a place which gives direction, which has to have a sense and a role of cultural and pedagogical responsibility, but also a political responsibility toward the schools and the city. This is why it should be 'a place not only of words but also of listening'. It is a link, yet again, between theory and practice. But where should it take its inspiration from? From the schools! From the schools and from the culture, indeed from the cultures and the most advanced research in all the disciplines. The great ability of the team is to keep abreast of things because of its ability to be attentive to the voices of all. It has to be able to listen to the voices of the auxiliary staff, of the parents, of the teachers, and has to be able to talk with them.

It's like taking the apologia of Menenio Agrippa and turning it around: no-one is just the head, stomach or the limbs, but in this exchange there is no hierarchy of individuals or predefined roles, but only a hierarchy of the values that come into play.

Clearly, of course, there are well-defined responsibilities and the decisive question refers to the strategy needed to manage them all. Since each worker, each teacher is responsible, then it is right that everyone should be in a position to carry out their tasks in the best way possible, and that there should also be differences and that these, in turn, should matter.

There should definitely be a hierarchy of responsibilities. But there shouldn't be a hierarchy that abolishes dialogue, exchange and, most importantly, respect. If, when we talk about respect, we have in mind teachers who take in six- or seven-month-old babies in the morning, and keep them for five, six or seven hours, one hopes that these teachers don't give too much thought to how much responsibility they are taking on every day! But then, this responsibility, just like the responsibility of the pedagogical team and of the central administrative office, must be recognised and recognisable, but also limited, respected and, most of all, 'participatory', in the sense that it should make people share in it. And this is not so very difficult, but it is necessary if your aim is to have teachers who participate with their colleagues, the children and the parents.

[*Added by CR while editing the book*: I want to emphasise here that there are, of course, different levels of responsibility, like for example that of the pedagogical director of the municipal early childhood services or the municipality's head of administration. But the most important task is to construct shared decision-making processes which make each protagonist not only aware of her or his own role, but also of their inter-dependence on the quality of work of others.]

Changing the subject, there is also the network of cultural affinities and exchanges. Would I be wrong in stating that in the definition of Reggio's methods and the objectives, the contribution of academic pedagogy has been less important than the contribution of individual figures or experiences which are not so easy to classify, like Bruno Ciari, Gianni Rodari and others? [Editors' note: *Gianni Rodari (1920–80) was a writer, poet, philosopher, political commentator and journalist. He contributed to a renewal in children's literature. One of his most famous books is* La Grammatica della Fantasia *(The Grammar of Fantasy), dedicated to the city of Reggio Emilia and which, in Malaguzzi's words, became 'a creative and teaching classic'. Malaguzzi also described the encounters with Rodari, as well as with Ciari, as 'of immense importance to us' (Malaguzzi, 2004: 12).*] *What degree of import- ance, at the initial stage, did you attribute to the ideas of activist pedagogical thinking, and to the work of Piaget? But subsequently, a lot of other things happened on the research field, didn't they?*

I agree with you, once again. The contribution of academic pedagogy was not very strong, except for our gratitude to the pedagogy of Maria Montessori, the activism of Dewey, of Agazzi, but I wouldn't call it, or it can't be seen in the same way as university academia . . .

It's the pedagogical side of the twentieth century cultural universe.

Precisely. I think what you say is true: there were people like Bruno Ciari, like Gianni Rodari and – we referred to him earlier – Lodi, but there were also artists which I'm not going to list to you now. I am also thinking of the strong impact of architecture and the neurological sciences. We were one of the major sources of inspiration for a kind of pedagogy which wasn't bound by a narrow historical tradition of pedagogy. The criticism I always heard from Loris Malaguzzi and made my own was that pedagogy in Italian universities was always reduced to the history of pedagogy and was not an active kind of pedagogy. I must say that to hear people say, up until the time of Malaguzzi's death, that his was a 'home-made' kind of pedagogy says a lot about the difficulties in recognising that our schools (as well as others, naturally) are schools where pedagogy lives. In addition to Piaget and the post-Piagetian school of thought, Bateson, Bruner, Vygostsky and others, there were also other disciplines like epistemology, the neurological sciences and others which were in full ferment, that made an important contribution to a kind of pedagogy that had to reckon with contemporary cultural reality. Our dialogue with university academics was much longer and more fruitful abroad: Stockholm, American universities. Of course, there are exceptions, but. . . . Perhaps it's a case of *nemo propheta in patria*, perhaps we haven't been able to talk the right way. The reproach from Italian universities was always: Reggio hasn't written very much. The criticism is that there is nothing 'academic', nothing official, there is no book that is a 'summation' of our work. Ours is still an academia that only values the written language. Our answer was the exhibit of 'The Hundred Languages of Children', putting forth another kind of writing, another language.

These considerations lead us to the question of the 'method', about which, if I'm not mistaken, a veritable pedagogical and academic discipline was formed; i.e. methodology. The impressions given on this subject by the usual analyses of the historical succession of 'methods' (Aporti, Froebel, Agazzi, Montessori, etc.) is that they each construct, in turn, a tight body of thought from which codified procedures are derived. A 'philosophical' part (however profound or otherwise), and an applied part, so to speak. I have an inkling that in the Reggio 'way' (this seems to me to be the most opportune translation: method as a way, similar to that used in Chinese Taoist philosophy) things go differently. Could you clear up the mystery of a method which is open and yet is unitary and consistent (if it is legitimate to call it so)? This seems to me to be both novel and disconcerting.

In my view, with your formulation of this question, you have captured once again what I think is an important difference. I have to confess to you, however, that I haven't had time to reflect on this question sufficiently and I would like to go back to this at a later date because it's important to provide a suitable answer to it. I think the issue of the 'way', which you emphasise – method as a way – could help us to perceive that it is not true, as people say, that there is no method in the municipal schools of Reggio Emilia, since without a method experience couldn't exist. There is an approach that requires – and it is probably the beauty and the difficulty of this story – to be constantly falsified in Popperian terms. And therefore it is a method that constantly seeks to generate its own doubts.

Hence the idea which I thought of for today's interview, which was to examine the idea of documentation. That is the strategy we have identified to try and be consistent in relation to the value of the subjectivity and the uniqueness of every individual. The great need to be consistent and therefore to constantly produce change – it's the paradox of this need – arose from, and has been proved more than ever by, the discussions held during all these years and by the latest contributions of the neurological sciences, which encourage us to personalise as much as possible ways and timeframes of learning.

The way the process of educability is achieved is determined by and has a determining influence on cultures. We believe, for example, that all individuals can learn to read and write: but the quality of this result will depend on the extent to which this learning to read and write is based on the times and the ways of the individual person and within a group context. Therefore, what we've tried to do has been to work out a methodology that would enhance the opportunity of capturing the strategies of each *individual* to learn, and to learn inside a particular context, therefore in relation to a *group*. This approach has hinged on documentation, which we should acknowledge as a way of trying to capture the subjectivities that interact in a group, and to create processes which can foster not so much teaching in the traditional sense, but rather the setting of contexts for learning to take place. In this, I find what you call the mystery of a way that is open while at the same time unitary, which tries to offer to each person in the group, and to each group as a sum of subjectivities, the opportunity of acquiring values and cultures (values expressed in cultures), according to each person's own subjectivity, but also with respect for being part of a group. This means that each year we ask our teachers to write a new 'statement of intents'; that is, what they intend to propose and why, to share with their colleagues, with the parents, trying not to make this declaration of intention a rigid plan but a progressive route which is negotiated in everyday life with the working group and the families.

I find in your description a recognition of the value of consistency, continuity, but also the need to live, therefore, a willingness to change. So, while a certain kind of insti-tutionalised school expects uniformity and predictability, or, from the opposite point of view, it practises 'artistic' improvisation, here we are facing neither the one nor the other.

Indeed, there is something in learning that, in a sense, equates with poetry and, without wishing to fall into mysticism, entails unpredict-ability. I'll give you an example, a very basic one really: in one of the schools they made a scrapbook to put together all their memories of the summer, one for each child, thinking that the following September they would develop the theme of sensory perception. They made this scrap-book, inviting each child to collect smells and scents, to record noises, etc., everything was set and arranged; and when we asked them what the most interesting thing that struck them during the summer was – and we were expecting to hear about the sun, the sunlight, the flowers, the sea; we were ready to take in all this – one child came out and said 'the crowds!', completely confounding our expectations. And all the others went: 'Yes, yes, yes, that's right, that's it!' They set off to go where we hadn't expected to go at all! So we shifted everything onto this thing. The unforeseen is part of life, indeed, I'm beginning to see that it's life itself.

Lastly, I'd like to go back to the concept of 'network'. I can't ignore the ever-growing tapestry of international relationships. The real importance of this seems to me to be the risk of rushed and trivial interpretations, which may be in line with the idea of exporting a 'product', therefore something exchangeable, as any other product, a serial product, etc. At this point, I think we need to clarify the issue.

As I was saying earlier, we should bear in mind that the encounter with these other cultures is for us primarily a way of importing questions and curiosity, an occasion of truly extraordinary richness which provokes us to develop professionally and reflect. These cultural differences some-times lead you to soar into inner worlds which you didn't suspect you ever had, and to experiences which you thought you hadn't had at that particular level. Therefore, we import, above all, a great deal of curiosity and a great number of opportunities for exchange.

What we've absolutely wanted to oppose is the temptation to start off by putting on display and circulating some kind of pre-packaged boxes, using a doubtful method of applying business to pedagogy. We therefore prevented the development of a mistaken approach to the concept of method which would have occurred by selling the 'Malaguzzi method' or the 'Reggio method'. Unfortunately, this is what happened with other experiences, so that you bought a set of notebooks, some furniture, and so on, and that was it.

We had a debate, if not something more, that wasn't easy to sustain because we weren't even very well equipped for arguing very much, and, in particular, we didn't know where this could lead. Then, gradually, the debate got clearer by going back to the origins and to the word 'education', which I believe is linked to ethical values, and, as such, a non-exportable concept. We think, rather, that the concept can be the source of exchanges and reflections, therefore today the argument is that every culture has to develop its own strategy in the field of school educa-tion. *Together*, we can try to share values which are universal, but at the local level, all the different actors – in Sweden, just as in Japan or Australia – will have to try to develop these values for themselves.

Some people loved the image of a seed. But Reggio isn't a seed that can be exported and transplanted. At the most, Reggio can lend itself to the metaphor of a mirror in which you can find an image of yourself. The exhibition is another occasion for reflecting on your own identity, your own values, your own image of school. The other thing we can share, in the sense that we didn't create it ourselves, is the image of the competent child. This – just as the image of the competent teacher – is one of those values which I don't think was invented by Reggio, it can already be found in some famous passages by Dewey . . .

Ideas which are already a century old . . .

Exactly, they are a century old and we, Malaguzzi and us, (this collective 'we' that you highlighted), had the courage to take them, make them part of our living experience, and support them in a place, in a context that was generous in this sense, and which welcomed them with generosity and made them its own, perhaps because it had them already. This is a little what other people do with us. They come here, they make us recognise what we have, what we are able to see, but also what we have not been able to see before.

Paradoxically, the Reggio approach exists beyond Reggio. For example, I would argue against the suggestion that the image of the rich and competent child was born in Reggio; no, it has a much wider genetic make-up, but here in Reggio it has a new courage and a new expression and an equally new identity. Therefore, it requires others to show the same courage, because to the people who are with us we can only ask them to have the courage to look inside themselves, to find and construct these and other values, in their own cultures. That's why I ask myself a lot of questions about the United States, I worry about Japan and a culture such as the Chinese, with which I'm not sure we'll be able to have a direct dialogue, if having a dialogue means more than speaking English or going from English to Korean. We'll have to be very careful to understand how others interpret us. To a culture like the Chinese the value of copying, for example, is different, it is a value.

Something else I would like to add is that we were born international, the idea is an international idea, our experience started to have a dialogue at the international level right from the start. Over time we have become more aware of these international origins.

Finally, I would ask you to raise the questions I didn't ask you, which are no doubt more important than the ones I had in mind.

I think your questions went in the most important directions, there is a coincidence between them and the research areas which I, together with my colleagues, have been working on recently. What might be worth insisting on is the fact that this is also a history of hard work, not so much to emphasise the hard work in itself, but to emphasise the quality of these schools where nothing is taken for granted or ignored, because there have been contradictions, there have been inconsistencies.

Then I'd also like it to be recognised that this story is also a history in the female gender. I'm thinking of Loris Malaguzzi and the theme of nostalgia for the future – by the way, Malaguzzi was a great cultivator of the future and hardly a cultivator of the past – and regarding this nostalgia of the future, I'm reminded of the fact that the exhibition and the book on the hundred languages of children, that was published in the United States (Edwards, Gandini and Forman, 1993) were supposed to be entitled 'Ariadne's thread'. This was to be an acknowledgment to all these women, all these Ariadnes, for being able to pull together so many extraordinary threads for so many years. Therefore I would at least like it to be recognised that this was a history of women. I think it's a very feminine story: let's consider their organisation of everyday life, also their patience – and I'm not sure if this is a secular or a religious quality – the women's patience, steadfastness, the strength of these hard working and dedicated young women who have been present throughout the generations. I'd like to recognise the merit of all these young women who, with salaries that are still inadequate, are capable of acts which today are sometimes even braver, even more full of the future and even more groundbreaking than they were some years ago. Because in this society of waste and ostentation, I'd like to say that Reggio is a history of the heroines of everyday life, or perhaps simply a history of women who every day have to be able to combine their role of protagonists of family life with the role of protagonists of a working life which they have felt to be important, because it is socially important, culturally important and politically important. I don't wish to assign any monopoly, it has been a history of teachers, auxiliary workers and cooks.

Which was also a way of enhancing the image of women, since this role as protagonist has also affected people's mental and symbolic images.

Absolutely. This also redeems the image of the woman teacher, which Malaguzzi held in great esteem; he had a truly enormous esteem and respect for teachers. There has been an affirmation of the dignity of the teacher. They say our teachers are *beautiful*. It's true, there are few places in the world where teachers in schools of early childhood, or anywhere else, are as beautiful, as dignified, as 'womanly' as they are here.

The same goes for the other professional figure – which we haven't perhaps talked enough about – the *pedagogista*. Here, too, they are mostly women who have been able to create this highly regarded professional position and who belong, once again, to this activist and active pedagogy. It is a pedagogy which needs people to act in the role of cultural mediators, something which is the teachers' job, but can also require mediators such as *pedagogistas* who are responsible for the relationship between the inside and the outside world.

Finally, allow me to make a comment. I am conscious of the partial nature of my account, of having omitted to mention facts and people. I am especially sorry if I haven't been able to express all the gratitude I feel for this history and its protagonists.

Chapter 14

Crossing boundaries

Reflections on Loris Malaguzzi and Reggio Emilia (2004)

What meaning and value do anniversaries have in our lives? What value might memory have in the process of searching for identity and future? These are two of the many questions we posed when we began reflecting on the meaning which celebrating 40 years of experience in Reggio municipal schools might assume in today's context. We stopped to think about the meaning of the verb 'celebrate', a verb which we feel is inadequate to represent our intention of looking to the future with the responsibility of the past.

We thought long about what kind of event or events might characterise and give meaning to this time. We opted to pluralise, to have different moments which, when put together, would be able to signify the event in the city, in the country and in the world. At the centre of our reflections were not so much the municipal schools but the values, concepts and structural choices which have characterised them. Values and concepts which have found inspiration, exchange and enrichment in their dialogue with other situations, other disciplines and other worlds of knowledge and culture.

'Crossing boundaries' was the metaphor which best described the sense of our journey and at the same time our hopes for the future. Crossing the cultural, psychological and geographical boundaries which sometimes hold us prisoner inside stereotypes, commonplaces and convictions; and which generate separateness, exclusion, isolation, absence of dialogue and dangerous forms of cultural racism.

'Crossing boundaries' was the name we gave to this international conference, held in February 2004, which in a certain sense was to represent our place for meeting with colleagues and friends from all over the world who wanted to be with us to construct and experience the event.

It took us more than a year to prepare because it had to be shared and carried out with the involvement not only of all the people working in municipal schools in the city, about five hundred in number, but also the involvement of parents and the entire city. It was to be another time for meeting and redefining identity through dialogue between protagonists who, in Reggio and other parts of the world, have searched and researched the meaning of educating today in national and international situations which are so complex and in many respects, difficult and contradictory.

Great efforts were made by teachers and *pedagogistas* to try and organise knowledge constructed together with children and parents into stories of images capable of offering reflection and questions for participants. There was great passion and the desire to open up again physical and mental spaces to others who, although they live in different situations, are extremely willing to place themselves at the centre of discussion through recounting these experiences.

It was a great opportunity for learning and a shared responsibility. All this created worries as well as constructive tension: can we do it? This was the question I asked myself and it became more pressing with the passing days. I had been asked to give a talk which would describe the search for identity through dialogue which has always characterised our experience since Loris Malaguzzi (who conceived and constructed the relational pedagogy orienting the Reggio experience) defined interaction and intercultural exchange as the element giving structure to our experience.

Preparing this talk was complex for me and in some respects difficult. The difficulty came first of all from the need to use synergy and synthesis to describe concepts and values structuring the experience. However there was another reason which made this talk extremely significant for me. That day (one of four days over which the conference was held) was dedicated to Loris Malaguzzi, on the tenth anniversary of his death. The sense of responsibility and the emotion of my memories of so many years spent together – 24 – made my throat constrict that morning. But the welcoming expressions of 1,200 people from all over the world, the smiles of so many familiar faces, the support of my colleagues accompanied me to the podium. And joy prevailed! It was contagious joy because we were all there together to remember Malaguzzi, the way he liked it: looking to the future and committing ourselves once again to a better quality of life for childhood around the world

There are in fact several ways of narrating the work of a scholar, of a philosopher, of a researcher; of a man like Loris Malaguzzi. Although, perhaps, as Sergio Manghi (1998) says, there are really only two. One is to think of the man and his work as if they were here in front of us, objectified and complete. The other is to think of the work in relation to ourselves, as part of us, work which also speaks of us, which continues and evolves with us and in us, and from which we take on meaning and responsibility.

In this phase of history, where the news too often describes and exalts the success of the individual over the group, the victory of the solitary leader saved by a miracle, people's uniqueness as separation and isolation rather than a strength and resource for dialogue, the truest, most sincere and relevant way I can think of paying homage to Malaguzzi is to speak of his extraordinary ability for promoting that sense of belonging, the educational project, that 'we' which has been capable of crossing boundaries, embracing dreams and building hope through encounter, through close exchange, through the angers and joys of transforming dialogue. Crossing boundaries: Malaguzzi loved to cross boundaries, he loved to inhabit the border areas. Not boundaries which have been established once and for all, or defined a priori; but boundaries perceived as places for meeting and exchange, where knowledge and action pursue and feed each other.

Together with him we shared many journeys and crossed many boundaries. We learned the 'art' of *creative transition* as Malaguzzi loved to define it. This helped us not to accept the boundary of his death as a limit or the dramatic interruption of processes and pathways we had constructed together.

I still remember the pain, the struggle ten years ago in imagining us existing without his presence or continuing to seek the path without his guidance. I still remember my sadness and difficulty and that of colleagues in the municipal schools. But mostly I remember the determination in our wish to carry on feeling and being 'we'.

We have tried to keep some values constant even when strategies and objectives often change. We have tried to elaborate an educational project which also has slower rhythms, when most of contemporary society seems oriented towards the short term and a constantly fluctuating instability. We committed ourselves to building a present which is aware of the past and responsible towards the future. And we especially tried to consolidate our awareness that we were the protagonists of a project which was not only about early childhood education, but about people, about mankind. This awareness helped us to understand that it was and still is necessary to make choices not only in pedagogy but in ethics and values too.

Pedagogy like school is not neutral. It takes sides, it participates in deep and vital ways in the definition of this project whose central theme is not mankind, but his relations with the world, his being in the world, his feeling of *interdependence* with what is other than himself. So pedagogy implies choices, and choosing does not mean deciding what is right compared to what is wrong. Choosing means having the courage of our doubts, of our uncertainties, it means participating in something for which we take responsibility.

We made these choices thanks to exchange and debate with colleagues and friends here in Reggio Emilia, in Italy and throughout the world.

I would like to express my and our gratitude for this to all those who have supported, shared and also criticised our choices.

With their help we have constructed our identity, an identity which is open to change. We have constructed the differences that we feel now, more than ever, to be the value we can offer; we are aware of, and responsible for, the fact that this way we are constructing a true concept of belonging.

In fact we are all connected, wherever we work, even in the most geographically and culturally distant and different contexts, to the same community of destiny, to a new and complex planetary anthropology.

What choices can I offer for your attention to try and give you the wider meaning that derives from these choices? Surely the first concerns the image of the child and the theory of learning, choices that have been reference points for us, guiding our experience, our journey. It is widely known that our choice, and one of the focal points of our philosophy, is the image of a competent child. 'What competencies is the child in possession of?' we asked ourselves, and to understand this we tried to meet the child, to see her or him, to understand her or him, to enter into a dialogue with her or him. A child is competent in forming relations, in communicating – I would dare to say in living. Each child born is a 'could be' of humanity, he is a possibility, the beginning of a hope, and is deeply influenced by the levels of awareness, the will, the courage and the politics of the country receiving him.

Children are not only our future, which we invest in by oppressing their dreams and freedom to be something other than we would wish them to be. They are our present. The child is not a citizen of the future; he is a citizen from the very first moment of life and also the most important citizen, because he represents and brings the 'possible', a statement that for me is completely without rhetoric. The child is a bearer, here and now, of rights, of values, of culture: the culture of childhood. He is not only our knowledge about childhood, but childhood's knowledge of how to be and how to live.

It is our historical responsibility not only to affirm this but to create cultural, social, political and educational contexts which are able to receive children and dialogue with their potential for constructing human rights. These are physical contexts but also mental contexts which require the deconstruction and overcoming of our preconceptions about childhood, the social reconstruction of a new culture of childhood, the construction of a new culture of mankind and a new identity for ourselves (educators, parents and other adults).

Children's ways of interpreting and experiencing give us different paradigms for thought, that is to say, different ways of feeling emotions and thinking which are disruptive and inconvenient because they put into question familiar ways.

And in an era of globalisation where we are coming to redefine the very concept of mankind, to start/restart from children, from their generous humanity, from trying to give new answers to their quest for meaning, might make it possible for us now, more than in the past, to have the courage to rewrite a new complex anthropology.

I am not proposing a romantic approach or an image of childhood which comes close to the creation of a world of innocence and purity. But I would like to emphasise this strong feeling of the need for a para-digmatic change, that Western thinking must adjust so that we can find, as we have never done in the past, vital energy from the relationship and dialogue with children and childhood.

Our interpretation of this concept of 'competent child' was connected with our sharing of values, in particular interaction and dialogue as essential qualities defining our relations with children and adults, with the city itself and with others in general. This value has had important implications for our choices.

The greatest effort Malaguzzi led us to make was in finding forms of organisation which were not only consistent with the theoretical posi-tions we had assumed, but able to guarantee the vitality and the bringing to crisis point of that same organisation, and its self-renewal. Organisa-tion which would guarantee us change, and sustain a logic not of repro-duction but of co-construction, that is to say – generative creativity. Organisation capable of listening and sustaining creativity up to the point where it takes on the value of risk and of adventure. There were trade unionist friends, politicians, people of good sense who understood that for an organisation or an educational system to be such, it cannot take on the logic of reproduction and standardisation but must be cap-able of embracing the surprises and disruptions of organisation created on a daily basis.

The 'pedagogy of relations', as Malaguzzi loved to define the peda-gogy enacted in our schools, found that exchange was easy and immedi-ate with that area of architecture defined as relational. This dialogue and exchange has been particularly fruitful and has never been exhausted, exactly because today – more than a dialogue – it has become a common research project, not only around school architecture but around chil-dren and adults and their ways of inhabiting the world. In the same way we chose to dialogue with all those people in various disciplines (psycho-logy, human sciences, biology, neurology, art and design) who agreed to carry out research with us, constructing questions together, experiencing journeys of research together which were respectful of each person's role, without preconceived hierarchies between academic knowledge and the knowledge of educators. Journeys which were also playful and entertaining, surprising and uncertain, because when researching into the world of children, it is really the children who must be the main protagonists of that research.

A researching school: a theme close to Malaguzzi's heart and ours – and to the hearts of others. I need to make this point in order to introduce a theme which represents a characteristic feature, and one of the most criticised, of our experience: *the construction of vocabulary* often as an alternative to more usual vocabulary. We can understand this criticism. But constructing our vocabulary was a fundamental element in the construction of our identity, above all because it was a way of constructing common values and meanings, of constructing choices, in order to be 'we' and to be able to offer an 'open identity' – an identity open to modification in the dialogue and encounter with the other.

Supporting this there has always been humour, when there is a strong risk of being too dogmatic. It is humour that often guides our criticism and self-criticism. And this too has been learned from children who, as we know, are capable of being extremely humorous.

We have tried to cross boundaries but also to inhabit them. In the face of historic antonyms – such as work-play, reality-imagination – we propose emotion *and* knowledge, creativity *and* rationality, *programmazione and progettazione*, teaching *and* research, individual *and* group, rigid science *and* plastic science.

We have tried to observe children and to observe ourselves with children. By doing this, we became aware and wanted to make visible that this dualistic way of thinking does not belong to children or to adults but to those who believe that 'scientific' means without emotion, without passion, without heart; those who believe that without these qualities science is truer and more objective. We have been able to see instead how reason and emotion, learning and pleasure, fatigue and joy, oneself and others, are not only capable of cohabiting together, but of reciprocally generating each other, supported by the strong force which comes from creative – and thus learning – freedom. The freedom of the unknown, of doubt, of the unfamiliar; a freedom children have if it is not restricted.

With these premises our choices become obvious around a problematic issue which has always been the subject of debate: the teaching–learning relationship. This is what Malaguzzi wrote on the subject: 'The aim of teaching is not to produce learning but to produce the conditions for learning, this is the focal point, the quality of the learning.' The key tool and structure we had for implementing this choice was documentation. Documentation, cited in many international texts on pedagogy as a tool for archiving and/or for the subsequent reconstruction of journeys already completed, is given an original interpretation in our work which places it within the process of teaching and therefore of learning.

Documentation 'in process', enacted and interpreted *during* research and not simply at the end, can guide the direction of the journey itself and encourage relations between children's learning structures and the subject of knowledge/learning itself that, in this kind of learning relationship, becomes an active subject. The learning strategy of the child redefines the identity of the subject of knowledge/learning itself as a reciprocal relationship. Documentation is seen not only as a tool for teaching but also as a structure for epistemology, since by favouring memory and reflection it can modify teaching and knowledge processes in children and in the group of children and teachers. So then, documentation is a part of reciprocal teaching and learning. If the teacher, besides her role of support and cultural mediation, knows how to observe, make documentation and interpret, she will achieve her highest potential for learning and teaching.

Recent reflections, shared with colleagues working in the Reggio experience and others, make it possible to bring to your attention some further areas of research we are exploring more deeply. For example, documentation processes, in the way we have described them, are by their nature also processes of evaluation (they give value to elements considered significant by making them visible). The documents produced are tools for evaluation and self-evaluation. They are an opportunity for reflection, interpretation, dialogue, negotiation and connection of theory to practice. Documentation becomes a strategy for evaluation understood as *the construction of shared meaning*.

Certainly for us documentation, or we might say the concept of visibility and sharing, was also an important cultural and political opportunity which gave us the strength to cross other boundaries and start up new exchanges. Documentation also revealed itself to be an effective way of constructing group identity, history and memories for journeys in which many people have participated.

All this required – requires – time. Time gives shape. We chose. We sought to give time to the children and to ourselves. We have said no to any form of precociousness, to starting children early at primary school or on reading and writing. We strongly defend the 0 to 6 project that guarantees children a time when they are not being pressured.

We were speaking of the concept of participation. The schools of Reggio Emilia, which were born of a true process of popular participation, together with other Italian experiences, are a declaration of participation by families, who constitute part of the schools' identity. Over the years it has become clear that participation is essential to processes of learning and identity in children and adults; it is a way of being a child, an educator, a parent. Participation, then, is a common journey which makes it possible to construct the sense of belonging to a community.

This is a time of great discussion about the reasons for the failure of participatory democracy in schools and elsewhere. We feel the obligation to share difficult aspects with others, but also to declare loudly and clearly that participation is an identifying feature of the very concept of school, education and democracy – and there can be no going back on this.

Each individual, in fact, expresses a unique cultural potential which schools and educational institutions must not only recognise and protect; they must also understand that they can only do this by building a context of interaction and exchange between these different 'uniquenesses'. Uniqueness manifests itself, is nourished, only through exchange. Viewed in this way, we realise that schools assume the character of an *agora* or meeting place, where a plurality of opinions and points of view guarantee secularity and where 'being educational' means being places for producing culture. Cultural production not only of a culture of childhood but above all of a culture produced by childhood.

Participation in the debate around themes such as 'the relationship between language and thought', 'the relationship between areas of knowledge', 'interdisciplinarity' and 'the community' was probably the starting point for one of Malaguzzi's most important works: *the theory of the hundred languages and the atelier*. Much has been written and much has been stated through our exhibition, videos and other material. But I feel it is necessary to specify that the hundred languages of children is not only a metaphor for crediting children and adults with a hundred, a thousand creative and communicative potentials. In our opinion the hundred languages represents a strategy for the construction of concepts and the consolidation of understanding. But above all it is a declaration of the equal dignity and importance of *all* languages, not only writing, reading and counting, which has become more and more obviously necessary for the construction of knowledge.

There is also the conviction, born of several years of experience, reflection and exchange, that creativity and poetry exist in every language, including those we define as scientific, as well as a strong aesthetic element (beauty) which acts as a connecting element in and between concepts. Beauty orients and attracts. It is the task of teaching (assisted by documentation) to sustain the meeting of languages that are enriched by exchange with other languages and discover their own limits, their own silences and their own omissions. It is beauty, 'the attraction of "being a part" ', it is the aesthetic of knowledge, Bateson would say.

It is an ecology of languages. An ecology where technological languages can be of fundamental support if we let the computer and other forms of technology become tools, media capable not simply of adding but of multiplying, able that is to create something new and unpredictable. It is our hope that they will be able to act as a support to creativity.

The *atelier* is a metaphorical space in schools which, taken as a whole, aims to support the development of communication and of the hundred languages. I believe there is a distinction to be made: the difference that I sense exists between *atelier* and studio workshops. It is not just a linguistic distinction, it is a difference in concept and pedagogy.

Workshops both outside and inside schools are much talked of today: and the debate is open. It is my suspicion that for many people workshops are something outside school and school learning, in the same way that creative languages are not thought to be part of knowledge. In Reggio Emilia the *atelier* has come to be developed more and more as a metaphor, not for creative languages but for a strategy of knowing, a way of structuring knowledge and organising learning. We do not have schools and the *ateliers* with the hundred languages like a kind of 'removable appendage'. We have 'schools of research' in which the *atelier* is an essential component in the sense that it is the essence of school as research.

We have been discussing children together, but we have always put children, boys, girls, adolescents, men and women together. These are thoughts that childhood has inspired, but childhood is not a separate phase of life or of human identity. Childhood is the loveliest metaphor for describing the possibilities of mankind, on the understanding that we let it exist, that we recognise it and that we cease all these processes of acceleration and imitation that, in denying childhood, destroy not childhood but man.

I am drawing to the close. I apologise for the limits and partial nature of these reflections. I have made choices of content and tried to use language that might be understood by the hundreds of people here present from many different cultures and pedagogies. I entrust the task of exploring more deeply the themes I have discussed to the visits to our municipal schools later today and to the sessions tomorrow. In each school you will find traces which are common to all the others; a fragment of the whole in each one.

That is Reggio Emilia: a kaleidoscope which mirrors and in which we can be mirrored (Batesonian self reflection). One thing that I hope I have been able to communicate is the intellectual honesty and passion of this experience and its protagonists near and far. Malaguzzi never concealed the great aspirations, hopes and expectations that he had for teachers. Those who knew him well will also remember how exacting, severe and rigorous he was (first and foremost with himself), but they also know that this was the outward sign of his deep respect and gratitude towards teachers. A respect which Malaguzzi always transformed into tangible gestures – battles shared, sweeping passions, generous public demonstrations and into small but essential details of everyday life (trusting in children meant and means trusting in teachers).

So respect for teachers' intelligence, ability and possibilities; a firm invitation to be the protagonists together with children in educational, cultural and political choices. Like the great respect he had for the intelligence of families who he looked to full of hope and optimism. I hope that together we, too, have been capable of offering this respect and trust and will continue to be capable of offering it, though we face a more difficult and contradictory future.

That is why dedicating a day to Loris Malaguzzi means also dedicating it to the teachers and schools of Reggio Emilia.

Chapter 15

In dialogue with Carlina Rinaldi

A discussion between Carlina Rinaldi, Gunilla Dahlberg and Peter Moss

The following chapter is based on a discussion between Carlina Rinaldi (CR), Gunilla Dahlberg (GD) and Peter Moss (PM) that took place on 28 March 2004 in Reggio Emilia. It provided an opportunity for Gunilla and Peter to raise a number of issues with Carlina about Reggio and its pedagogical work. The discussion was taped and subsequently transcribed and edited by all three participants. Some additions were made in subsequent discussions to elaborate parts of the original discussion.

Left politics and the early women's movement: the historical context of Reggio

GD: As all of us know, pedagogical experiences have to be understood in relation to the economic, social and political context. So we would like to hear about your thoughts on the history of your experience in Reggio. In particular could you give us ideas about the importance of left politics, as well as the Union of Italian Women (Unione Donne Italiane – UDI) for your experience? [Editors' note: The UDI, founded in 1945, brought together women from diverse political backgrounds – from communists to liberals – to work for the emancipation of women at a time when Italian women did not have the right to vote or for maternity leave and faced serious job discrimination. UDI worked at a national level, but its work at local level was particularly valued allowing many women to discuss their rights, as well as the rights of children and families, and so become more active protagonists in civil society.]

CR: The roots of our experience are in the socialist ideas that took hold in our area of Italy in the late nineteenth century and early twentieth century. The first school for young children in our area, the Villa Gaida, was opened in 1912, inspired by the Socialist mayor of Reggio. He wanted a school that clearly expressed important ideas in socialist thinking – education as a tool, a weapon against poverty, ignorance, arrogance; education as a tool for freedom. In many ways, these were also the expression of the basic values of the French Revolution – Liberty, Equality, Fraternity. As proof of the power of these ideas, the first act of the Fascist governor of our province, in the early 1920s, was to close this school and others like it.

But to understand the role and influence of the left, you must also talk of women. For these left ways of thinking also supported women's struggle. Women were always natural protagonists, but within the family, not outside. As socialism became more influential from the end of the nineteenth century, so too women became more aware of their own rights, the rights of women. Women played an important part in the socialist movement, which also recognised women as the subject of rights – at least theoretically as there was some contradiction in how male politicians often treated women mainly as wives and mothers!

An increasing awareness of the rights of women was also linked to an increasing awareness of the rights of children. As women became more protagonists in society and more aware of their rights, they began to demand as a right a place to leave children so they could work – but it had to be a public place, a quality place. It was the women who established the idea of quality as a right.

So we could say that it was the Socialists – or going back further, the French Revolution – that opened people's minds to the possibility of change, and through this women helped to build a concept of quality public services as a right.

Especially after the end of the Second World War, the women's movement developed the idea of the school for young children as a public place. This idea was supported by the UDI, which provided a space to develop the idea, it was a sort of catalyst. But it was also supported by farm workers, an exploited group who were influenced by left politics. It was in this very lively atmosphere that the municipality of Reggio (which then had a Communist Party majority) took the decision to innovate and open the first municipal school, the beginning of 40 years of experience.

It is important, therefore, to recognise that it was not just the Communist Party which had the courage to innovate. It was in many ways the people, the citizens, who were aware of their rights, were supportive and participatory – real protagonists.

PM: Why did the municipal preschools start in Reggio in the mid-1960s, and not earlier?

CR: There were perhaps two main reasons. It took time for the left parties to come to engage with new ideas about the school. Partly this was because – as I said before – they had ambivalent attitudes towards women and the idea that young children could have a good life even if they were not all the time with their mothers. And partly because there was an uneasy relation between the left and the world of schools and education, a relationship in which the left did not feel confident or competent, almost you might say they had a feeling of inferiority or subordination. This took time to overcome, to the point for example where a municipality like Reggio governed by the left could open its own municipal schools and be prepared to support educational innovation and experimentation.

But the other reason was that the times changed. From the late 1950s, Italy went into a period of economic and social transformation, we call the economic boom. There was migration to the North and to larger towns and cities, from the countryside and the South. More women, in the North and Centre, entered the labour market, including those who had young children. Add to this, as we have already spoken about, a growing awareness among women of the value of quality services and of rights, and you can see that the period up to 1963 was a period of new demands and expectations, with rising pressures on local administrations to develop services.

And when places like Reggio came to develop municipal schools of early childhood, some of the ground had been prepared by UDI, which had been organising schools for young children since the end of the war, places like Villa Cella which left such an impression on Malaguzzi. [*Editors' note*: see page 146 for more information on Villa Cella.] These experiences, of schools organised by this organisation of women, helped to break an historical and deep-seated association between schools and religion, the idea that schools must be religious institutions, and the religious idea of schools as places of 'assistance' for children and families in need. We can trace Malaguzzi's claim that children were the subject of rights rather than the subject of needs, to that important work of the women's movement, which paved the way for our experience in Reggio.

'Our Piaget': theory as tool or prison

GD: Who and what have been important influences for you in your work and how do you see the relationship and tension between theory and practice?

CR: While you were asking this I was immediately going back to the pages written by Loris Malaguzzi in the book *The Hundred Languages of Children* (Edwards, Gandini and Forman, 1993) where he talks about *our* Piaget, *our* Vygotsky, *our, our*. We talked about 'our', 'our', 'our' to try to avoid being a prisoner of any definition – any pre-definition – that obliged you not to play the game of life with the children, with the teacher and with the school. I don't know if I am really clear enough. What I mean is a theory which tells you what the end result should be.

It is important to avoid any prediction. In the exhibition 'The Hundred Languages of Children' there are some words of Loris about a concept of being. He says this exhibition is against all pedagogy whose purpose is in some way to predict the result, which is a sort of predictor that pre-determines the result, and that becomes a sort of prison for the child and for the teacher, and for the human being.

PM: So, when you say our Vygotsky, our Piaget, this is about avoiding this imprisonment?

CR: Yes, imprisonment is right, exactly. When I started to work with Loris he was struggling with Piaget, grateful to Piaget as a guide, but also trying to come away from him. I don't know if he was feeling the vibration of post-Piagetian thinking – social positivism, you know? I don't know, but I think that he was feeling the dialogue with the children. And in the seventies, the children opened up a lot of new possibilities. In terms of Piaget they gave us the courage of having a big crisis regarding the phases. And documentation was coming out. It was a tool for challenging the theory with the practice, for working with the idea of visibility. Because when you start to see that there is a child that does not crawl but starts to walk, then you question the theory.

GD: So when you talk about 'a big crisis regarding the phases', you mean the stage theory from Piaget?

CR: Yes.

GD: Theory in this case becomes a kind of normalisation.

CR: Exactly.

GD: Or imprisonment, which is a very interesting word.

CR: That is why although Reggio may be postmodern in its perspectives, we are not for postmodernism, because 'isms' are risky. Because they simplify and lock you in prison again. Instead your freedom is to challenge.

GD: Yes, all the time.

CR: You are being postmodern. Because to be postmodern means to challenge.

PM: So you want theory to be a tool.

CR: Absolutely, I want each school to use theory, really, for interpreting, and not to be used, as we say, by theory. [*Editors' note*: unless otherwise mentioned, 'school' in this chapter refers to the municipal early childhood centres in Reggio.]

GD: Yes, I think that's a very good answer, and I like this idea of imprisonment very much, that concept. In our book [Dahlberg, Moss and Pence, 1999] and in my [university] department we have struggled with developmental psychology because it feels like teachers are having all the time the Piagetian stages in the back of their minds, even when they read documentation. And we talk about child development psychology in our book as part of a dominant discourse and a product of modernity, that governs teachers and also all of us. Is that something you discuss regularly in your practice?

CR: Absolutely, very much. And particularly now that I work at a university, I see how conservative these theories are, in terms of maintaining power and giving power to certain perspectives. I think that really documentation is the best tool for making the teacher aware of their own theories, that they have from their background, not only their academic background but also their cultural background – something that is in the society, is in the television, is everywhere. And this is something that Reggio understands very well, how these theories build the image of the child. Documentation was and is still the only tool that I can see for creating crisis in terms of knowledge, professional development, identity and everything.

Creating crisis: the importance of the unexpected and uncertainty

PM: Could you say a bit more about what you mean by 'creating crisis', and whether you view that as something that is important and desirable?

CR: I think my first personal crisis came after one year of working with Loris – there was Loris and I was then the only *pedagogista*. After one year I thought that I had learned everything, that in a new school year you repeat what you have done the year before, you know? So the big crisis came this second year when finally I understood much more about what we were using at that time – that was a diary written by the teacher. That was one of the first attempts at documentation, in which the teacher was invited to write something every day, or twice or three times a week, about one event that had pushed them to reflect because it was unexpected. So 'crisis' and 'unexpected' were absolutely linked.

And the culture of unexpectedness and uncertainty for me and for us came out from having on the one side the cultural stereotypes and on the other having the freedom of challenging them. But this meant, from a psychological perspective, accepting as a woman and as a teacher the issue of crisis and making mistakes.

The big crisis as a teacher is to be in crisis. A few days ago I was [working with a group of teachers in another country]. They are starting to struggle with documentation, and one teacher said that she came away from this feeling that it is also moral and ethical to show the children that she does not know everything, and she has doubt and she has uncertainty.

It has something to do with an acceptance of the crisis of your knowledge. Because there is a relationship between the identity of your knowledge and your own identity. I don't know if I am clear. But documentation will help you to value this crisis as a positive moment of encounter, a generative element. The crisis becomes the place of encounter.

PM: So crisis is partly about recognising that you don't know, that you are uncertain, but then being able to accept that . . .

CR: Yes, as a quality that you can offer, not only as a limitation. And that is very problematic in a culture in which there is punishment when you have a crisis, when you have doubts, and when you make a mistake. You have to really change your being, to recognise doubt and uncertainty, to recognise your limits as a resource, as a place of encounter, as a quality. Which means that you accept that you are unfinished, in a state of permanent change, and your identity is in the dialogue. And that is, I think, in this culture, for a teacher, for a person, for a human being, a personal and professional crisis.

Dialogue, interdependency and transformation

GD: I think we could dwell a little bit more on this because I think this is so important. I think what you talk about now really challenges education, it's a totally different idea of education. And I also heard you saying your identity is in the dialogue. I have never heard you talk about that before, it's the idea of identity being relational.

CR: A big moment in my life was September 11, in term of crisis as an educator, and as a person. Because in that moment I became aware, more aware of my personal responsibility as a human being. And also because I saw the crisis of that society and also the way in which they reacted, telling themselves and me that we have to continue. This idea that nothing is changed, we have to continue, we have to continue with our normal life. And I started to scream, literally to scream, to the students that this normal life, this normality has produced this phenomenon. Why can't you be challenged by this event as an educator? That means as a person. To be a person means to be an educator, and what does it mean to educate today? I thought that the only thing, the only perspective, was to really believe in dialogue and interdependency. This could be the only way for hope. The idea of dialogue – I looked in the dictionary for its Latin and Greek roots – understood as having a capacity for transformation.

PM: Dialogue is a central idea of yours?

CR: It is of absolute importance. It is an idea of dialogue not as an exchange but as a process of transformation where you lose absolutely the possibility of controlling the final result. And it goes to infinity, it goes to the universe, you can get lost. And for human beings nowadays, and for women particularly, to get lost is a possibility and a risk, you know?

PM: So, for you, dialogue is not just about exchanging words. It is about transformation. Seeing things, understanding things in a different way.

CR: Exactly. And, that is why in Reggio we talk about a different kind of community as a possible solution, we talk about 'metropolis' as a place where different cultures can live together – but only if we have the courage to open up to the concepts of hybridisation and transformation. With real dialogue, I think, there are possibilities of this future.

PM: Would you actually define education as being a process of dialogue?

CR: Absolutely. I feel that the boundary between you and the child has to be maintained in the dialogue. You have to feel the link but at the same time, they are also the other.

GD: It seems you have this idea of radical dialogue, which is built on contestation and opening to the other without a fixed goal to reach.

CR: That is why the child is indispensable, an incredible resource. Because the child's search for meaning in life pushes you, if you dialogue with him, into the universe because there are no limits. And that is also why there is hope for the future.

PM: You were talking about uncertainty and risk when you went into dialogue. Does that also imply you need a condition of trust to enable that to happen? Because it sounds a dangerous thing.

CR: I don't know if trust is a condition for dialogue or the result of dialogue. Dialogue, for sure, supports trust, because without trust you cannot dialogue. And dialogue is an ethical issue and also the essence of life.

GD: So when you say it is the essence of life, that is your way of expressing what most natural scientists talk about today, the importance of connections?

CR: Certainly, connections ... connections as interdependency. The ethical is in defining connection as interdependency. The ethics come here – in interdependencies. And dialogue is another definition of connectedness and can be thought of more in terms of an interdependency. This I feel after September 11 – that the only future is if we can talk more, feel more, live more: interdependency and dialogue. This offers the possibility of welcoming contrasts, differences and different perspectives.

PM: Are there contrasting values between dialogue and interdependency and economic thinking?

CR: For sure there is dialogue and interdependency in the language of economy – which we might think of as one of the hundred languages!

But I don't know if economy can welcome these kinds of concepts as I understand them. For this idea of dialogue, as I use it, contrasts with economic thinking which sets limits on dialogue because you have to predetermine and predict outcomes. That makes me feel suffocated.

One word in the language of economy that we should maybe challenge more is investment. Because it's a key word now. Our government [in Italy] is much more aware today of the discourse of children as an investment for the future. But it's so easy to forget, as they are becoming seen more and more as investments, that children are citizens of the present, they are persons and childhood is really one of the best periods of life. It is not a 'pre' something. It is not a sickness. It is not an investment.

Rights and negotiation

GD: How do we understand the concept of children's rights in Reggio? Because I know that Malaguzzi wrote about these three rights: of children, parents and teachers.

CR: Yes. You have to remember when he wrote this, what kind of debate he was engaged with, because all writing and speeches you do in dialogue with something. And I think he wrote about these rights in contrast to needs. That is essential. And he was discovering how everything can change if you look at the individual as a subject. So the concept of subjectivity and intersubjectivity was emerging at this time as a cultural debate and also a political debate. And it was in this context that the concept of rights came out in contrast with the concept of needs. The concept of citizenship based on needs and based on rights is completely different. So the perspective has changed completely. But what are the sources of rights? Obviously they are negotiated and they come out of the context.

PM: So you used the term that rights are 'negotiated'; could you just explore that a bit more? Who negotiates, how?

CR: What can we say about rights and negotiation? I think, again, they are completely interdependent. I struggled a lot, in discussing with Loris and my colleagues, to find the difference between negotiation and the Latin concept of *in medio stat virtus* ('in the middle there lies the best'), which is a very conservative definition. I tried to understand what is the difference between this definition on the one hand, and on the other negotiation and transformation and radical dialogue, as you called it.

PM: Right. And do you find a difference?

CR: Negotiation is not a matter of finding the middle or the in-between. Real negotiation, I think, for me goes directly to dialogue. There is no way to escape transformation. In negotiation the two sub-jects have to accept to change, partially at least, their own identities. I don't think that negotiation is simply a transaction, in which I get this and you get that.

GD: So, negotiation for you is not compromising.

CR: It's not that, exactly. Compromising, this kind of negotiation, is more based on an economical idea of negotiations.

GD: So negotiation for you is not an exchange, 'I give you this and you give me this'?

CR: No, no. This is a more simplistic level, which may be good for peace but it is not this.

PM: But, again, when you speak of negotiation you seem to have this idea – which was what you were talking about with dialogue – that you might get something you did not expect once you start negotiating. Suddenly something happens.

CR: Yes, yes, absolutely. You go into the unknown.

GD: When you talk about rights, how do you relate to the UN Convention on the Rights of the Child? Because usually when people talk about children's rights, there is an assumption that it is related to the UN Convention.

CR: I feel strongly that when I talk about children I talk about human beings, and when I talk about human beings I talk about children. I know that I run a risk here, in a society where children are never included in the definition of human being and civil rights. And it's true that politically now we have to continue to talk about children and child-hood. But I think that when we have to discuss rights, we have to discuss rights of human beings. To discuss the rights of children on a different table, separated from the table at which we discuss about human rights, I think this also is risky.

PM: So you would want to talk about children first and foremost as human beings?

CR: Exactly! Because human beings need children, not because children need to be identified as human beings.

PM: I'm still fascinated by this discussion of rights. Perhaps I can try a concept on you and hear your response. It sounds to me as if you are saying that the discussion about rights in Reggio is a process of continually defining the position of children in society? It's about their relationship to the society.

CR: To the society. And at the same time it also defines the adults.

GD: You cannot separate out the child from the concept of human beings. Is that what you're saying?

CR: Exactly. I'm being careful not to identify children with adults, but to recognise them both as a part of humanity. Because only if we create this link is there hope for human beings.

Individuality, difference and interdependency

GD: If I understand you right, you stress the concept of interdependency all the time in negotiation and dialogue, which also for us means that you transgress the fairly individualistic neo-liberal idea.

CR: Absolutely! This is the risk. I am often going to the United States, which I think of as a friend about whom I have mixed feelings. Because the culture is so individualistic, and it's invading everything.

GD: If we get into this question of difference, actually, today lots of people say that difference has become the new dominant discourse, which can seem to be very individualistic also. So how do you relate to that?

CR: It is only because of you – and I thank you! – that I am different. I mean, I am not blonde, but alongside you [GD] I look blonde because you are not blonde. I am female because he [PM] is a male. And I can discover this individuality because you exist. Thank you! And because we are interdependent. You make my difference in negotiation, this kind of negotiation.

PM: We're talking about interdependence and dialogue and negotiation, and you're saying that it's through them that we support and develop difference. And it's also as we talk that we understand where we have differences.

CR: Absolutely. For some of them [differences] we need the courage to have a big discussion. But some others will come out from mundane discussions. So perhaps I will feel stronger in my identity after this conversation today.

It may also be that we can cultivate some of our differences through our solidarities. We have been talking about our links with partners all over the world, and maybe what you and other partners have done for us in Reggio has been not only to offer solidarity but to support our differences. In dialogue you don't become a Reggio! You are Peter, you are Gunilla, you are not Reggio.

This is what I adore. You [Gunilla and Peter] have given so much to us because you maintain your own identity. So there is solidarity while maintaining our differences. And the fact is that I have to go more and more to other countries to understand Reggio, this is coming more and more evident to me.

The challenge of transgression

GD: You do not really bring in the concepts of gender, class and ethnicity into your discussion. Why?

CR: I had a period in which the gender issue was one of my main concerns, and it still is important. But I try, maybe too much recently, to put gender among many other dimensions of difference. Some differences are more related to power than others. Historically this is the case for gender, as well as race. Our world today is dominated by this Western, white, male society that is also capitalistic and imperialistic. By male, I also mean a certain kind of relationship, that, in my opinion, excludes dialogue and negotiation, and imposes a domination over others.

GD: Are these issues that you bring into your daily practice in Reggio, like when you work with the pedagogy of listening? Do you have that discussion when you listen to the children? Do you deconstruct gender and class issues in your discussion with the teachers?

CR: Yes. In Reggio we have an organisation that allows us to challenge the differences among ourselves and with others, and to support the differences, an organisation of the environment and an organisation for working in groups. So, again, dialogue is an essential way for confronting and discussing differences. Sometimes it becomes very hard, for example when we talk about religious differences.

When we started to talk about schools, our schools, we [in Reggio] are talking about pluralism *in* the school. Now [in elementary schooling in Italy] we are talking more about pluralism *between* schools, you know? So the family has to have the right to choose which school to use for their child. And so, the different cultures are less open to be challenged.

PM: You are saying that education policy means that people group themselves together, and that makes dialogue between different families and groups more difficult?

CR: We make our towns more like metropolises in which you have the Jewish community, the Christian community, the Muslim community. I respect different religions, but religion can really suffocate dialogue. In this respect I feel that in some ways young children can be a resource because they are allowed, we are allowed to develop dialogue. But in the same time, it's not seen as a cultural value. And the culture does not seem to be able to really listen to the children, to the deep contribution they can make if treated as protagonists.

It seems to me that one of the crises facing us today is the challenge of transgressions, of being able to sit around the table and to challenge.

Theory, practice and research

GD: I would like to ask you more about theory, in particular it would be interesting to hear your relationship to Dewey, whom Malaguzzi talks a lot about in The Hundred Languages of Children. *At the same time, I once heard you saying that you find pragmatism a bit problematic. It's also relevant because a lot of interesting discussions today about interdependence and dialogue relate to pragmatism and communitarianism.*

CR: Some writings of John Dewey, but also of others like Montessori, Vygotsky, Freinet and Bruner, influenced Reggio, definitely. Maybe we have to struggle more about pragmatism. I go back again to Locke and the origins of English philosophy, and the pragmatic approach, the richness of this – and the poverty that came after. Because I don't know how in the debate between pragmatism and idealism there came the separation between theory and practice. Why did this separation come about? What purpose did it serve? What kind of power relations does it express?

Theory and practice should be in dialogue, two languages expressing our effort to understand the meaning of life. When you think, it's practice; and when you practice, it's theory. 'Practitioner' is not a wrong definition of the teacher. But it's wrong that they are not also seen as theorists. Instead it is always the university academics that do theories, and the teachers . . . they are the first to be convinced of it. In fact, when you invite them to think or to express their own opinions, they are not allowed to have an opinion. The way they become theoretical is to quote Bruner, Dewey, Piaget.

So you always have that separation between theory and practice. But, I mean, when you do practice, it's because you have a theory. When you take a picture, you have a concept. And at the same time, when I think it's because there is a practice behind it.

GD: Do I understand it right, what you are saying is that Dewey has been understood in terms of a simplified dualism. A dualistic idea, so learning by doing became only practice.

CR: Brava, brava! This is it exactly. This happened to Dewey, to Maria Montessori. This is why I became crazy when [an academic] told me, 'I am the theoretical thinker.'

GD: Implying the teachers are the practitioners.

CR: And the teachers have to find the practice.

PM: So there are at least two problems with the concept of practitioner. One of which is that it implies a hierarchy, in which the 'practitioner' is below. But the other one is that you can't imagine a practice that is separated from theory.

CR: Very well summarised.

GD: Which is part of a dualistic tradition going back hundreds of years.

CR: Absolutely. And again it is an issue of power.

PM: But then – from your perspective – theory is just everywhere? I mean, the world is full of theory. It's everywhere. We cannot live without theory.

CR: We cannot live without theory or practice. We need to be theoretical practitioners, and to be thinkers. And to give to the children the value and the experience of being a thinker.

GD: This is very important, because being in the university, we are in this tradition of separating theory and practice, this is the discourse we live in. We are supposed to go to the teachers and inform them about research, and that is what we actually have transgressed and struggled with [in my department], because the teachers already are theorists.

CR: That is why I have written so often about the teacher as a researcher. As I wrote, it's not that we don't recognise your [academic] research, but we want our research, as teachers, to be recognised. And to recognise research as a way of thinking, of approaching life, of negotiating, of documenting. It's all research. It's also a context that allows dialogue. Dialogue generates research, research generates dialogue.

GD: Yes. And as I also understand, which I think many people do not understand, you have a total research process because you systematise what you find.

CR: Absolutely. But can you find a university teacher who can learn from a practitioner? Very rarely! That is why Malaguzzi was never recognised and I think will never be recognised as a researcher. But to do good practice means to continue to do research, to continue the theory, and this is what they [universities] don't challenge. But we [in Reggio] are, first of all, researchers.

GD: I don't know if I told you this, but when I came here [to Reggio] the second time to look into documentation, I had the opportunity to be fairly close to Malaguzzi. So we were together, and the last day he looked at me and said, 'Gunilla, I think I would be really happy to have a project together with you.' And I looked at him and then he said, 'You know, you are in the university and I think our experience could really connect to your work in your university.' So I got the feeling that he thought I was another kind of researcher, and he also saw the possibility to open up into the university.

CR: And he felt very much the importance anyway of university – but not as it is. But as it can be. And it's closely connected to democracy, this whole topic.

The hundred languages: the fantastic theory

CR: And there is something else that is full of democracy, the theory of the hundred languages of children. It should be developed more and more, because it's fantastic. Nobody has understood – maybe Malaguzzi too – the power of this theory. I am trying to go back and reconstruct Malaguzzi's research and also, I can say, our research, and remember when he started to talk about 'the hundred languages of children'. It was related, again, to a certain debate about the importance of verbal and written languages, but also to the study of the brain, and to ideas about learning processes like learning by doing also from Dewey. You see many influences, including the wider political and cultural debate, for example the debate about how privileging these two languages were, how in some way they supported the power, not only of certain knowledges, but also of certain classes.

I see the hundred languages as a lake with many, many sources flowing into it. I think that the number of a hundred was chosen to be very provocative, to claim for all these languages not only the same dignity, but the right to expression and to communicate with each other.

But also what I find fascinating, and I'm trying to develop, is this idea that multiplicity can help us again with dialogue, through a dialogue among the different languages. That means interconnection, inter-dependency, that can help each language to become more aware of its own specificity, and to support the conceptualisation and the dignity of the others. So, to take an example, when you draw you can support not only your graphic language, but also your verbal language. Because you make the concept deeper. And when the concept becomes deeper, the languages are enriched – again you have this kind of permanent process.

And also in this theory there are the traces, often autobiographic. Malaguzzi was a man with a lot of different interests. He lived the concept of inter-disciplinarity, you know. He was familiar with disciplines that again are able to challenge each other, he could see how science is linked with art, and art is really linked with mathematics. Power needs boundaries, so when you challenge disciplinary boundaries, as Loris did, you challenge power.

GD: So that means, his idea of interdisciplinarity is not about just adding disciplines. You're putting disciplines into confrontation. And through that something new again may come.

CR: Yes, it's not only to add. It's again a transformation.

Becoming a competent teacher

GD: We know that you are now working in the University of Modena and Reggio with teacher students. Could you comment on your experience there in relation to your ideas of what is needed for becoming a competent teacher in your schools?

CR: What I try to do with the students is to help them to encounter their own image of the child, to reflect on it, to understand the implications for education of the image of the child they have – in terms of values, strategies, the quality of relationship with the children, and so on. What is also absolutely important is to support them to discover the connection between theory and practice, and to give them the feeling, the emotional feeling, that their place – their metaphorical place – is the connection, the meeting place between theory and practice. I think here there is the meaning of teaching.

In fact in my experience in the university, students study the history of pedagogy, different psychological theories, all at a rather abstract level. So it is very hard for them to discover that pedagogy and psychology are tools for their dialogue with the child. It is hard for them to understand didactics – the practice of teaching – as a place of encounter because didactics is not well considered in University – it is a Cinderella subject.

PM: What about the role of documentation?

CR: I think the only way of developing a new behaviour can be with documentation. I would like to see the university students spending much more time studying and reflecting in the schools with the children, learning with a pre-school teacher, with the university teachers able to look at the same learning processes of a child, not only from a psychological and pedagogical perspective, but also for example with the mathematics professor accepting the challenge that every child can offer. So, I see more and more the school really as a forum, a place of encounter and dialogue where the culture is challenged. And where also university teachers can go and learn and teach, as well as the pre-school teachers, the university student and the children. Teaching then can be developed in a system that is open, challenging, and accepting of crisis.

So I think it is important for the students to be more supported to understand the fundamental role of documentation, the great opportunity it offers to become a competent teacher. But also, in my opinion, they should be invited to reflect more about the relationship between education and freedom, education as an opportunity to become more aware of our differences and so our freedom to express them. For me freedom means interdependency, and this means helping students to understand the ethical value of team working as an expression of interdependency as a value.

To become a competent teacher is also to have the possibility to discover another value, interdisciplinarity. And it also means to become involved in the culture of their own place and time – to be contemporary. This means being aware of both local and global, to become more aware of the school and their place in the school but also of their wider social and cultural role as teachers. Their role as teacher is not just in relation to the school, not just limited to within the walls of the school, but also in relation to the wider society and culture. They must always think outside the school and of the link between the school and outside.

Students need to know more about contemporary languages, and their use as tools. I also think that the competent child can help the teacher become competent. The hundred languages of the children have to become the hundred languages of the teacher. The teacher can have a hundred languages if she or he can discover her competence by listening and not only talking. The teacher can be competent in expressing and communicating with the hundred languages and using a hundred media when she or he can connect – theory and practice, time and space, hands and mind, school and society, dreams and passion, strength and joy.

The power of documentation

GD: Now you bring documentation in again, and documentation is placed in this kind of forum. As you know, internationally today there is a big discussion, and also practice, of using documentation or portfolios. We can see this in Sweden, even in the Swedish preschool curriculum they say that the teachers should use pedagogical documentation. I would like to ask you how you view that development in relation to a critique of pedagogical documentation, not a critique which I think shows a close knowledge of your experience, but which, from my perspective, shows a superficial knowledge about pedagogical documentation. And that critique could be spelt out as the power to see is the power to control. So, if you use pedagogical documentation, you control the child, you see everything the child is doing.

CR: Very good question. I would like to start with the discussion about the relationship between a good education, control and seduction. Because education has a lot to do with both: control and seduction.

There is reciprocal control in education – you control the child and the child controls you. The children have to control us, because the good meaning of imitation is to control, it is to take power from power. So I'm not scandalised by the word control. It is absolutely a good word, control is really a good word in education. The problem is that you, as a teacher, have much more power than the child has, the problem is how you use the power that you have.

But the real issue in documentation, with which I am trying more and more to struggle, is who is observing and who is observed. And I see a lot of reciprocity. When you take a picture or you make a document, in reality you don't document the child but *your* knowledge, *your* concept, *your* idea. So it's more and more visible – your limits and your vision about the child. You show not who that child is, but your thought. You don't show the child, but the relationship and the quality of your relationship, and the quality of your looking at him or her. That is why it's so dramatic because the king is naked!

There was this teacher in a group [in another country] with whom I am working on documentation. I asked about the difficulties and the good and the bad feelings that they have, and she said 'When I look at the documentation, it's like when I look at myself in the mirror, I feel embarrassed.' So in some way she told us that she can see not the child but her limitations in the relationship with the child, her own theory, her own perspective. So she said it was for her like looking in the mirror, she can see that she is fat. That was a very strong way of telling the difficulties.

And that is also ethical, because thanks to documentation the child also becomes aware about the teacher's perspective. It's more honest and more visible, because it's always in terms of expectation and valuing. So I can see what you value in my learning processes. I don't see what I do, because what I do is something that I have to develop in my learning process. I see what you see about my doing, my thinking.

GD: I think that's a very good answer, actually. And the context in which peda-gogical documentation is carried out must be very crucial; if it's an individualistic and competitive context or if it's a context that places value on dialogue, negotiation and interdependency.

CR: Absolutely!

What does it mean to be inspired by Reggio?

PM: This question is one you must often have been asked. What do you think people in other places are doing when they talk about being inspired by Reggio?

CR: It's a huge issue, understanding this amazing phenomenon. Reggio is a metaphor and a symbolical place. Being in relation with Reggio allows people to hope, to believe change is possible. It enables you to cultivate dreams, rather than being a utopia. Because utopia is something very good but perfect, but dreams are something that you can have one night. And there is also a feeling of belonging to something that is about education in its widest sense, as a hope for human beings. And Reggio is a place of encounter and dialogue, and not only with Reggio but with many related protagonists. So Reggio makes room for people to dialogue, it provides an excuse to do this.

GD: That's an excuse, yes I recognise that idea.

CR: Dialogue as friendship, dialogue as an encounter with yourself, dialogue as a place where you can admit what you know about yourself but you don't want to admit when you are at home, dialogue as a place in which to tell to her what I think she should do at home but she does not do. When a team of people come to visit us in Reggio, we can be a place where colleagues can have an excuse for talking about some topics that at home they are not allowed to talk about. Here, they are apparently talking about Reggio, but really they talk about themselves. Being here provides this good excuse to talk about education, about the meaning of being a citizen and a human being. Everything we have been talking about.

PM: So, in a nutshell it's all about people entering into a dialogue with Reggio. Do you need certain conditions? Are there certain things you need to have before you can enter that dialogue? Do you need to have something in common before you can come into dialogue with people?

CR: I think the values. And more than values is attention to listening and an openness to negotiate.

PM: So if you have a preschool in another country that says it is working with Reggio Emilia ideas, ideally you would say they are coming into a relationship with you, of dialogue.

CR: As you know, they cannot do a Reggio. Perhaps we should make more clear that Reggio itself is an interpretation of Reggio! The only thing that we can share with the others is our values and the reason why and the way in which we try to challenge ourselves. So, that's why we have the courage, really the courage, to talk with people from South Africa, Albania or China. We have nothing to teach. The risk we have to avoid is the imperialistic approach, for us and them to believe that everything we touch becomes gold and is perfect.

PM: So the danger is you come into an imperialist relationship in which you think you can make things good for them, and they too think you can do that.

CR: Exactly, exactly. That means that you don't think you know what is right and what is wrong. Obviously at the same time they should not be left alone, they need to feel part of a network of hope, of possibility, of support. And they need also, maybe, sometimes to have really concrete tools, but this does not mean necessarily buying Reggio furniture and equipment.

But it is indispensable for us to combine this dialogue with others with our internal dialogue because they are part of the same research. But at the same time, it's so hard to find enough time. Because we want a real dialogue.

PM: You talked about sharing values, which I think is about listening and dialogue. But do they need to share certain understandings with you, for example about what knowledge might be, or what we might understand by learning?

CR: Sorry, maybe I made a mistake using only the concept of value, because for me this is a value, as well as an understanding. It is a value to choose among the many ways in which we conceptualise knowledge, or to choose a particular way to talk about learning. It is a value because you're choosing, you're taking responsibility.

PM: So that's a very important point, when you talk about value, it is because there are always values in the choices you make.

CR: And to take responsibility means challenging your choice. You need to do research and to have confrontation. And this is something that we should do much more about. I think that, for example, we have been limited in developing international exchange. I would like to have more seminars in which our overseas friends can come here, we can show our research, we can have comments and we can ask them to bring here the best work from their countries. And also to have more confrontations with people from other disciplines on certain topics, for example to discuss the meaning of documentation with a neurologist or to discuss and debate the building of identity with a psychologist or to talk with economists about how children are strongly related to economy. Or, again, to have small symposia about important questions, for example about citizenship today, so we can challenge each other from our different perspectives. Another area for working with people from other disciplines and countries could be the theory of the hundred languages as an amazing support to creativity, learning processes and democracy. Because I feel that they are very strongly related.

So this is how I would really like Reggio to develop our network further. And I hope that we will be able to do this more when our Centre for International Research is open.

PM: Are there other directions that you would like to see Reggio take over the next few years? New ideas, new areas of work?

CR: New directions mean other dialogues. Because I hope that Reggio could be more able to talk without losing, as I said before, its own identity. To talk with politicians all over the world. To talk about assessment. Evaluation, though, is a perfect example of the difficulties of participating in a debate, in giving our perspective in a language that is not the usual one, and not to be seduced by the questions that push you to create another evaluation system, push you to say 'we could add this bit and this bit and this bit'.

And, to work more, as I just said, with other disciplines, other areas of human knowledge. And to work in other places too. For example with the people that work in the hospitals, with the paediatricians, with everybody.

PM: Could you imagine in ten years' time the hospital in Reggio working, say, with pedagogical documentation?

CR: Why not? Yes, with the patients.

Reacting to Reggio

PM: We've been talking about how Reggio is found in many parts of the world. I suppose what seems interesting is that it is so big in the United States, which you could say has a very different context to this part of Northern Italy.

CR: I have the courage to say that we are in dialogue with the United States. There is a strong interdependency. They are transforming us, but we are maybe changing something. But they are still the imperialistic society and they are conditioning all of us.

PM: Are there ways in which that close relationship with the United States, and indeed other English-language countries, could change you in ways that would worry you?

CR: Yes, by normalisation. Because in the effort of trying to understand what we are, and what is 'the Reggio approach', and to classify us, they make us out for example to be 'an emergent curriculum' or to fit some other type of curriculum. No, we are not! There is this need of capturing the secret. So in some way they are accusing us of not being able to narrate in a clear way what we are and why we are what we are. And so they push us to find a clear language – or a language clear for them.

That could be good, but it means also being more conformist. We cannot be classified with a label, in the way in which language is used to order the world. So, that has created some alarm in one way. The second way is when they start to ask us to provide scientific proof that we are functioning effectively – evidence. And the third way is when they try and standardise our ways of working into a programme: first of all you do this, then that, then something else.

GD: So when people are asking you questions, you often answer, 'It depends.'

CR: We try to avoid the idea that for each question there is one clear answer. Often you have to say, 'It depends.' And that's to introduce the concept of context, which makes many people crazy.

GD: That's interesting. Because when I tell this story to Swedish audiences, that when you get questions you often answer 'it depends' and then you elaborate, usually Swedes love that you say that. And they say they can really understand it. And it's so beautiful that Swedes can understand that your work is contextualised.

PM: You're saying here are two European societies who actually share a certain paradigm, or way of thinking.

CR: And also the English, anyway, are much more sensitive in term of listening to our philosophical explanations and agree with our theoretical approach. But some visitors really disagree and are disturbed. They are disturbed by the fact that we say, 'it depends', that we introduce a relativeness and they don't like long answers. They want quick, quick! I think it must be cultural.

Where's the evidence?

PM: Imagine I'm an English government minister, and I've come to Reggio for a day, to find out about Reggio, and I say to you, 'Look, in England we are very focussed on services having good outcomes. What are your outcomes? What is the evidence that Reggio works?' How do you respond to that sort of question?

CR: So, I would ask her 'What is for you the outcome for preschool education? And what does education mean for you?'

PM: You would turn the question back?

CR: Absolutely. First of all because I really think in terms of dialogue it is absolutely correct and necessary. Because I feel that in Italy, in my own language, and in Reggio too, that words are losing meaning in an amazing way. So we can be using the same word for very different concepts. So I would really like to understand the idea, the concept behind these questions. Is 'education' being used for example to mean being a good citizen or being prepared for the school? So I would like to negotiate the question, because if I negotiate the question, I negotiate the concept behind the question – and the answers that are behind the questions. Because, in general, when you formulate a question you already have an answer in mind.

PM: Right. But were you saying in a way that the idea of outcome could be important?

CR: Yes, it could be. But really, I would like from a politician, an economist, or whoever else it is asking me about outcomes, to have the right to discuss their opinion. I think that a society, a community has a right of expecting outcomes, because this is also the meaning of the school. But I would like to have a round table, or many round tables, meeting on a regular basis, to discuss about outcomes.

PM: To discuss about how we should understand the term?

CR: Exactly. The term and also, when you have decided what you mean by outcome, what kind of freedom I have then to negotiate locally.

Process and/or outcome

PM: What is striking to me is that you talk a lot about making the learning processes visible – documentation. And you're very strong on that side. Do you see a distinction between the processes and the outcomes?

CR: No! Maybe I'm completely wrong, but personally I don't see one. Because I understand that a society needs an outcome, but the outcome for me is also the process. And this is harder to negotiate. Because I think that the problem of politics, the problem of society, is that the process is often not valued and supported.

PM: So is there, then, a dualism, a false distinction between process and outcome? Can any moment of the process be an outcome?

CR: What I feel today is a society of fragmentation, fragmentation not as a possibility, but as a loss of meaning. We are losing the possibility of reflecting, and finding meaning, building meaning. Constructing meaning is the right word. Everything is a show! Everything is entertainment. I am not against episodes or events. I am against a culture that isolates them, and does not allow you to have time for reflecting and understanding, and constructing meaning in your own life, and with others. This is why making learning visible can be risky because it can be misunderstood, it can become a show.

PM: So if the English minister came to me after this discussion, I would try to say that in Reggio I think that there can be no distinction between process and outcome because there is no idea of a final place, or a final answer. I would add that you are talking about a way of living which is about looking and thinking, and reflecting.

CR: That's a good issue. There is again a dream here, a dream of a different society, you know. And a hope. Not for a different school but a different society. But it's not a final solution. That is why it is not utopia. Because utopia is something perfect. Our utopia should be in crisis! It should have the courage to be in crisis!

PM: Otherwise it can become a totalitarian model?

CR: I think so. You know, I am not dreaming about humanity having a final boundary or a goal, but every moment can be thought of as a step. There is also an idea related to religion, in which God can at any moment invite you to make a synthesis of your life. The Christian God tells you that every moment you have to be ready . . .

PM: To meet your maker.

CR: Yes. At any moment, you should be able to give an account of yourself. And in some way, it's the way in which we look at the process as also an outcome, as a part of something that has a value in itself. So we are not only working for some final goal, every moment has to find its own significance. You know it's not bad as a concept. I like it. Every moment is rich.

GD: Because if you have a very clear goal when working with children – either you accept the child or negate the child.

CR: Exactly, exactly. Yes. Instead I have to have the right to negotiate every moment, and that is the concept of process. So, it has to be clear that there is something that gives me hope, something I strive for, but at the same time it is not yet perfect. Something that needs to be continuously challenged. Reggio, in a way, is a process of being permanently challenged. Because it's in dialogue with a changing context.

Evaluation and regulation

PM: Would I also be right, if the minister came to me, to say that in Reggio you have to take some responsibility for evaluating your work? You must take a view about your work.

CR: Absolutely. With pedagogical documentation, and maybe also some other tools. That's another reason why documentation is important. It's a permanent process of evaluation. If I can negotiate the outcome, and if I can include the process, documentation is a good tool. But I know it's hard to suggest that for a national system.

PM: That's a really interesting point. You can talk about Reggio and your wonderful work. But what do you do about Italy or Britain or some other country as a whole, because not everywhere will be like Reggio? Therefore do you need to have regulation and control or curriculum, these sorts of normalising things? What's your view about the role of regulation if you look, say, in Italy as a whole?

CR: Is it possible to combine documentation with some test that I would like to be part of? The big problem is what does it mean today to be

Italian, to be European, to be in dialogue with the world? So, the competences for me are much more in the area of social skills, our social behaviour. I would like to know more about the way in which children are able to learn in a group and as a group. I would like to know much more about the way in which they can discuss and debate about topics; how they find sources; about the way in which they develop their citizenship. How can I measure this? I have to trust. The key word is still to trust, in my opinion, and will continue to be so.

PM: To trust whom in this case?

CR: To trust the teachers, to trust the community.

PM: This is very difficult. Are you saying that really you think that it is each community that must take responsibility for the work of education?

CR: No, not only, but also.

GD: So how do you find the idea of grading in the school system. What we can see today, for example in England, is specific goals that are laid down for ever younger age groups of children. The aim is to grade children, to ensure they do not lag behind.

CR: I think it's terrible.

GD: Why do you think that, because the ideology behind it is that it is related to social justice, so the teacher can see if any child is lagging behind so this child can get support.

CR: It is related to the computer, to the idea of the child as a computer with inputs and outputs. I mean, I feel this is terrible. When I test a performance, it's not the subject that is valued, it's the test. And what kind of justice is this? If this child does not have this performance. First of all, how can you know? And if I am a good teacher, I should know that Peter is not able to draw. If I live with him I document. I don't need a test! Or, this test can simply confirm what you already know. If it reveals something, it does not reveal something about the child, but about the context. The process of real evaluation is much harder.

GD: Much more difficult and complex. Yes.

CR: Education is really about being passionate together. To have feelings together. To have emotions together. And documentation can help you to discover passion, feeling and emotion. [Working with a group of teachers recently in another country] they said that the best and very brightest moment for them is when they document a child being able to do something for the first time. They felt passion, the word passion was the word that they used.

The question of curriculum

GD: Carlina, related to this is this idea that we hear very often in our countries, and that you mentioned earlier, that you are working here in Reggio with the emergent curriculum. How do you relate to that idea that you are?

CR: As a reaction against people who classify us in Reggio as working with an emergent curriculum, I have been thinking about a concept that might be called a 'contextual curriculum'. Our interpretation of the concept of curriculum starts from the assumption that children have a stunning mastery of many languages and an appreciation that 'other minds' can share their own different beliefs and theories. While still in the first years of life, they also develop powerful theories about the physical, biological and social world, theories that can be understood as interpretations through which children construct and give meaning to the world around them. These theories are enriched and challenged through dialogue with others. Above all, children acquire an awareness of their capacity to think, to have an opinion and to build 'theories' (that is to think and interpret reality) and of the importance of dialogue with others in order to build their own knowledge and identity.

If the curriculum is conceived as a path or journey, it will be a path or journey that has, in our opinion, to sustain these competences as fundamental values for knowledge and for life. It should favour competences for learning, the learning to learn through reflection and self reflection, through the 'hundred languages'. A curriculum of this kind can be defined as 'contextual' in the sense that it is determined by the dialogue among children, teachers and the environment surrounding them. It can arise from a proposal by one or more children or teachers, from a natural event or from something found in the news. But the emphasis on context also values participatory strategies and the possibility that not only families but the community to which children belong could participate in curriculum. I use the concept of 'participation' here in its sense of each subject being capable of influencing and being influenced by other subjects, so participating in the destiny of each and of all.

PM: Although you are talking now about a particular concept of curriculum, I have the feeling that you are, at the very least, ambivalent about 'curriculum', that it is perhaps not a concept that you or Reggio would choose to use because it does not relate well to your values and practice.

CR: Yes, you are right. My attempt to develop the idea of 'contextual curriculum' arises from my wish to be understood by those who use the language of curriculum and believe in the importance of curriculum. For us in Reggio, *progettazione* is a word that is very dear to us, and is something different from curriculum. *Progettazione* is a strategy, a daily practice of observation–interpretation–documentation. When I speak of 'contextual curriculum', I am really attempting to explain the concept of *progettazione*.

What has to be guaranteed is that learning is seen not only as an individual activity, which can be documented by a single test, but rather as a group activity. For example children who grow up together at school seek the opinions of their friends and stimulate their friends to express their own points of view. They feel the thoughts of others as an integral part of their own thinking, and seek them out; it seems as if the mind is uneasy if it has no opportunity for sharing. Children want to involve everybody and soon they learn how to do it applying different strategies. Children who don't speak Italian yet and children with disabilities are comfortably and meaningfully integrated into activities.

When you consider others as part of your own identity, then their different, sometimes divergent, theories and opinions are seen as a resource. The awareness of the value of these differences and of having dialogue among them increases. The 'hundred languages' are useful both to understand and to be understood.

Instead of formal teaching of a predetermined curriculum (writing, reading, counting, etc.), to be evaluated using some testing procedure, both teachers and children document their own daily activities and learning in symbolic systems with which they are comfortable. In this process of investigation, documentation (photos, videos, notes, recordings, etc.) carries out its fundamental role: to facilitate reflection and self-reflection on children's and teachers' learning processes and the professional development of teachers.

This process will be enriched by the exchange and dialogue with the parents and the social environment. Perhaps, and most important, teachers, parents and children work together each day to build the kind of community in which they want to live.

The question of time

PM: Doesn't everything you do in your schools in Reggio, your whole concept of the school and the process of education, imply a particular attitude towards time, an attitude which struggles to be less time governed.

CR: Yes. Today there is too little talk about schools and time. For me it is important that for a school to be a place of life, then it needs the time of life, and that time of life is different, for example, to the time of production. In production, the most important element is the product. But, as we said already, in a school what is important is the process, the path we develop. The educational relation needs to be able to make time, it needs to be slow, it needs empty time.

The etymology of the word 'school' links the concepts of school and time. Let me explain further. The Latin *schola* (*scholē* in Greek) means leisure, free time, time to spend in studying and reflecting. And time is indispensable for this. In any formative relationship, time is the necessary element for creating the relationship. So a school that forms is a school that gives time – time to children, time to teachers, time for their being together. There has to be the possibility in schools, of any kind, the possibility in any group, to create connections but also to live differences and conflicts.

Is it legitimate today, when everything seems to go towards ever greater speed, in fact towards super-speed, to admire slowness, empty time, pauses? It is not a contest between speed and slowness, but about having the courage to rediscover the time of human beings. And the child can help us, he or she can help us to feel again the time that is inside us and the time that we are. We are made of time, we are the shape of time. The question is to be able to listen to this time of ours and to propose it not only as a right, but as a social and cultural value – a value that children offer to us.

Public responsibility for school

GD: It would be interesting for us to hear your ideas about the importance of Reggio being a public and municipal project. And how do you see the relationship between public and private in services for children?

CR: Today we talk of the crisis of the welfare state, though for me there never was a crisis of the welfare state but only of the economy to support the welfare state. There is also a development of more neo-liberal concepts, with much more focus on the private, related to a crisis of communist society. But I still think that it is a duty of public authorities to create schools, because they are, as I have said many times, not only a way in which to express and to construct a culture of childhood, but also in a more general way a place for culture.

Personally I am convinced that education has to be public. Absolutely, I have no doubt about this because of everything we have shared before. Public in terms of money. But also public in terms of schools being a place of differences, of dialogue among differences. I am very worried about – I told you earlier – the idea of schools for different groups: the Jewish School, the Catholic School, the Arabic School, the school for a particular social group, for boys or girls only. We need schools which provide a physical, public place for dialogue. It is a big risk if children grow up reflecting only on themselves, with only a particular group.

My idea of the school is a pluralistic concept. I strongly believe that pluralism is indispensable.

PM: And you said that public also means that the money is public?

CR: I can accept also philanthropic money for the schools in Reggio.

PM: In addition to public funds?

CR: Exactly. If philanthropic money does not impose any conditions such as, 'I want to have only this kind of children. I want to have only these kinds of values.' So, money can be neutral in some ways, if there is a strong identity in the schools.

PM: Does it matter if the public authority, the municipality, manages and runs the school? Or is that less important?

CR: I believe in the basic principle that we built in Reggio, that Malaguzzi was very supportive of, too – that the community must take responsibility for the quality of the school. I had the luck to live in a place in which it was possible not only to have the community involved in the school, but to have the community express the best values in its schools. So that is maybe the reason why I believe that schools, not only for young children but all schools, have to be able to be local and global.

This also influenced my ideas about evaluation. That is why documentation, why research, why the risk of assessment are so important.

Because if you don't take a risk in evaluation, you don't change. Evaluation is a part of the process by which we challenge ourselves with the children in a kind of solidarity of love.

For me, the only reality now is in the dream, because I think that I am here because of the reality outside and because of the dreams that I have here. They are concrete, my dreams, you know, concrete like the newspaper of this morning, concrete in that they are vivid, motivating, they give me passion. And what could be is part of the dream.

PM: The idea of the dream is really important in all your thinking and all your work?

CR: Yes, dreams. Because they are full of metaphors, of symbols, they are welcoming. They do not have the arrogance of the scientific, they do not have to be proven. Dreams are a risk, so too is documentation and the dialogue with other countries. Maybe because life is a risk. They are a risk and a strength.

Bibliography

Arnheim, R. (1954) *Art and Visual Perception: A Psychology of the Creative Eye*, Berkeley: University of California Press.

Arnheim, R. (1992) *To the Rescue of Art: Twenty-Six Essays*. Berkeley: University of California Press.

Ausubel, D.P. (1968) *Educational Psychology: A Cognitive View*. New York: Holt-Rinehart and Winston.

Balducci, E. (1990) *L'uomo planetario*. Firenze: Cultura della Pace.

Bateson, G. (1972) *Steps to an Ecology of Mind*. San Francisco: Chandler Publishing.

Bateson, G. (1979) *Mind and Nature: A Necessary Unit*. New York: E.P. Dutton.

Bateson, G. (1996) *Questo è un gioco*. Milano: Raffaello Cortina.

Bateson, G. and BATESON, M.C. (1987) *Angels Fear: Towards an Epistemology of the Sacred*. New York: Macmillan.

Bauman, Z. (1993) *Postmodern Ethics*. Oxford: Blackwell.

Bauman, Z. (1997) *Posmodernity and Its Discontents*. Cambridge: Polity Press.

Bauman, Z. (2001) *The Individualized Society*. Cambridge: Polity Press.

Bauman, Z. and Tester, K. (2001) *Conversations with Zygmunt Bauman*. Cambridge: Polity Press.

Becchi, E. (ed.) (1979) *Il bambino sociale: privatizzazione e deprivatizzazzione dell'infanzia*. Milano: Feltrinelli.

Becchi, E. (1982) 'Metafore d'infanzia', *Aut Aut*, pp. 19f.

Becchi, E. (1994) *I bambini nella storia*. Bari: Laterza.

Becchi, E. (1994) 'Prima o dopo Kant nella ricerca empirica?', *Cadmo*, 4, pp. 3–5.

Becchi, E. (ed.) (1999) *Manuale della scuola del bambino dai tre ai sei anni*. Milano: Franco Angeli.

Becchi, E. and Bondioli, A. (eds) (1992) *Gli asili nido in Italia: censimenti e valutazioni di qualità*. Bergamo: Juvenilia.

Becchi, E. and Bondioli, A. (eds.) (1997) *Valutare e valutarsi*. Bergamo: Junior.

Beck, U. (1986) *Risikogesellschaft. Auf dem Weg in eine andere Moderne*. Frankfurt: Suhrkamp.

Berandi, F. (1994) *Mutazione e cyberpunk: immaginario e tecnologia negli scenari di fine millennio*. Genova: Costa e Nolan.

Berger, P.L. and Luckmann, T. (1966) *The Social Construction of Reality: A Treatise in the Sociology of Knowledge*. Garden City, NY: Doubleday.

Bertin, G.M. (1951) *Introduzione al problematicismo pedagogico*. Milano: Marzorati.

Bertin, G.M. (1953) *Etica e pedagogia dell'impegno*. Milano: Marzorati.

Bertin, G.M. and Contini, M.G. (1983) *Costruire l'esistenza. Il riscatto della ragione educative*. Roma: Armando.

Bertoldi, F. and Serio, N. (eds) (1999) *Oltre la valutazione. Idee e ipotesi a confronto*. Roma: Armando.

Bertolini, P. (1988) *L'esistere pedagogico. Ragioni e limiti di una pedagogia come scienza fenomenologicamente fondata*. Firenze: La Nuova Italia.

Bertolini, P. and Dallari, M. (eds) (1988) *Pedagogia al limite*. Firenze: La Nuova Italia.

Bocchi, G. *et al.* (1983) *L'altro Piaget. Strategie delle genesi*. Milano: Emme Edizione.

Bocchi, G. and Ceruti, M. (eds) (1985) *La sfida della complessità*. Milano: Feltrinelli.

Bocchi, G., Ceruti, M., Fabbri, D. and Munari, A. (1983) *Epistemologia genetica e teorie dell'evoluzione*. Bari: Dedalo.

Bondioli, A. (1996) *Gioco e educazione*. Milano: Franco Angeli.

Bondioli, A. (ed.) (2001) *AVSI. AutoValutazione della Scuola dell'Infanzia*. Milano: Franco Angeli.

Bondioli, A. (ed.) (2002) *Il progetto pedagogico del nido e la sua valutazione*. Bergamo: Junior.

Bondioli, A. (ed.) (2002) *La qualità negoziata. Gli indicatori per gli asili nido della Regione Emilia Romagna*. Bergamo: Junior.

Bondioli, A. (ed.) (2002) *Il tempo nella quotidianità infantile: prospettive di ricerca e studio di casi*. Bergamo: Junior.

Bondioli, A. and Ferrari, M. (eds) (2002) *Manuale di valutazione del contesto educativo*. Milano: Franco Angeli.

Bondioli, A. and Ferrari, M. (eds) (2004) *Verso un modello di valutazione formativa. Ragioni, strumenti e percorsi*. Bergamo: Junior.

Bondioli, A. and Ghedini, P.O. (eds) (2000) *La qualità negoziata*. Bergamo: Junior.

Bondioli, A. and Mantovani, S. (eds) (1987) *Manuale critico dell'asilo nido*. Milano: Franco Angeli.

Bondioli, A. and Savio, D. (eds) (1994) *Osservare il gioco di finzione: una scala delle abilità ludico-simboliche infantili (SVALSI)*. Bergamo: Junior.

Borges, J.L. (1956) *Ficciones*. Buenos Aires: Emece Editores.

Borghi, E., Canovi, A. and Lorenzi, O. (eds) (2001) *Una storia presente. L'esperienza delle scuole comunali dell'infanzia a Reggio Emilia*. Reggio Emilia: Edizioni RSLibri.

Boselli, G. (1998, 2nd edn) *Postprogrammazione*. Firenze: La Nuova Italia.

Branzi, A. (1996) *La crisi della qualità*. Milano: ArtBook.

Bronfenbrenner, U. (1979) *Ecology of Human Development: Experiments by Nature and Design*. Cambridge, MA: Harvard University Press.

Brown, A.L. (1997) 'Transforming Schools into Communities of Thinking and Learning about Serious Matters', *American Psychologist*, 52 (4), pp. 399–413.

Bruner, J.S. (1964) *On Knowing: Essays for the Left Hand*. Cambridge, MA: Harvard University Press.

Bruner, J.S. (1971) *The Relevance of Education*. New York: Norton.

Bruner, J.S. (1974) *Toward a Theory of Instruction*. Cambridge, MA: Harvard University Press.

Bruner, J.S. (1977) *The Process of Education*. Cambridge, MA: Harvard University Press.

Bruner, J.S. (1983) *Savoir faire, savoir dire: Le développement de l'enfant*. Paris: Presses Universitaires de France.

Bruner, J.S. (1983) *In Search of Mind: Essays in Autobiography*, New York: Harper & Row.

Bruner, J.S. (1986) *Actual Minds, Possible Worlds*. Cambridge, MA: Harvard University Press.

Bruner, J.S. (1990) *Acts of Meaning*. Cambridge, MA: Harvard University Press.

Bruner, J.S. (1996) *The Culture of Education*. Cambridge, MA: Harvard University Press.

Bruner, J.S. (1998) in G. Ceppi and M. Zini (eds), *Children, Spaces, Relations: Metaproject for an Environment for Young Children*. Reggio Emilia: Reggio Children.

Bruner, J.S. (2002) *La fabbrica delle storie. Diritto, letteratura, vita*. Roma: Laterza.

Bruner, J.S. (2004) 'Reggio: A City of Courtesy, Curiosity and Imagination', *Children in Europe*, 6, p. 27.

Cagliari, P. (1994) *La partecipazione: valori, significati, problemi e strumenti*. Reggio Emilia: Comune di Reggio Emilia.

Caillois, R. (1958) *Les jeux et les hommes: le masque et le vertige*. Paris: Gallimard.

Calvino, I. (1972) *Le città invisibili*. Torino: Einaudi.

Calvino, I. (1988) *Lezioni americane*. Torino: Einaudi.

Camaioni, L. (1980) *La prima infanzia*. Bologna: Il Mulino.

Camaioni, L. (ed.) (1993) *Manuale di psicologia dello sviluppo*. Bologna: Il Mulino.

Camaioni, L., Bascetta, C. and Aureli, T. (1988) *L'osservazione del bambino nel contesto educativo*. Bologna: Il Mulino.

Caronia, L. (1997) *Costruire la conoscenza*. Firenze: La Nuova Italia.

Ceccato, S. (1987) *La fabbrica del bello*. Milano: Rizzoli.

Ceppi, G. and Zini, M. (eds) (1998) *Children, Spaces, Relations – Metaproject for an Environment for Young Children*. Reggio Emilia: Reggio Children.

Ceruti, M. (1989) *La danza che crea*, Milano: Feltrinelli.

Ceruti, M. (1995) *Evoluzione senza fondamenta*. Bari: Laterza.

Chomsky, N. (1957) *Syntactic Structures*. Paris: Mouton.

Chomsky, N. (1968) *Language and Mind*. New York: Harcourt Brace and World.

Chomsky, N. (1980) *Rules and Representations*. New York: Columbia University Press.

Clark, M.S. and Fiske, S.T. (eds) (1982) *Affect and Cognition*. Hillsdale, NJ: Erlbaum.

Cornoldi, C. (1995) *Metacognizione e memoria*. Bologna: Il Mulino.

Dahlberg, G. and Moss, P. (2005) *Ethics and Politics in Early Childhood Education*. London: Routledge.

Dahlberg, G., Moss, P. and Pence, A. (1999) *Beyond Quality in Early Childhood Education and Care: Postmodern Perspectives*. London: Falmer Press.

Dal Lago, A. and Rovatti, P.A. (1993) *Per gioco: Piccolo manuale dell'esperienza ludica*. Milano: Raffaello Cortina.

Deleuze, G. and Guattari, F. (1999) *A Thousand Plateaus: Capitalism and Schizophrenia*. London: Athlone Press.

Deleuze, G. and Parnet, H. (1987) *Dialogues*. London: Athlone Press

Derrida, J. (1999) *Adieu to Levinas*. Stanford, CA: Stanford University Press.

Dewey, J. (1916) *Democracy and Education*. New York: Macmillan.

Dewey, J. (1929, 2nd edn) *My Pedagogic Creed*. Washington: Progressive Education Association.

Dewey, J. (1933, 2nd edn) *How we Think: A Restatement of the Relation of Reflective Thinking to the Educative Process*. Boston, MA: Heath and Company.

Dewey, J. (1940) *Education Today*. New York: Putnam.

Dewey, J. (1959) *Experience and Education*. New York: Macmillan.

Dreyfus, H.L. and Dreyfus, S.E. (1986) *Mind over Machine*. New York: The Free Press.

Edelman, G.M. (1989) *The Remembered Present*. New York: Basic Books.

Edelman, G.M. (1992) *Bright Air, Brilliant Fire: on the Matter of the Mind*. New York: Basic Books–HarperCollins.

Edwards, C., Gandini, L. and Forman, G. (eds) (1993) *The Hundred Languages of Children*. Norwood, NJ: Ablex.

EUROSTAT (2003) *The Social Situation of the European Union: 2003*. Luxembourg: European Commission.

Fabbri, D. (1990) *La Memoria della Regina*. Milano: Guerini e Associati.

Fabbri, D. and Munari, A. (1984) *Strategie del sapere: Verso una psicologia culturale*. Bari: Dedalo.

Fodor, J.A. (1983) *The Modularity of Mind: An Essay on Faculty Psychology*. Cambridge, MA: MIT Press.

Fodor, J.A. (1987) *Psychosemantics: The Problem of Meaning in the Philosophy of Mind*. Cambridge, MA: MIT Press.

Foerster, H. von (1984) *Observing Systems*. Seaside, CA: Intersystems Publications.

Freinet, C. (1960) *Education through Work: A Model for Child Centered Learning*. Lewiston, NY: Edwin Mellen Press.

Freire, P. (1967) *Edução como prática da liberdade*. Rio de Janeiro: Paz e Terra.

Freire, P. (1996) *Pedagogia de autonomia. Saberes necessários à prática educative*. São Paulo: Paz e Terra.

Freire, P. (1998) *Pedagogia do oprimido*. São Paulo: Paz e Terra.

Fullan, M. (1991) *The New Meaning of Educational Change*. New York: Teachers College Press.

Gadamer, H.G. (1972, 2nd edn) *Wahrheit und Methode: Grundzüge e. philos. Hermeneutik*. Tübingen: Mohr.

Galimberti, U. (1997) *Il corpo*. Milano: Feltrinelli.

Galimberti, U. (1999) *Psiche e techne. L'uomo nell'età della tecnica*. Milano: Feltrinelli.

Gandini, L., Mantovani, S. and Pope Edwards, C. (eds) (2003) *Il nido per una cultura dell'infanzia*. Bergamo: Junior.

Gardner, H. (1985) *Frames of Mind: The Theory of Multiple Intelligences*. New York: Basic Books.

Gardner, H. (1985) *The Mind's New Science*. New York: Basic Books.

Gardner, H. (1989) *To Open Minds*. New York: Basic Books.

Gardner, H. (1994) 'Foreword: complementary perspectives on Reggio Emilia'. In C. Edwards, L. Gandini, and G. Forman (eds), *The Hundred Languages of Children: The Reggio Approach to Early Childhood Education*. Norwood, NJ: Ablex.

Gardner, H. (1999) *The Disciplined Mind. What All Students Should Understand*. New York: Simon and Schuster.

Geertz, C. (1973) *The Interpretation of Cultures: Selected Essays*. New York: Basic Books.

Gergen, K.J. (1985) 'The Social Constructionist Movement in Modern Psychology', *American Psychologist*, 40 (3), pp. 266–75.

Gergen, K.J. (1991) *The Saturated Self: Dilemmas of Identity in Contemporary Life*. New York: Basic Books.

Gergen, K.J. (1992) *Towards a Postmodern Psychology*. In S. Kvale (ed.) *Psychology and Postmodernism*. London: Sage.

Gergen, K.J. (1994) *Reality and Relationships: Soundings in Social Construction*. Cambridge, MA: Harvard University Press.

Gergen, K.J. (1995) *Social Construction and the Educational Process*. In L.P. Steffe and E.J. Gale (eds) *Constructivism in Education*. Hillsdale, NJ: Erlbaum.

Gergen, K.J. (2000) 'Verso un vocabolario del dialogo trasformativo', *Pluriverso*, 5 (2), pp. 100–13.

Giddens, A. (1990) *The Consequences of Modernity*. Cambridge: Polity Press.

Giudici, C., Krechevsky, M. and Rinaldi, C. (eds) (2001) *Making Learning Visible: Children as Individual and Group Learners*. Reggio Emilia: Reggio Children.

Goleman, D. (1995) *Emotional Intelligence*. New York: Bantam Books.

Gombrich, E.H. (1966) *The Story of Art*. London: Phaidon Press.

Hall, E.T. (1966) *The Hidden Dimension*. Garden City, NY: Doubleday.

Harris, J. (1998) *The Nurture Assumption*. New York: The Free Press.

Hawkins, D. (1974) *The Informed Vision: Essays on Learning and Human Nature*. New York: Agathon Press.

Heshusius, L. (1994) 'Freeing Ourselves from Objectivity: Managing Subjectivity or Turning toward a Participatory Mode of Consciousness?', *Educational Researcher*, 3, pp. 15–22.

Huizinga, J. (1939) *Homo ludens: versuch einer bestimmung des spielelementest der Kultur.* Amsterdam: Pantheon akademische verlagsanstalt.

Johnson, G. (1991) *In the Palaces of Memory.* New York: Alfred A. Knopf.

Kant, I. (1945) *Pedagogia, a cura di N. Abbagnano.* Turino: Paravia.

Katz, L. and Cesarone, B. (eds) (1994) *Reflections on the Reggio Emilia Approach.* Urbana, IL: ERIC/EECE.

Katz, L. and Chard, S. (1989) *Engaging Children's Minds: The Project Approach.* Norwood, NJ: Ablex.

Kellog, R. (1969) *Analyzing Children's Art.* Mountain View, CA: Mayfield Publishing.

Kumar, K. (1995) *From Post-Industrial to Post-Modern Society: New Theories of the Contemporary World.* Cambridge, MA: Blackwell Publishers.

Lanzi, D. and Soncini, I. (1999) 'I significati dell'educare oggi'. Lecture presented at the International Symposium *Learning About Learning*, Reggio Emilia, 16–18 June 1999.

Levy, P. (1994) *L'intelligence collective: pour une anthropologie du cyberspace.* Paris: Découvert.

Luria, A.R. (1976) *Cognitive Development. Its Cultural and Social Foundations.* Cambridge, MA: Harvard University Press.

Lussu, G. (1999) *La lettera uccide.* Roma: Stampa Alternativa e Graffiti.

Lyotard, J.F. (1979) *La condition postmoderne: rapport sur le savoir.* Paris: Éditions de Minuit.

Malaguzzi, L. (ed.) (1971) 'Esperienze per una nuova scuola dell'infanzia'. In *Atti del seminario di studio tenuto a Reggio Emilia il 18–19–20 marzo 1971.* Roma: Editori Riuniti.

Malaguzzi, L. (1975) 'Il ruolo dell'ambiente nel processo educativo', In *Arredo Scuola 75 – per la scuola che cambia.* Como: Luigi Massoni Editore.

Malaguzzi, L. (1993) 'For an Education Based on Relationships', *Young Children,* November, 1993, pp. 9–13.

Malaguzzi, L. (1994) 'History, Ideas and Basic Philosophy'. In C. Edwards, L. Gandini and G. Forman (eds) *The Hundred Languages of Children: The Reggio Approach to Early Childhood Education.* Norwood, NJ: Ablex Publishing.

Malaguzzi, L. (1995) *Una carta per tre diritti.* Reggio Emilia: Comune di Reggio Emilia.

Malaguzzi, L. (1996) *The Hundred Languages of Children: Catalogue of the Exhibition.* Reggio Emilia: Reggio Children.

Malaguzzi, L. (2004) 'Walking on Threads of Silk: Interview with Loris Malaguzzi by Carlo Barsotti', *Children in Europe,* 6, pp. 10–15.

Manghi, S. (ed.) (1998) *Attraverso Bateson. Ecologia della mente e relazioni sociali.* Milano: Raffaello Cortina.

Mantovani, S. (1975) *Asili Nido: psicologia e pedagogia.* Milano: Franco Angeli.

Mantovani, S. (1983) *La ricerca in Asilo Nido.* Bergamo: Juvenilia.

Mantovani, S. (ed.) (1997) *Nostalgia del futuro: Liberare speranze per una nuova cultura dell'infanzia.* Bergamo: Junior.

Mantovani, S. and Musatti, T. (eds) (1983) *Adulti e bambini: educare e comunicare*, Bergamo: Juvenilia.

Mantovani, S., Restuccia Saitta, L. and Bove, C. (2000) *Attaccamento e inserimento: stili e storie delle relazioni al nido*. Milano: Franco Angeli.

Maturana, H. (1991) 'Science and Daily Life: The Ontology of Scientific Explanations'. In F. Steier (ed.) *Research and Reflexivity*. London: Sage.

Maturana, H.R. and Varela, F.J. (1980) *Autopoiesis and Cognition: The Realization of the Living*. Dordrecht: D. Reidel Publishing Company.

Maturana, H.R. and Varela, F.J. (1992) *The Tree of Knowledge*. Boston: Shambala, New Science Library.

Melucci, A. (1989) *Nomads of the Present: Social Movements and Individual Needs in Contemporary Society*. Philadelphia, PA: Temple University Press.

Montessori, M. (1950) *La scoperta del bambino*. Milano: Garzanti.

Morin, E. (1977) *La méthode: La nature de la nature*. Paris: Editions du Seuil.

Morin, E. (1982) *Science avec conscience*. Paris: Editions du Seuil.

Morin, E. (1999) *Les sept savoirs nécessaires à l'éducation du future*. Paris: UNESCO–Seuil.

Morin, E. (1999) *La tête bien faite: repenser la réforme, réformer la pensée*. Paris: Editions du Seuil.

Munari, A. (1993) *Il Sapere Ritrovato: Conoscenza, Apprendimento, Formazione*. Milano: Guerini e Associati.

Munari, B. (1977) *Fantasia*. Bari: Laterza.

Munari, B. (1981) *Da cosa nasce cosa*. Bari: Laterza.

Musatti, T. (1986) *Early Peer Relations: The Perspectives of Piaget and Vygotskij*. In E. Mueller and C. Cooper (eds) *Process and Outcome in Peer Relationships*. New York: Academic Press.

Musatti, T. (1987) *Modalità e problemi del processo di socializzazione tra bambini in asilo nido*. In A. Bondioli and S. Mantovani (eds) *Manuale critico dell'asilo nido*. Milano: Franco Angeli.

Musatti, T. (1993) 'Meaning between Peers: The Meaning of the Peer', *Cognition and Instruction*, 2, pp. 241–50.

Musatti, T. and Mantovani, S. (eds) (1983) *Bambini al nido: gioco, comunicazione e rapporti affettivi*. Bergamo: Juvenilia.

Musatti, T. and Mantovani, S. (eds) (1986) *Stare insieme al nido: relazioni sociali e interventi educative*. Bergamo: Juvenilia.

Musatti, T. and Mayer, S. (1990) *Les jeux de fiction dans la cour: transmission et propagation de thémes de jeu dans une collectivité de jeunes enfants*. In H. Sinclair and M. Stambak (eds) *Les jeux de fiction entre enfants de trois ans*. Paris: Presses Universitaires de France.

Musatti, T. and Mayer, S. (eds) (2003) *Il coordinamento dei servizi educativi per l'infanzia. Una funzione emergente in Italia e in Europa*. Bergamo: Junior.

Musatti, T. and Picchio, M. (2003) *Il monitoraggio della qualità dei servizi integrativi per bambini piccolo*. Roma: Istituto di Scienze e Tecnologie della Cognizione, Consiglio Nazionale delle Ricerche.

Neisser, U. (1967) *Cognitive Psychology*. Englewood Cliffs, NJ: Prentice Hall.

Piaget, J. (1951) *Play, Dreams and Imitation in Childhood*. London: Routledge.

Piaget, J. (1964) *Six études de Psychologie*. Paris: Editions Gouthier.

Piaget, J. (1970) *Psychologie et epistemologie*. Paris: Denoël.

Piaget, J. (1970) *La situation des sciences de l'homme dans le système des sciences-Psychologie-problèmes généreaux de la recherche entredisciplinaire et mécanism communs*, Paris: Mouton.

Piaget, J. (1975) *L'équilibration des structures cognitives*. Paris: Presses Universitaires de France.

Piaget, J. (1977) *Naissance de l'intelligence chez l'enfant*. Neuchâtel: Delachaux et Niestlè.

Piaget, J. (1977 *Construction du reel chez l'enfant*. Neuchâtel: Delachaux et Niestlè.

Piccinni, S. (2004) 'A Transforming City: Interview with Sandra Piccinini by Amelia Gambetti', *Children in Europe*, 6, pp. 4–5.

Pierantoni, R. (1998) *Verità a bassissima definizione. Critica e percezione del quotidiano*. Torino: Einaudi.

Plato (1986) *Lettere, a cura di P. Innocenti*. Milano: BUR.

Plato (2000) *Tutti gli scritti, a cura di G. Reale*. Milano: Bompiani.

Polanyi, M. (1958) *Personal Knowledge: Towards a Post-Critical Philosophy*. Chicago, IL: University of Chicago Press.

Pontecorvo, C. (ed.) (1993) *La condivisione della conoscenza*. Firenze: La Nuova Italia.

Pontecorvo, C., Ajello, A.M. and Zucchermaglio, C. (eds) (1995) *I contesti sociali dell'apprendimento*. Milano: Ambrosiana-LED.

Popper, K.R. (1969) *Conjectures and Refutations*. London: Routledge.

Popper, K.R. (1972) *Objective Knowledge: An Evolutionary Approach*. Oxford: Clarendon Press.

Popper, K.R. (1994) *Alles Leben ist Problemlösen: Über Erkenntnis, Geschichte und Politik*. Munchen: R. Piper.

Popper, K.R. (1994) *Knowledge and the Body–Mind Problem: In Defence of Interaction*. London: Routledge.

Putnam, R. (1993) *Making Democracy Work: Civic Traditions in Modern Italy*. Princeton, NJ: Princeton University Press.

Rabitti, G. (1994) *Alla scoperta della dimensione perduta. L'etnografia dell'educazione in una scuola dell'infanzia di Reggio Emilia*. Bologna: CLUEB.

Read, H. (1943) *Education through Art*. London: Faber and Faber.

Readings, B. (1996) *The University in Ruins*. Cambridge, MA: Harvard University Press.

Rinaldi, C. (1994) *I pensieri che sostengono l'azione educative*. Reggio Emilia: Comune di Reggio Emilia.

Rinaldi, C. (1999a) *L'ascolto visibile*. Reggio Emilia: Comune di Reggio Emilia.

Rinaldi, C. (1999b) *Le domande dell'educare oggi*. Reggio Emilia: Comune di Reggio Emilia.

Rinaldi, C. (1999c) *I processi di conoscenza dei bambini tra soggettività ed intersoggettività*. Reggio Emilia: Comune di Reggio Emilia.

Rinaldi, C. (2000) 'Organization as a Value', *Innovations,* Fall 2000, pp. 2–7.

Rinaldi, C. and Cagliari, P. (1994) *Educazione e creatività.* Reggio Emilia: Comune di Reggio Emilia.

Rinaldi, C., Giudici, C. and Krechevsky, M. (eds) (2001) *Making Learning Visible: Children as Individual and Group Learners.* Reggio Emilia: Reggio Children.

Rodari, G. (1973) *Grammatica della fantasia.* Torino: Einaudi.

Rogers, C.R. (1951) *Client-Centered Therapy: Its Current Practice, Implications and Theory.* Boston, MA: Houghton Mifflin Company.

Rogers, C.R. (1969) *Person to Person: The Problem of Being Human.* Lafayette, CA: Real People Press.

Rorty, R. (1989) *Contingency, Irony and Solidarity.* Cambridge, MA: Cambridge University Press.

Rose, N. (1999) *Powers of Freedom: Reframing Political Thought.* Cambridge: Cambridge University Press.

Rousseau, J.J. (1969) *Emile.* Paris: Gallimard.

Shaffer, M.R. (1990) *Il Bambino e I Suoi Partner* (The Child and his Partners). Milano: Franco Angeli.

Schaffer, H.R. (1996) *Social Development.* Oxford: Blackwell.

Schneider, M. (1951) 'Die historischen Grundlagen der musikalischen Symbolik', *Musikforschung,* 4, pp. 113–28.

Schön, D.A. (1983) *The Reflexive Practitioner.* New York: Basic Books.

Sclavi, M. (1989) *A una spanna da terra.* Milano: Feltrinelli.

Sclavi, M. (2003) *Arte di ascoltare e mondi possibili.* Milano: Bruno Mondadori.

Scuola di Barbiana (1967) *Lettera a una professoressa.* Firenze: Libreria Editrice Fiorentina.

Stein, E. (1980) *Zum Problem der Einfühlung.* Munchen: Kaffke.

Süskind, P. (1994) *Das Parfum.* Zurich: Diogenes.

Tanizaki, J. (1998 *In Praise of Shadows.* New Haven, CT: Leete's Island Books.

Tyler, R.W. (1949) *Basic Principles of Curriculum and Instruction.* Chicago, IL: University of Chicago Press.

Usher, R. and Edwards, R. (1994) *Postmodernism and Education.* London: Routledge.

Varela, F.J., Thompson, E., Rosch, E. and Blum, I.C. (1991) *The Embodied Mind: Cognitive Science and Human Experience.* Cambridge, MA: MIT Press.

Vattimo, G. and Rovatti, A. (eds) (1983) *Il pensiero debole.* Milano: Feltrinelli.

Vecchi, V. (1993) 'The Role of Atelierista'. In C. Edwards, L. Gandini and G. Forman (eds), *The Hundred Languages of Children.* Norwood, NJ: Ablex.

Vygotskij, L.S. (1960a) *Istorijarazvitija vyssih psihiceskih funktcij.* Mosca.

Vygotskij, L.S. (1960b) *Razvitie vysich psichiceskick funkcij.* Mosca.

Vygotskij, L.S. (1970) *Izbrannja psichologicakia issledovaya.* Mosca.

Vygotskij, L.S. (1978) *Mind in Society.* Cambridge, MA: Harvard University Press.

Vygotskij, L.S. (1986) *Thought and Language.* Cambridge, MA: MIT Press.

Watzlawick, P., Beavin, J.H. and Jackson, D.D. (1968) *Pragmatics of Human Communication: A Study of Interactional Patterns, Pathologies and Paradoxes*. London: Faber and Faber.

Weick, K. (1969) *The Social Psychology of Organizing*. Reading, MA: Addison-Wesley.

Zolla, E. (1994) *Lo stupore infantile*. Milano: Adelphi.

Index

acculturation 66–7
administrators 41
aesthetics 78, 81, 102
Agazzi schools 146, 161
Agrippa, Menenio 160
alterity 17, 19
anniversaries 168
architecture for schools 78, 79–81, 82, 88
Arcobaleno *nido* 58
Ariadne's thread metaphor 54–5, 166–7
assessment 69, 71–2; *see also* evaluation
astronomy 148–9
atelier 175, 176
atelierista x, 59, 78, 98, 102, 147, 153, 154
audiovisuals 63; *see also* documentation
authority 91
auxiliary staff 149, 150–2, 154–5, 160

Bartoli, Ione 144
Bateson, G. 11, 81, 122, 176, 177
becoming 8, 80
belonging, sense of 19, 20
Bertani, Eletta 144
Bini, Giorgio 145
body 93, 150
Bologna 145
Borghi, Ettore 143–4
brain 124, 138–9
Bruner, Jerome 1–2, 12, 58, 122, 126, 157, 190
business methods 2, 165

Cagliari, Paola 155
Calvino, Italo 122
care-taking 106
celebration 168
Centre for International Research 199
Ceppi, G. 79
change/continuity 104–5
child development 84
childhood: culture of 3, 171; politics of 12–13; possibilities 176; as social category 13, 145; society 91; *see also* image of child
children 66–7; as actors 152; as citizens 12, 106, 171; communication 48; competence 84, 92, 105, 111–13, 123, 165–6, 172; drawings 115–16; grading 204; knowledge 81; learning process 74; lunch 78; meaning 130–1; motivation 84; and parents 26–7, 33, 47; peers 127–8, 206; public institutions 27, 80; questioning 112; respect 58; rights 77–8, 123–4, 180, 187–8; sexuality 92, 93; space 87; strong 108, 112, 123; as subjects 70; theory-making 112–14, 171–2; transition from *nido* to *scuola dell'infanzia* 109–10; *see also* image of child
Children, spaces, relations (Ceppi and Zini) 79
Ciari, Bruno 145, 161, 162
class issues 189
co-construction 6, 11, 17, 125–6, 172

co-creators 125–6
collectivity 9
collegiality 28, 60, 133–4
communication: children 48;
    documentation 57–8; family 38–9,
    47; individuals 31; information 45;
    interaction 55; management
    councils 48; staff/parents 38, 47–8
community 157, 159, 175, 184–5
competence: children 84, 92, 105,
    111–13, 123, 165–6, 172;
    professionalism 50; teachers 72–3,
    194–5
complicity concept 113
compromise 187
conflict 156
consensuality 51
context 200, 203
continuity 41–2, 104–5, 107, 108, 164
Continuity in Children's Services 102
control 195–6
controversy 127
co-protagonists 126
country outings 43
creativity 119–20; co-creators 125–6;
    drawings 115–16; language 175–6;
    learnings 120; play 117–18;
    questions 113; valued 102; *zerosei*
    103
Creativity as a Quality of Thought 102
crisis 183, 202–3
crossing boundaries 168–9, 173
'Crossing boundaries' conference
    168–9
cultural factors 22, 37, 70, 83–4, 156,
    163
curriculum 21, 116, 131–2, 200,
    205–6

Dahlberg, Gunilla 8, 13, 14, 15, 16,
    178, 182
danger 94–5
day-trips 43
decentralisation 29
delegated decrees 156
Deleuze, Gilles 3, 7–8
democracy 16, 130, 140–1, 175,
    192–3
Derrida, Jacques 15

developmental psychology 182
Dewey, John: active learning 6, 11,
    161; democracy 141; experimental
    school 3, 158; as influence 77, 190
dialogue 1; conflict 156; context 203;
    education 185; family 60, 155–6; as
    friendship 197; identity 169;
    interdependence 185–6, 188–9,
    199–200; solidarity 94; staff
    meeting 135; theory/practice
    190–2; transformational 76, 184–5
'Dialogues' 62
Diana school 58, 61–2, 157–8
didactics, participatory 69, 73
difference: cultural 156; identity 189;
    interdependence 9, 188; normality
    139–40; of opinions 155–6;
    recognition 95–6; respect 94, 108;
    school 208; subjectivity 139; values
    140
disciplinarity 7
dissensus 17
documentation 62, 68–71, 174;
    communication 57–8; curriculum
    206; democracy 130; education
    204–5; evaluation 61, 62, 71–2,
    203–4, 208–9; interpretation 70–1;
    listening made visible 100;
    observation 129–31, 139; parents
    59; pedagogical 15–16, 19, 194–6;
    protagonists 61–2; re-cognition 58;
    re-visiting 58–9; reciprocity 57, 100;
    research 98, 137, 149; search for
    meaning 63–4; self-reflection 196;
    subjectivity 163; teacher's diaries
    183
Domus Academy 77, 78–9
drawings 115–16
dreams 209

early childhood services 10, 19, 103,
    144, 145, 152–3
Eco, Umberto 122
education 2, 3–4, 29; becoming 8;
    care 106; control 195–6; dialogue
    185; documentation 204–5;
    ethical/political dimensions 2, 165;
    freedom 50, 194–5; politics of 12;
    public 208; research 148; values

138; *see also* school
educators x, 36–8, 59, 97–8; parents
    36, 38; primary role 59;
    professionalism 37; Reggio Emilia
    97–8; *see also atelierista; pedagogista;*
    teachers
Edwards, C. 54, 166, 181
Emilia Romagna 103
emotion 95
England 200–1, 204
environment 77–8, 86, 99, 134
ethics 2, 12, 165, 196
Eurostat 33
evaluation 61, 62, 71–2, 203–4, 208–9
'evenings in the kitchen' 43
everyday activities 159

Fabbri, Donata 122, 128
family 47, 90; communication 38–9,
    47; component parts 32, 91;
    dialogue 60, 155–6; *nido* child 33;
    non-*nido* using 44–5; participaton
    151–2; school 89; society 31–6, 91;
    and staff 39–41; *see also*
    grandparents; parents
Fascism 157, 179
fatherhood 34, 90
fertility rates 33
Forman, G. 54, 166, 181
formazione 137
Foucault, Michel 13
freedom 50, 173, 194–5
Freinet, Célestin 77, 145, 190
Friends of Reggio Children
    Association 144
friendship 94, 197

Galardini, Annalia 103
Gambetti, Amelia 122, 137, 156
Gandini, Lella 54, 61, 121–2, 166, 181
Gardner, Howard 3–4, 61, 76, 122,
    158
gender issues 189
genetic mutation 79–80
Gergen, Kenneth J. 76
Giaroni, Loretta 144
Giudici, C. 62
globalisation 90, 139, 172
grading 204

La Grammatica della Fantasia (Rodari)
    120, 161
grandparents 32, 43
group learning 99, 127–8, 132,
    149–50
group meeting 42
group parties 43
Gruppo Nazionale Nidi 25
Gruppo Nazionale Nidi Infanzia 25, 159
Guattari, Felix 7–8

Harvard Graduate School of
    Education 61
Hawkins, D. 122
holiday diary 109
hope 19, 20–1, 60
humour 173
hundred languages of children
    concept 7, 175, 192–3; *atelierista*
    154; multiple intelligences 61; as
    pedagogy 17, 65–8; peers 127;
    self-reflection 205
The Hundred Languages of Children
    (Edwards, Gandini and Forman) 54,
    166, 181
'The Hundred Languages of
    Children' exhibition 18–19, 59,
    162, 165, 181
hygiene 151

identity: anniversaries 168; body 150;
    cultural 70; dialogue 169; difference
    189; individual 109; learning
    105–6; memory 68–9; paternal
    152–3; Reggio Emilia 102; sexual
    92; space 83; teachers 48
image of child 83–4, 91, 105, 122–4;
    community 157; learning 171;
    pedagogy 151; student teachers
    194; theory 182
images 39, 115–16
in-depth study group 43
individual 9, 31, 109, 125, 139, 141
intelligences, multiple 61, 66
interdependence: dialogue 185–6,
    188–9, 199–200; difference 9, 188;
    freedom 195; pedagogy 10, 170
interdisciplinarity 136, 193, 195
international networks 164–5, 166

interpretation: children's theories 112,
    171–2; documentation 70–1;
    language 122; listening 65;
    observation 129; reality 123;
    reasoned 57; teachers' theory 75
interviews 42, 43, 109–10, 144
intradisciplinarity 77
isolation 33, 45, 47
Istoreco 144

Kaminsky, Judith 121–2
knowledge 7, 13; body 93; children 81;
    co-construction 126;
    compartmentalisation 120;
    construction of 124; controversy
    127; fields of 136; individual 125,
    141; rhizome metaphor 7–8; social
    125; transmission of 90
Krechevsky, Mara 61, 62

language:
    contamination/hybridisation 67,
    99; creativity 175–6; culture 22;
    documentation 16; ecology of 176;
    graphic 193; interpretation 122;
    meaning 201; thinking 6, 175;
    translation 75; verbal/non-verbal
    37, 39, 193; vocabulary 173
languaging 11–12
learning: active 6, 11, 161; aesthetics
    81; children/adults 74; creative
    120; environment 134; identity
    construction 105–6; image of child
    171; listening 114–15; peers 206;
    reciprocal 57; space 77; teaching
    126–7, 173–4; unpredictability 164;
    values 141; see also group learning;
    learning by doing
Learning about learning symposium 97
learning by doing 191, 193
legibility 71, 84
Levinas, Emmanuel 14
listening 115–16; to children 116–17,
    128, 131; documentation 100;
    emotion 95; interpretation 65;
    learning 114–15; Malaguzzi 149;
    reciprocity 116–17, 126; see also
    pedagogy of listening
loneliness 33, 47

lunch for children 78

Making Learning Visible (Giudici,
    Krechevsky and Rinaldi) 62
Malaguzzi, Loris 4, 5–7, 9, 122;
    Borghi 143; breadth of interests
    148–9; celebration of 168–70;
    Dewey 190; early childhood 145;
    Gardner 61; The Hundred Languages
    of Children 181; image of child 83–4;
    listening 149; municipal schools
    25–6, 53, 144–6; nostalgia for the
    future 166; organisation 159;
    progettare 55–6; relational pedagogy
    169; respect 59–60, 177; rights of
    child 77–8; teachers 73, 147;
    teaching/learning 127; see also
    hundred languages of children
    concept
management councils 44, 48–9
managerialism 10, 40
Manghi, Sergio 169
Mantovani, Susanna 53
Maturana, Humberto 5, 11–12
meaning: context 84; language 201;
    search for 56, 63–4, 111, 112,
    130–1, 143–4; socialisation 111
Melucci, A. 13–14
memory 68–9
men in early childhood services 152–3
metaphor 75–6, 209
method 162–3, 165–6
Montessori, Maria 6–7, 77, 98–9, 161,
    190
Montessori schools 146
Morin, Edgard 122
Morrow, Leslie 122
Moss, Peter 8, 14, 178, 182
mothers 34, 37, 47–8
Munari, Alberto 122, 128
municipal schools 208; architects 78;
    auxiliary staff 149, 150–2, 154–5,
    160; Gardner 61; Malaguzzi 25–6,
    53, 144–6; Reggio Emilia x, 2,
    144–6, 179, 180–1

national law 1044 25, 27
needs/rights 123, 180, 186
negotiation/rights 186–7

neoliberalism 10, 19, 207–8
network system 158–9, 164–5, 166
neurons 124
new cultural geography 20
new social movements 13–14
Newsweek 157
nidi x, 37; care-taking/education 106;
  closure threats 179; as
  communication sysem 27–8;
  cooperative-run 158; family 33;
  individual demand based service
  36–7, 97; law 1044 25, 27; network
  system 158–9; non-using families
  44–5; participation 30; *scuole
  dell'infanzia* 86, 103, 107, 109–10,
  151; society 30, 37; staff 36–42;
  staff pay 106; valuing the person
  150–1
normality 139–40
Nostalgia del Futura conference 53–4
nostalgia for the future 110, 166
nursery schools 144, 146–7

objectivity 11–12
observation 128, 129–31, 139
organisation 28, 39, 40, 44, 159
Other 15, 139
outcomes 201, 202–3

parents: and children 26–7, 33, 47;
  documentation 59; loneliness 33,
  47; needs 36; psychological
  constraints 41; resistance 40–1; role
  26, 34–5; and school 26, 89, 156–7;
  space 87–8; statements of intent
  164; and teachers 36, 38, 42–3,
  47–8, 89, 135, 157; *see also*
  fatherhood; mothers
Parma 102, 103
Parnet, H. 7
participation 29–30; auxiliary staff
  154–5; co-responsibility 40;
  community 175; democracy 140,
  175; family 151–2; influence 205;
  management councils 48–9; *nidi* 30;
  organisation 44; professional
  development 49–50; protagonists
  10–11; *scuole dell'infanzia* 30;
  selection criteria 42; social

management 49, 50–1; staff 154–5
parties 43
pedagogical team 160, 161
pedagogista x, 54, 97–8, 102, 103, 167
pedagogy: academic 161, 162;
  architecture 79, 80–1; business
  methods 165; image of child 151;
  interdependence 10, 170;
  partisanship 139; research 97, 98;
  teachers 99–100
pedagogy of listening 12, 14–15, 17,
  64, 65–8, 113, 140
pedagogy of relationships 113, 172–3
peers 127–8, 206
Pence, Alan 8, 182
Piaget, Jean 5–6, 7, 118, 122, 161,
  181–2
Piagetian school 159
Piccinini, Sandra 144
Pistoia 102, 103
play 117–19
postmodernism 182
poverty 32
power 13, 125–6
process-based approach 147, 202–3
professional development 28, 141–2;
  auxiliary staff 150; collegiality 60,
  133–4; *formazione* 137; individual
  141; parent--teacher relations 135;
  participation 49–50; process-based
  approach 147; re-cognition 131;
  teachers 25–6, 110, 135–6
professionalism 37, 47–8, 50
progettazione xi, 28, 72; and curriculum
  206; dynamics 132–3; Malaguzzi
  55–6
progettualità 107, 108
programmazione xi, 28
project work 7, 132–3
Project Zero 61, 62, 76
protagonists 10–11, 51–2, 61–2, 81
public institutions 27, 80
public services 10, 36–7, 97, 179
Putnam, R. 9

questioning by children 112, 113

race 156
re-cognition 58, 69, 130, 131

re-visiting 58–9, 68
Readings, Bill 14–15
reciprocity: control 196;
    documentation 57, 100; interviews
    144; learning 57; listening 116–17,
    126; relationships 141
reflection 62, 102; *see also* self-
    reflection
Reggio Emilia 1–2, 3–8, 9; *atelier* 176;
    community 18–19, 184–5; Domus
    Academy 77–9; early childhood
    services 10, 144; educators 97–8;
    Gruppo Nazionale Nidi Infanzia 25,
    159; identity 102; image of child
    91; as inspiraton 197–9;
    international visitors 121–2; local
    place 20; methods 162–3, 165–6;
    municipal schools x, 2, 144–6, 179,
    180–1; radical politics 8–11; space
    77; time 18; values 138, 165–6, 198;
    women's active participation 9,
    166–7
relations-communications 28–9, 43
relationships: creativity 113; emotion
    95; listening 65–6; pedagogy of 169,
    172–3; reciprocity 141; time 18
religion 189–90, 202–3
research 17–18; documentation 98,
    137, 149; education 148;
    pedagogical 97, 98; school 101,
    173; teachers 192
resistance 40–1
respect 55, 58, 59–60, 94, 108, 177
responsibilities: democracy 16;
    parenthood 34–5; personal 184;
    public 207–9; shared 40, 169; staff
    160–1
rhizome metaphor 7–8
Ricco, Paola 122
rights: aesthetics 102; children 77–8,
    123–4, 180, 187–8; continuity 104;
    hierarchy 112; needs 123, 180, 186;
    negotiation 186–7
Rinaldi, Carlina 1, 2, 13;
    becoming/education 8; crisis 183;
    'Dialogues' 62; *Making Learning
    Visible* 62; presentations 21–2
risk 94
Rodari, Gianni 122, 162; *La*

Grammatica della Fantasia 120, 161
Rose, Nikolas 17
rules/sexuality 93

safety 86, 94
St Louis Reggio Collaborative 137
scaffolding 68, 99
school: ageing environment 86;
    architectural design 79–81; as
    construction site 126; curriculum-
    led 116; democracy 140–1;
    difference 208; and family 89; as
    living organism 85–6; maternal
    152; parents 26, 89, 156–7;
    political/ethical practice 14–16;
    research 101, 173; socio-political
    experimentation 79; as system
    85–7; time 207; values 128; *see also
    nidi; scuola dell'infanzia*
science 4–5
scuola dell'infanzia x; individual demand
    based service 36–7, 97; male
    identity 152–3; *nidi* 86, 103, 107,
    109–10, 151; participation 30; staff
    pay 106
selection criteria 42
self-certification 34
self-determination 32
self-evaluation 59
Self/Other 9, 139
self-reflection 177, 196, 205
sex education 93
sexuality 92, 93
Shaffer, M.R. 84
social capital 9
social constructionism 6, 8, 11, 13,
    122, 123, 126
social experimentation 18–19
social management 47, 49, 50–1
social postitivism 181
socialisation 78, 111
socialism 9, 178–9
sociality 67
society: childhood 91; fragmented 31,
    202; *nidi* 30, 37
Soglia, Giuseppe 157
solidarity 94
space: architecture 80; identity 83; for
    individuals/gatherings 85; Japanese

86; as language 82–3; learning 77; legibility 84; for meeting 85; organisation of 87–8; process-oriented 88; Reggio schools 77; teachers 87; time 134–5
staff: continuity 41–2; equality 150; and family 39–41; male 152–3; *nidi* 36–42; and parents 38, 42–3, 47–8, 157; participation 154–5; pay 106; professionalism 47–8; resistance 40; responsibilities 160–1; self-confidence 40; social management 51; timetabling 159–60; working mothers 47–8; *see also atelierista;* auxiliary staff; *pedagogista;* teachers
staff meeting 135, 147–8
statements of intent 163–4
Una storia presente (Istoreco) 144
student teachers 194
study groups 121
subjectivity 9–10, 27, 128, 138–9, 163
Sweden 148, 160, 195, 200

teachers x, 54–6, 59; and children 125–6, 134, 148–9; competence 72–3, 194–5; ethics 196; identity 48; Malaguzzi 73, 147; Montessori 98–9; and parents 36, 38, 42–3, 47–8, 89, 135, 157; *pedagogistas* 102; pedagogy 99–100; professional development 25–6, 110, 135–6; research 192; respect 55; role 59; space 87; statements of intent 163–4; theory 75, 191–2; uncertainty 183–4; women 167; working pairs 134, 153–4; *see also* documentation
teacher's diaries 149, 183
teaching/learning 126–7, 173–4
theory 75, 112–14, 182, 191–2
theory/practice 17, 56–7, 100, 102, 190–2
thinking: divergent/convergent 117–18; language 6, 175
time 18, 134–5, 207
timetabling 159–60
trade unions 41

transformation 76, 79–80, 105, 184–5
translation 75

UN Convention on the Rights of the Child 187
uncertainty 183–4
Union of Italian Women (UDI) 178
United States of America 156, 199–200
Università Statale di Milano 53
universities 161–2, 192
unpredictability 164, 173
utopian thought 20

values: difference 140; education 138; 'The Hundred Years of Children' exhibition 165; learning 141; Reggio Emilia 138, 165–6, 198; school 128
Varela, F. 11–12
Vecchi, Vea 103
Vercalli, Emanuela 122
Villa Cella preschool 146, 180
Villa Gaida *nido* 149, 157, 178–9
Villetta school 62
violence 94–5
vocabulary 173
Vygotsky, Lev 6, 7, 122, 126, 181, 190

Washington 156
welfare state 25, 29, 207
Winner, Ellen 61
Wittgenstein, Ludwig 60
women: Reggio Emilia story 9, 166–7; role changes 90
women's movement 179, 180
working conditions 134
working sessions 43
workshops 43, 176

zerosei project 102, 103–4, 151, 158, 174
Zini, M. 79
Zini, Tullio 78